Husrev Tabak is currently Assistant Professor in the Department of International Relations at Recep Tayyip Erdogan University, Rize, Turkey. He completed his PhD in Politics at the University of Manchester and his MA in Politics and Sociology at University College London. His publications include "Islam, Nationalism and Kurdish Ethnopolitics in Turkey" in the *Peace Review*, "Methodological Nationalism and the Study of Foreign Policy in Turkey" in *Uluslararası İlişkiler (International Relations)*, and "Manifestations of Islam in Turkey's Foreign Policy" in *Turkey: Opportunities and Challenges*.

"This book presents an excellent account of the changing relationship between Ankara and the Kosovar Turks. Skilfully deploying international norm theory, it traces out how the former's shift towards what has been called 'post-Kemalist' policy frameworks has been internalised and resisted by Kosovo's Turkish-speaking community. In doing so, it offers a series of insightful findings on the ideational consequences of Turkey's contemporary foreign policy. It is therefore a key resource for anyone interested in both Turkey's relations with its kin communities in the Balkans and the over-arching role of norms in international relations."

Tim Jacoby, Professor, University of Manchester

"Turkish internal and external politics has been drawing an ever increasing amount of scholarly attention, yet there are still few studies shedding light on the links between domestic and foreign policy. Stemming from the National Outlook ('Milli Görüş') movement, the JDP has been trying to create a new set of religiously, culturally and historically inspired norms within internal politics, orienting its selective 'democratisation' course towards these new norms. Husrev Tabak's book provides an original academic framework, showing how new cultural and religious norms have impacted on Ankara's treatment of the Turkish community in Kosovo. So far, the topic of 'Outside Turks' has been understudied. This book examines 'Outside Turks' in terms of the interconnections between internal and external politics. The comprehensive fieldwork makes it a reference book for scholars who work on the nexus between domestic and foreign policy, Turkish foreign policy, minorities in the Balkans and the JDP's understanding of values and norms. It is also highly recommended for all those who would like to gain an in-depth view of Turkey's Outside Turks policies and how they have been changing in the recent decades."

Birgül Demirtaş, Professor,
TOBB University of Economics and Technology, Turkey

THE KOSOVAR TURKS AND POST-KEMALIST TURKEY

Foreign Policy, Socialisation and Resistance

HUSREV TABAK

I.B. TAURIS

LONDON · NEW YORK

Published in 2017 by
I.B.Tauris & Co. Ltd
London • New York
www.ibtauris.com

Copyright © 2017 Husrev Tabak

The right of Husrev Tabak to be identified as the author of this work has been asserted by the author in accordance with the Copyright, Designs and Patents Act 1988.

Every attempt has been made to gain permission for the use of the images in this book. Any omissions will be rectified in future editions.

References to websites were correct at the time of writing.

Library of Modern Turkey 26

ISBN: 978 1 78453 737 1
eISBN: 978 1 78672 055 9
ePDF: 978 1 78673 055 8

A full CIP record for this book is available from the British Library
A full CIP record is available from the Library of Congress

Library of Congress Catalog Card Number: available

Typeset in Garamond Three by OKS Prepress Services, Chennai, India
Printed and bound by CPI Group (UK) Ltd, Croydon, CR0 4YY

MIX
Paper from
responsible sources
FSC   FSC® C013604
www.fsc.org

To ümmühan, ersin mirza and ayşe mira...

CONTENTS

LIST OF ILLUSTRATIONS

Figures

Appendix Figures

Table

LIST OF ABBREVIATIONS

ADD	Kemalist Thought Association
AKEA	Association for Culture, Education and School
CUP	Committee of Union and Progress
D-8	Developing 8
DIYANET	Presidency for Religious Affairs
DM	Diplomatic mission member respondents
EULEX	European Union Rule of Law Mission
FPA	Foreign Policy Analysis
HDP	Peoples' Democratic Party
HÜDA-PAR	Kurdish Free Cause Party
IHH	Humanitarian Relief Foundation
IP	International Politics
IR	International Relations
JDP	Justice and Development Party
KDTP	Democratic Turkish Party of Kosovo
KFOR	Kosovo Force
KKTC	Turkish Republic of North Cyprus
LE	Local elite respondents
MABED	Mamusha Research, Science and Education Association
NATO	North Atlantic Treaty Organisation
NGO	Non-Governmental Organisation
NMP	Nationalist Movement Party
OIC	Organization of Islamic Cooperation
PKK	Kurdistan Workers' Party

PM	Prime Minister
RPP	Republican People Party
SVN	Scoping visit notes
TC	Republic of Turkey
TDK	Turkish Language Council in Turkey
TDP	Turkish Democratic Party
TIKA	Turkish Cooperation and Coordination Agency
TRT	Turkish Radio and Television Corporation
TÜMED	Turkey Alumni Association
UNMIK	United Nations interim administration
WP	Welfare Party
WWI	World War I
WWII	World War II
YTB	Presidency for Turks Abroad and Related Communities

ACKNOWLEDGEMENTS

This is the first book in the English language exclusively devoted to the study of the ethnic Turkish community in Kosovo. I would therefore like to thank several members of this community who have kindly taken part in my research and shared their knowledge and rich personal archives. Among them, Bayram Pomak deserves the most gratitude. I am indebted to him for acting as my main point of contact with the community and for guiding me throughout my fieldwork in Kosovo. Along with him, Bedrettin Koro, Mehmet Bütüç and Ferhat Derviş humbly and generously shared their experiences, thoughts and personal archives. Mehmet Bütüç, the owner of the now closed *Yeni Dönem* newspaper, kindly gave me the last remaining copies of the *Yeni Dönem* newspaper for my personal use; I, however, as a sign of respect for the history of the community in Kosovo, handed them over to the Kosovo National Archives in Pristina where they are now preserved. Refika Sulçevsi, another member of the ethnic Turkish community, kindly arranged the registration of these materials in the archives. She also kindly helped me to study the archives of the *Tan* newspaper, the last copies of which were restored and archived with the help of Turkey's development agency, TIKA. There are also others who helped me during my fieldwork and deserve mentioning here. I wish to thank in particular Mürteza Büşra, Nimetullah Hafız, Raif Kirkul, Tahir Luma, Ethem Baymak, Enver Baki, Refki Taç, Cüneyt Ustaibo, Nuhi Mazrek, Ela Kasap, Müferra Şinik, Levent Buş and Cengiz Çesko for their hospitality during my fieldwork. Nevzat Hüdaverdi, a teacher and a former manager of the *Tan* newspaper, and Müveddet Bako, a retired teacher and the founding president of the first political party for the ethnic Turkish community both passed away after I completed my fieldwork; they were ever so kind in sharing their publications and invaluable personal histories with me. I pray they rest in peace. I would finally like to express my gratitude to Cengiz Kovaç for kindly arranging the cover photo of this book.

The preparation of this book took more than four years, and my wife Ümmühan and my son Ersin Mirza have shared the difficulties and pressures of the entire research period and suffered more than I did. My gratefulness to both is endless. This book is dedicated to both of them as a sign of my appreciation.

FOREWORD

Turkey's foreign policy, during the times of the Justice and Development Party (the AKP) government, has become a very popular theme of books, articles and PhD theses, among many Turkish and non-Turkish scholars of International Relations, in trying to account for the country's more assertive, post-Kemalist, neo-Ottoman paradigm shift. What makes this book stand out from most of the existing studies is the original way in which it approaches the matter and the intellectual sophistication of the narrative. Husrev Tabak's book is solid International Relations reading, in that it discusses a single country, Turkey, and a single empirical case, ethnic Turks in Kosovo, while, at the same time, it frames it very effectively into the wider context of foreign policy analysis. This is an impressive piece of work which delivers effortlessly on both conceptual and empirical grounds. It is a PhD thesis turned into a book, coming from a fresh, young academic mind, who approaches the subject matter with responsibility and respect. I was very fortunate to be the external examiner of the final thesis; from the first few pages I realised that this was going to be an impressive reading, which kept its density, seriousness and firmness until the last page.

This book is a convincing story of how norms and identities in post-Kemalist Turkey's foreign policy are shaped, diffused and received among ethnic Turks abroad. Indeed, the foreign policy philosophy of the AKP has been often defined in "missionary terms", by either presenting Turkey as a model to other Muslim countries in the Middle East or as peace builder in post-conflict zones like Bosnia or Kosovo, in the Balkans. Husrev goes beyond the strategic and realist discussion of the

AKP's foreign policy and examines its normative side, steeped in what he calls the new values of "de-ethnicised nationhood", "Ottomania", "Turkish Islam" and "Islamic internationalism". Tabak points out rightly that in the post-Ottoman European lands, Turkey, traditionally, felt a sense of protective duty vis-à-vis its Muslim "cousins", most of whom were remnants of the Ottoman Empire, and how Outside Turks were historically a central concern of Turkey's foreign policy, since the beginning of the Turkish Republic, especially during the communist years of totalitarian oppression. With the end of the Cold War, a new normative Muslim agenda started to infiltrate Turkey's secular foreign policy in the Balkans, which became consolidated during the reign of the AKP years.

The author in his extended fieldwork in Turkey and Kosovo traced the understanding of the new AKP normative foreign policy, by looking at three stages: norm production, norm propagation and norm internalisation. As such, the normative analysis of Turkey's foreign policy is not just an intellectual discussion but becomes the actual interaction between the producers of foreign policy norms (Turkish domestic political agents), and the consumers of these norms in Kosovo (ethnic Turks). I noted with interest this multidimensional discussion including the discrepancies in the agendas between domestic producers of norms and outside ethnic recipients of the new post-Kemalist normative transition, the latter suspicious of the new religious orientation. Beyond this "homeland–diasporic" friction, we also get a better insight into the internal diversity of the local communities in Kosovo, and the relations between ethnic Turks and mediating Kosovar authorities.

There are many things I appreciated about this book which I read as a thesis in one breath, but more importantly I would like to point out three successes. How a single focused case study can generate wider conceptual and theoretical thinking and become effortlessly generalisable with other cases; in that sense the book goes beyond Turkish exceptionalism. Empirically, there is important new information which relates to our introduction to the local Turkish communities in Kosovo, who are given an independent critical voice to challenge the new religious influences of the mother country. Finally, the Kosovar story becomes the story of many other similar cases of Turkey's engagement with Ottoman Turks elsewhere in other Balkan environments.

I am very impressed by the professionalism, consistency and control of this book project. As a PhD thesis it was a great example of the candidate's journey, containing all the steps that every student should take when writing a thesis. As a book it is an original contribution to the literature, and adds not just a new dynamic study on Turkey, but very crucially a convincing case study of foreign policy analysis.

Othon Anastasakis
Director of South East European Studies (SEESOX)
University of Oxford

CHAPTER 1

INTRODUCTION

Turkey has an historical interest in tuning in what it considers the "Outside Turks" communities[1] with the homeland, particularly the ones residing in the Balkans. The traditional (Kemalist) approach to these communities, which were mostly defined by religious identity, manifested itself in the form of state engagement to build national consciousness among these communities with an exclusive focus on ethnic identity. The traditional approach achieved a great deal of success until the 1980s. For instance, the Turkish-speaking Ottoman remnant communities in Bulgaria, Romania, Greece and Cyprus all became proud bearers of an ethnic Turkish identity. Nonetheless, after the 1980s Turkey was ruled by post-Kemalist governments,[2] such as the parties of Turgut Özal[3] and Necmettin Erbakan,[4] something which affected the ways in which Outside Turks were approached by the state. In this sense, Outside Turks slowly begun to be viewed more in a cultural and religious sense, rather than in purely ethnic terms. This change in approach has soared since the rise to power of the Justice and Development Party (JDP) and was soon reflected in the Outside Turks communities. This change involved a number of government institutions with overseas (post-Kemalist) missions, such as the Turkish Cooperation and Coordination Agency (TIKA), the Presidency for Turks Abroad and Related Communities (YTB), the Presidency for Religious Affairs (Diyanet) and the Yunus Emre Institute. These institutions are the most ardent supporters of the post-Kemalist cause and are mostly interested in promoting and protecting the religious and Ottoman cultural identity of the Outside Turks. Within this scope, for example, multicultural and multi-ethnic forms of attachments are championed, a firm emphasis is placed on inter-ethnic relations among Muslim communities during the Ottoman times, and the safeguarding of Muslim identity and practices, history and culture have all become priority concerns. This book, therefore, raises questions about the implications of these changes in policy and their influence on Outside Turks communities, with a particular focus on Kosovar Turks.

This empirical scrutiny on Kosovar Turks is in fact a foreign policy analysis and brings together domestic changes and their overseas implications. In other words, it addresses domestic norms and how they are integrated into foreign policy by analysing the ways in which the Turkish governments, ever since the early Republican era, particularly the JDP governments, have dealt with Kosovar Turks as an Outside Turks community. It, accordingly, gives accounts of the ways in which domestic norms have guided Turkey's approach to Outside Turks and traces the conduct of post-Kemalist policy towards the Outside Turks, before exploring the implications of such a policy for Kosovar Turks. The study focuses on both the formation and conduct of Turkey's policy towards the Outside Turks and approaches foreign policy as a bridge between a domestic locality and an international locality, through which domestic norms become internationalised and begin to function in a foreign setting.

Turkey's Involvement in the Affairs of Outside Turks

The peculiar adventure of the notion of *Outside Turks* began with the territorial shrinking of the Ottoman Empire and with the remaining Turkish-speaking communities left outside of this empire before and after its eventual collapse. Even before the final collapse of the Ottoman Empire in the twentieth century, the Ottomans had a history of acting as 'protectors' of Muslim communities after territory had been lost to newly-independent states. Yet, it was only towards and during World War I (WWI) that the Ottoman Empire and the intellectual circles within the Empire embarked on political programmes and manifestations aimed at liberating the Turkic communities from imperial domination and to create a bridge between Turkish-speaking communities living inside and outside the country (Landau 1995: 29). Nonetheless, the losses resulting from WWI and the de facto collapse of the Ottoman Empire created novel circumstances under which the 'inside' and 'outside' demarcation with regard to Turkish-speaking communities was solidified. Ultimately the National Pact of 1920[5] reified the notion of 'Outside Turks' both as a *condition* to be experienced outside Anatolia as a category of Turkey's foreign policy and as communities to be moulded according to the new culture, identity and value-system of the homeland – that is, Turkey (Tüzün 1998: 28). The Republic of Turkey was thus established and its borders were drawn via the act of leaving hundreds of thousands of Turkish-speaking communities outside the borders, while still having a will to intervene in the affairs of those communities.

Turkey has, therefore, been involved in the affairs of these Turkish-speaking Muslim communities sometimes due to its responsibility as the successor of the Ottoman Empire, sometimes due to a Pan-Turkist ideological motivation, yet mostly with the 'transformative' motive of keeping these communities in tune with the developments in their homeland, Turkey. Historically, the first two have represented a passive form of engagement, in which Outside Turks communities were, for instance, supported in their fights for ethnic rights or given shelter from state oppression. The latter approach to Outside Turks, during the Kemalist era, represented Turkey's will to transform the religiously organised and acting Turkish-speaking Ottoman remnant communities into nationally behaving ethnic Turkish communities. Yet, with the advent of the post-Kemalist turn, Turkey aimed to rehabilitate these 'ethnically acting' and 'ethnically thinking' communities through the introduction and recalling of an invented Ottoman multi-cultural experience as model for organising inter-ethnic relations. The transformative motive for the both Kemalist and post-Kemalist approaches, in this fashion has resulted from – as pointed out brilliantly by Uzer – the idea that Outside Turks communities are a "cultural–political extension of the mainland" (2010: 111).

During the Kemalist era, the transformative motive led Turkey to alter and fight against Outside Turks' attachment to Ottoman cultural and identity practices. These communities were, accordingly, asked to embrace national and ethnic identities at both the personal and communal level. This was what the Kemalist regime embarked on in domestic politics too: building an ethnic nation out of the ashes of a multi-ethnic and multi-religious Islamic empire. Turkey's desire to privilege national identity and culture in its relation with Outside Turks remained by and large consistent up until late 1980s and, for instance, saw the Turkish-speaking communities in Cyprus, Greece, Romania and Bulgaria gain an ethnic and national consciousness. In Cyprus, Kemalist principles were even placed in the Constitution of the Turkish state, which was de facto founded in the northern part of the island in 1983. After the 1980s, but particularly after the coming to power of the JDP in the 2000s, however, there were increasing aspirations in Turkey to shift towards a consideration of these communities in line with the Ottoman–Islamic conception of nationhood, geography and Turkishness. The societal and official positions mostly departed from the dominant Kemalist political frames in imagining societal links outside Turkey. Thus, the post-Kemalist posture came to imagine the Turkish nation and Outside Turks along cultural and religious lines, rather than in a purely ethnic sense. This was part of a broader surfacing of practices in domestic and foreign policies, which are at ease with the imperial, multinational and multicultural legacy of the Ottoman Empire – as opposed to Kemalist notions of a nation state based on a single nation, which nonetheless has ties with ethnic kin overseas. In this fashion, for instance, religious identity, rather than ethnic identity, is considered indisputably consistent in building relations with overseas ethnic kin communities. Despite the shift in comprehending Outside Turks, therefore, the will to mould these communities according to the culture, identity and value-system of the homeland continued uninterruptedly.

Nonetheless, this shift in approach to Outside Turks occurred within a broader post-Kemalist turn in domestic politics. In the scope of this turn, the Kemalist claims to the cultural, ethnic, religious and language homogeneity of the country have lost ground while its multicultural and multi-ethnic structures have officially been admitted (Çağaptay 2012b, Akyol 2013, Gürbey 2006, Kadıoğlu 2007, Kirişçi 2006, Kirişçi 2009b). This is the juncture when the post-Kemalist Turkey mostly departed from the dominant Kemalist political frames in state–society relations and in imagining societal links outside Turkey. This book accordingly explores the implications of such changes for Outside Turk communities, in this case those in Kosovo.

Moreover, due to Turkey's global diplomatic opening, Outside Turks communities are now in regular contact with Turkey's diplomatic mission members (local embassies, TIKA, Yunus Emre Institute,

Diyanet), humanitarian organisations (such as Turkish Crescent, IHH, Deniz Feneri, Kimse Yok mu), religious groups (such as the Gülen movement, Süleyman Efendi Group (Süleymancıs), Erenköy movement, Menzil movement) and migrant solidarity associations. They altogether deliver services and run activities in interaction with Outside Turks communities on the ground in most of the overseas localities the ethnic Turkish communities are resided. Therefore, the possible impact of these different elements on those communities due to this high level of direct contact deserves scrutiny and this is the aim of this book.

The Path of Scrutiny

The analysis in this book is based on my PhD research conducted between 2011 and 2015 and fieldwork between 2012 and 2014 in Kosovo and Turkey in the scope of which members of the Turkish diplomatic mission, members and representatives of Turkey's religious organisations, and elite members of the local ethnic Turkish community were interviewed. The interviews with both the practitioners of the post-Kemalist foreign policy and it's "receivers" enabled me to trace both the implementation and implications of such policy. Moreover, I consulted documents throughout such as parliamentary records, newspaper archives (*Tan* 1969–99, *Yeni Dönem* 1999–2008, *Kosovaport* 2010–14, *Kosova Haber* 2010–14), locally published monographs, literary books, textbooks, bulletins, journals. Furthermore, for the purpose of understanding more sensitively the norms, values, tacit social rules, culture and daily routines of the ethnic Turkish community, throughout the fieldwork, I visited many places and attended several events. I visited schools which either gave Turkish classes or taught entirely in Turkish to observe how ethnic Turkish students learned about their nationality. To observe Turkey's institutional presence in Kosovo and the ethnic Turkish community's level of attachment to them, I attended the events organised by TIKA or Yunus Emre Institute and often visited the mosques and artefacts which were renovated or re-built (many had been destroyed during the war in the 1990s) by Turkey. I also visited religious groups from Turkey in secular and Qur'anic schools and attended the kermises and halaqa meetings[6] organised by them. All these observations, document analysis and interviews were conducted to seek answers to the below questions inquiring the implications of

Turkey's post-Kemalist approach for Outside Turk communities, in this case those in Kosovo:

1. How have post-Kemalist changes in domestic politics been reflected in Turkey's attitudes towards Outside Turks?
2. How are Turkey's post-Kemalist domestic norms transferred to the Outside Turks locality in Kosovo?
3. How are these norms understood by the Kosovar Turks and what are the implications of these norms on this community?

In responding to these questions, this book is organised into nine chapters. Chapter 1 has introduced the enquiry and outlined the conceptual and practical boundaries of the book. Chapters 2 and 3 elaborate the Kemalist and post-Kemalist Outside Turks policies respectively thus provide the accounts of the past and present of Turkey's policy towards the Outside Turks. Chapter 4 contains the literature upon which the theoretical framework is built on and demonstrates how an analysis of norms can be used to explore the abroad implications and influences of domestic change. Chapter 5 introduces the historical and political context of the Kosovar Turkish locality and provides the accounts of the past and present of Kosovar Turks. Chapters 6, 7 and 8 provide empirical evidence generated from the fieldwork. Chapter 6 elaborates the emergence of post-Kemalist norms concerning Outside Turks and illustrate the ways in which they are translated into foreign policy acts. Chapter 7 explores the post-Kemalist foreign policy's conduct towards the Kosovar Turkish community and looks at the ways in which emergent post-Kemalist norms concerning Outside Turks have been transmitted to the Outside Turks locality in Kosovo. Chapter 8 queries both the implications of post-Kemalist norms on Kosovar Turks and the local responses to them. Chapter 9 summarises the main findings, addresses the research questions, and discusses the wider implications of the findings.

CHAPTER 2

KEMALIST POLICY TOWARDS THE OUTSIDE TURKS

Outside Turks' Reification

The peculiar adventure of the notion of *Outside Turks* began with the territorial shrinking of the Ottoman Empire and the remaining Turkish-speaking communities left outside of this empire before and after its collapse. In the twentieth century, the Ottomans had a history of acting as "protectors" of Muslim communities after territory had been lost to newly independent states. Yet, it was only towards and during World War I that the Ottoman Empire and the intellectual circles within the Empire embarked on political programmes and manifestations aimed at liberating the Turkic communities from imperial domination and creating a bridge between Turkish-speaking communities living inside and outside the country (Landau 1995: 29). Nonetheless, the losses resulting from WWI and the de facto collapse of the Ottoman Empire created novel circumstances under which the "inside" and "outside" demarcation with regard to Turkish-speaking communities was solidified. Ultimately the National Pact of 1920 reified the notion of "Outside Turks" both as a *condition* to be experienced outside Anatolia, as a category of foreign policy, and as communities to be moulded according to the new culture, identity and value-system of the homeland, Turkey (Tüzün 1998: 28). The Republic of Turkey thus was established and its borders were drawn via the act of leaving hundreds of thousands of Turkish-speaking communities outside the borders, while still having a will to intervene in the affairs of those communities. Therefore, the idea of Outside Turks came to depend on three developments: (1) the territorial shrinking of the Ottoman Empire, (2) the building of Turkey as a nation state with an imagined cross-border nation, and (3) the presence of a form of ideology in the "inside" that promoted the transforming of the "now-outsiders", that is, the mainly Turkish-speaking Ottoman remnant communities.

The nineteenth century was for the Ottoman Empire an era of dissolution as Greece, Serbia, Montenegro and Romania became independent states; Bosnia became part of Austro-Hungary; Crimea and the south Caucasus became part of Russia, the North African provinces became colonies of France, Britain and later Italy, and by the early twentieth century Bulgaria and Albania had also become independent states. As a result, on the eve of WWI the Ottomans had control over only Anatolia (including partly the Caucasus), Eastern Thrace and the Arabian Peninsula. This shrinking brought about, on the one hand, the territorial separation of some of the (Turkish-speaking) Muslim inhabited areas of the Ottoman Empire and on the other the mass migration from the *outside* into the *inside*. Immigrants would easily become the *insiders*; yet in dealing with those that remained outside of the country, the Ottoman Empire acted as a legal protector for these newly Muslim minority communities in newly established states. Accordingly, in the London Protocol of 1830 the Ottoman Empire was present as a signatory party and as the *legal protector* of the Muslim communities in the newly established Kingdom of Greece (Tüzün 1998: 11). Later, this was also enshrined in the 1881 Treaty of İstanbul, in the 1913 Treaty of Athens and then finally in the 1923 Treaty of Lausanne.

Concomitant to the territorial shrinking of the Ottoman Empire, the second development that contributed to the reification of the notion of Outside Turks was the surfacing and later institutionalisation of a "Turkist" national thought and its legacy on the new republic and its imagination of a cross-border nation.

The initial thinking of an historically present figure of the "Turk" and the nation it signifies was the product of Turkology studies in the West during the mid-nineteenth century. This generated a considerable inferential influence among the Ottoman elites, intellectual circles and statesmen (Tüzün 1998: 13). The discovery of the early eighth century inscriptions in Orkhon Valley in Mongolia in 1899 further reinforced the idea of the presence of a historical Turkish consciousness and ideal, along with its own language and civilisational trajectory. The "scientific" findings regarding the Turkish language, consequently also inspired and sparked a great deal of interest about the history of the Turks prior to the Ottoman Empire and towards the communities with which the Ottoman Turks arguably had a shared history, language and common ancestry (race) (Isyar 2005: 344). With the "scientific" guidance of the Turkology studies and as part of a 'Turkist awakening", language purification, standardisation, and simplification efforts took place at the behest of Ottoman statesmen and intelligentsia and with it a vast number of publications on Turkish history (pre-Islamic) and language began to appear towards the end of nineteenth century (Gürbüz 2003: 502).

It was however in the early twentieth century that Turkist thought, with its cross-border aspirations, was truly institutionalised. Yet, this was had with the huge influence of Turkic intellectuals in Russia. To this end, as historical records show, the Turkist cultural and political awakening was had very early among the Turkish-speaking intellectuals at the time living under Russian rule (see Landau 1995 and Soysal 2002). They were the first to speak of a Pan-Turkic ideology and the idea of culturally and linguistically uniting the Turkish-speaking communities throughout the continent. It was their promotion of the idea of "Turkism" that highly influenced the intellectual and bureaucratic circles in the Empire. They were, in a sense, filling the transnational gap between the Ottoman elites and the central Asian (in Turkistan) Turkic people that in turn strengthened claims produced by the Turkology studies in the minds of Ottoman intellectual circles.

Their efforts in the linguistic realm were envisaged as a necessary way to bridge the Turkic communities together. This began in earnest thanks to journalistic endeavours and was later followed by efforts to increase the literacy level among the Turkic groups and to unify (thus standardise) the Turkic languages through language reforms. The journals were disseminated throughout the Turkic world (including the Ottoman territories) with İsmail Gaspıralı one of the most prominent figure in this. Gaspıralı was striving to create a united Muslim thus *Turkic* voice in Russia and was holding firm to the motto "unity in language, thought and action". He published a newspaper called *Tercüman (Interpreter)* in Crimea that was also "read in the Ottoman Empire and was often quoted by the Turkish Press" (Gürbüz 2003: 507, Köksal 2010: 200, Turan 2000). Indeed, he was an inspitiring pioneer for the successor Pan-Turkists and his motto became the official motto of many succeeding organisations and publications.

The efforts made through publications (journals, books, booklets and bulletins) later took the form of intellectual collaboration when some of those influential Turkist intellectuals (émigrés) fled to the Ottoman Empire (İstanbul) due to the oppressive nature of the regime in Russia due also to their involvement in the political machinations to awaken an Islamic uprising among Muslims living under the Russian rule (Tüzün 1998: 14). Some of these figures included Şehabettin Mercani of Kazan (1818–89), İsmail Gaspıralı of Crimea (1851–1914), Zerdabi Hasanbey of Baku (1842–1907), Mirza Feth Ali Ahundzade of Sheki/Azerbaijan (1812–78),[1] Yusuf Akçura of Simbirsk/Russia (1876–1935), Ahmed Ağaoğlu of Shusha/Azerbaijan (1869–1939) and Hüseyinzade Ali Turan of Salyan/Azerbaijan (1864–1941) (Tüzün 1998: 14–15). These intellectuals had an important role in reifying both the Turkist mind-set and the notion of "Outside Turks" both in late Ottoman era and later in Republican Turkey. Indeed, some of these figures also participated in the nation- and state-building activities of the Republican governments after 1923 (Soysal 2002).

Therefore, with the involvement of these émigrés, İstanbul became the centre for debates about Turkism; with the support of these intellectuals, Turkist circles began to found associations with several cross-border branches and to publish newspapers with cross-border circulation (Tüzün 1998: 20, Üstel 1996: 53, Üstel 1997, Üstel 2002a, Akçura 1904 (1976)). The first association of this kind was Türk Derneği (The Turkish Association) founded in 1908 in İstanbul and with branches in Rusçuk (now in Bulgaria), Budapest, İzmir and Kastamonu (Gürbüz 2003: 508; Turan 2000). Following this, in 1911 Türk Yurdu Cemiyeti (later Türk Ocağı or Hearth of the Turks) was established and soon became a place of attraction for adherents of Pan-Turkism (Landau 1995: 39). Türk Ocağı began publishing the *Türk Yurdu* as its official journal with an aim to generate a Turkish nationalist spirit and sense of unity in cultural norms initially among the Ottoman Turks, yet had the broader aim of spreading this throughout the Turkic world (Gümüşoğlu 2002: 270). The *Türk Yurdu* was distributed to all Turkic lands so as to disseminate the Pan-Turkist ideal based on an imagined common Turkish culture, history and language (Üstel 1996: 55, Gümüşoğlu 2002). Thus, similar to Gaspıralı's *Tercüman*, the *Türk Yurdu* functioned as a channel to inform Turkic communities about each other's developments (Üstel 1996: 55). To this end, the Türk Ocağı functioned as a sort of "liaison bureau" for the various committees coming from the "Outside Turks" communities into İstanbul (Üstel 2002a: 264). By the same token and with a similar motive, the Committee of Union and Progress (CUP) – a political organisation which political power to rule the Ottoman Empire after 1913 – also displayed a "commitment (as a part of their active propaganda campaign) to the problems of Turkic groups in the Caucasus, Crimea, and Azerbaijan" (Landau 1995: 45). The CUP opened branches in the Caucasus and Turkistan, distributed pamphlets in Afghanistan, in Russian and Chinese Turkistan; and even sent agents (of the secret Teşkilat-ı Mahsusa organisation) to Afghanistan, the Volga region, and Azerbaijan in order "to preach Pan-Turkism", and ordered "Ottoman embassies and consulates ... to take part in this propaganda campaign" (Landau 1995: 50–4). Together with this, the CUP warred in the Caucasus so as to open a corridor between the Ottoman Empire and the Turkic people of Turkistan. The Bolshevik Revolution of 1917 was considered by some in the Ottoman Empire as a chance to realise the Pan-Turkist dream, yet Germany prevented this from happening and the dream was never fulfilled.

To this end, the late Ottoman era witnessed the coming of a new mind-set[2] that aimed at "promoting the solidarity or union of groups physically in different states, but [argued to be] bound to each other by a 'common or kindred language, race, or tradition or by some other postulated tie'" (Landau 1995: 180). Such a frame of mind generated a concern in foreign policy towards the mostly Turkish speaking co-religious communities living abroad, who later on became the members of a cross-border nation (Tüzün 1998: 15). The new republic continued to refer to this "concern" for "co-nationals" abroad after the Liberation War (1920–22). This was the case despite the territorial limits defined in January 1920 by the promulgation of the National Pact (Misak-i Milli) by the last Ottoman Parliament – something which was also embraced by the Turkish Parliament in Ankara in April 1920.

Accordingly, as noted above, in the Treaty of Lausanne (1923) Turkey was an official legal protector in Western Thrace and Hatay.[3] Right after the signing of the treaty, moreover, Turkey embarked on population exchanges with Greece, in the scope of which the Turkish-speaking residents of Greece were sent to Turkey in return for Greeks living in Anatolia who were sent to Greece. With a similar motive, in 1925 Turkey signed agreements[4] with Bulgaria and Yugoslavia to facilitate the migration of Turkish-speaking communities to Turkey. The new republic was, in this sense, "a more welcoming harbour than the Ottoman Empire had ever been" (Eissenstat 2001: 44).

Pan-Turkism's contributions to the reification of the notion of Outside Turks cannot be ignored, as it shaped the "cognitive maps" of intellectuals and statesmen in the Ottoman Empire and later Turkey towards co-national Turks left outside the country. Nonetheless, the official position after the establishment of Turkey with its cross-border nation was however never built on the idea of Pan-Turkism, since this would imply irredentist aims.[5] With the establishment of Turkey, in this fashion, the building of outside Turks and the development of relevant policies was based rather on seeing Turkey as a homeland for the Turkish nation and the outside Turks as a sort of cultural extension which would be moulded according to the new culture in the homeland. The third development which led to the idea of Outside Turks gaining currency in Turkey, therefore, is the presence of a transformative motive towards the Turkish-speaking Ottoman remnant communities. Turkey thus worked to socialise Turkish-speaking communities into Kemalist principles and to secure the parallel development of their national identities to mirror the homeland. This was an alternative to pan-Turkist path of working to unite all Turkic people yet involved intervening into the affairs of Outside Turks.[6]

Based on the third motive, therefore, the early Kemalist era will to intervene and its endeavours to 'tune in' these communities to developments inside Turkey were the result of a stance which aimed to both "buil[d] its own identity, [while also] aim[ing] at transforming the 'Outside Turks' accordingly" (Karadeniz 2011: 345). In this sense, in the scope of building for itself a new identity, the founding Kemalist cadre launched a nation-building project in Turkey in the scope of which both the geography and the people within the borders of the new country were re-imagined. While Anatolia was imagined as ancient Turkish territory, the "Islamic-Turkish-Self" was redefined and rebuilt as a National-Turkish-Self (Zürcher 1999, Kutay 1993: 102–3). Society was to be moulded, indoctrinated and engineered accordingly. This nation-building project, however, did not confine itself within the borders of Turkey and Turkish-speaking Ottoman remnants were also targeted. Outside Turks communities, in this fashion, "operate[d] as a cultural-political extension of the mainland" (Uzer 2010: 111). This was necessary to secure parallel development of their national identity in their "home" abroad. It was on this basis that the Outside Turks were asked to emulate and adopt the Kemalist principles of the revolution – that is the value-added representations of the "new" Turk created in Turkey by Kemalist rulers. This nationalist framing and moulding is admitted by Tevfik Rüştü Aras, Minister of Foreign Affairs, in a parliamentary speech delivered on 18 June 1932:

> another notion that can be said as unique to Mustafa Kemal's Turkey's foreign policy is that its domestic and foreign affairs are the same. It is nationalist both in domestic affairs and foreign affairs .... We mean, we do not have separate policies, Turkey does not have two voices on this regard. It is the same in both domestic and foreign realms ... [To this end] protecting the culture of our citizens outside the borders [Outside Turks], sustaining their attachment to the homeland, [and] protecting and safeguarding their well-being are our duty.
>
> (Tevfik Rüştü Aras 1932: 166)

As argued by Aras, Turkey was in the business of building inside and outside Turks in a simultaneous manner. Regardless of the ideological positioning of the government, however, such a motive has always been present in Turkey. During and after the Kemalist rule, despite the changes in ideological orientation of the policy makers, governments have spent efforts to mould the Outside Turks according to the new culture, identity and value-system of the homeland.

As a final point, it should be noted that the clarity of the concept of "Outside Turks" was not always straightforward. This is because the meaning of "Outside Turks" has been blurred historically due to the internal imprecision of to whom the state (both Ottoman Empire and Turkey) calls "Turk", to the diversity of the Turkic people towards whom nationalistic claims were attributed to, and to the formation of vast Turkish labour-migrant communities throughout Europe by the 1960s.

Accordingly, firstly, during the Ottoman Empire period, "the Turk" as a communal identification, mostly lacked an ethnic connotation.

The term referred mostly to a religio-cultural identity. By the time of the new Republic, however, the Kemalist regime attributed an ethnic meaning to "Turk" and asked Turkish-speaking communities to do so, too. In line with this, Turkey accepted their migration to Turkey, yet also accepted along with ethnic Turks from Bulgaria or Macedonia, Muslim Albanians, Bosniaks and Torbeshis from Yugoslavia which were all granted Turkish citizenship (Kadirbeyoglu 2009, Çağaptay 2001). They were considered as suitable for "Turkification", yet this was not the case for all of the remnant communities, as Albanians, Bosnians or Torbeshis were not considered part of Outside Turks. We see a reverse motive only by the 1990s as the ethnic diversity of the meaning of "Outside Turks" was discovered.

The second blurring factor has been the idea of uniting the Turkic world (in the name of the Turkish race) despite its diversity in terms of ethnicity, religion, geography, dialect and historical experience. The simultaneous presence of multiple and sometimes competing Turkish nationalisms[7] and their selective appeal to these *determinants* has generated competing discourses, missions and projects – yet this diversity in nationalisms did not strengthen the formulation of the policies. On the contrary, the competing nationalisms embarked on different determinants (ethnicity, religion, geography, dialect or historical experience) of the Turkic world hence the subjects of the policy and its extent have kept changing. For the Pan-Turkists, for instance, the "racially" Turkic people of Turkistan, the Caucasus and East Europe (including the Turkish-speaking Christian Gagauz of Romania) were the addressee of the concept during WWI, WWII and at the end of the Cold War. On the other hand, the governments or official bodies (both Kemalist and post-Kemalist governments) in Turkey have traditionally curtailed the scope of their Outside Turks policy to the Ottoman Balkans and Cyprus as the initial sphere of activity and responsibility.

To this end, the connotation of the concept of Outside Turks became an issue of dispute. The *Outside Turks* is the literal translation of its Turkish equivalent *Dış Türkler*. The *dış* means "the outside" and semantically denotes the presence of a distinction between the insider and the outsider. The above-mentioned Pan-Turkists have constantly argued that *Outside Turks* have been ruled out by the Turkish governments because they have historically been regarded as *the outsider* and thus their status will not change until they are united to the homeland and become *insiders*.[8]

The official policy circles however most of time confronted such complaints by arguing that Turkey takes good care of its kin communities everywhere.

The final blurring factor is the mass labour migration from Turkey to Europe by the 1960s. When their numbers reached the millions, they were incorporated into the scope of Outside Turks by various governments (Karadeniz 2011). Yet labour-migrants of Turkish-descent in Europe have been the least developed category under the notion of Outside Turks.

In sum, the aforementioned developments in the development of the Outside Turks and the 'blurring points' have altogether worked to reify Outside Turks. Today, the notion of *Outside Turks* designates three distinct communities, as the Constitution of Turkey's Presidency for Turks Abroad and Related Communities suggests: Turkish citizens living abroad (*Türk vatandaşları*), ethnic Turkish communities living outside Turkey (*soydaşlar*), and kin communities living in the Balkans, Caucasus and Central Asia (*akraba topluluklar*[9]) (*Turkish Official Gazette*, 06/04/2010: Article 5978). In line with this division, the communities I am referring to as *Outside Turks* are the second category of people: ethnic Turkish communities (*soydaşlar*) living in the Balkans and Cyprus who declare themselves as Turkish-by-blood, speak the Turkish language in daily life, chose education in the Turkish language for their children, possess Turkish culture, have strong attachment to the Ottoman past and are recognised by Turkey as ethnic Turks. They practise their ethnicity in their literary writings, cultural events, education and the media. Practising Turkishness, for them, is a way to protect their identity and to sustain a sense of belonging to a cross-border nation.[10]

Kemalist Approach to Outside Turks

In the new Republic, the will to intervene in the "now-outside-Turkish" remnant communities was in a broader sense generated by three distinct motives. In the first instance, Turkey signed agreements with several countries to facilitate the immigration of Muslim communities to Turkey, resulted from the responsibility Turkey bore towards the former subjects of the Empire. The second motive was Pan-Turkist ideals. Pan-Turkism however found minor place in official policy formation and it was overwhelmingly restricted to ultra-nationalist circles. As has already been introduced above, in the new Republic, the most consequential and constitutive motive for intervening in the "now-outside-Turkish" remnant communities was introducing the Kemalist project underway in Turkey to Turkish-speaking Muslim communities, something which was particularly influential in the Balkans and was generated by a belief that Outside Turks communities are the cultural–political extension of Turkey. Accordingly, via the process of asking Outside Turks to adopt Kemalist principles, the "new Turk" created in Turkey was intended to be rebuilt abroad. This new Turk was secular in daily life, public appearance and education; s/he was nationalist in education, language and history; ethnically conscious and acting in a nationalist manner; and had a sense of belonging to the new Turkish state rather than to the caliphate or sultanate. In making Outside Turks communities emulate this new model of Turkishness, the state sought to transform the Islamically conscious communities into communities which thought "nationally" and employed several instruments to do so. These included diplomatic missions, financial aid and equipment or Kemalist missionaries (*Kemal's teachers*) with these mostly targeting education and the media to achieve such transformation.

In education, the focus was initially on building schools which taught Turkish and which adopted the Latin script (Boyar and Fleet 2008: 781, İsmail 2001b). In this vein, while Turkey funded the building of new Turkish schools in Romania, Turkish primary and high schools "which taught along Kemalist lines" in Bulgaria, Romania, Cyprus and Greece were mainly supplied with textbooks and education materials (Köksal 2010: 207, Anzerlioğlu 2006: 45, Köstüklü 2011: 537, Dağıstan 2002). Moreover, in Bulgaria, Turkey's diplomatic mission approached the government "in a friendly manner" to convince them to officially change the alphabet from Arabic to Latin in Turkish schools (Boyar and Fleet 2008: 781, Köksal 2010: 207). This effort yielded a result a year later and in 1930 the Bulgarian government circumscribed the use of Arabic script in schools, though this was in effect only until 1934 (Boyar and Fleet 2008: 781). In Romania, the Turkish Ambassador, Hamdullah Suphi, in exactly the same manner, negotiated with the Romanian Ministry of Education to replace the Arabic alphabet used in Turkish community with the Latin alphabet (Anzerlioğlu 2006: 32). He also requested from the ministry that Turkish history classes were included in the curricula of Turkish schools (Ibid.: 32). In a similar vein, as admitted by the Romanian Army's Chief of General Staff, it was the Turkish ambassador from whom they learned that the Orthodox Christian Gagauz people settled in Romania were not Bulgarians but Turks in origin (Ibid.: 45). Similar notices were given to the Ministry of Education in Romania through which Gagauz students' entrance to Turkish schools was facilitated (Ibid.: 45). A parallel energy was expended by the diplomatic missions to enable the opening of more Turkish schools in countries where Outside Turks were settled (Ibid.: 45). Moreover, as further motivation, gifts were personally sent by Mustafa Kemal to Turkish schools, as was the case in Romania for instance (Hablemitoğlu 1999).

Moreover, the Kemalist transformation of Outside Turks communities was also attempted via "Kemal's teachers" (*Kemal'in Öğretmenleri*) who were sent to Bulgaria, Greece, Cyprus and Yugoslavia (Hablemitoğlu 1999, Sonyel 1995: 176, İsmail 2001b). For instance, in Romania alone, Turkey sent 80 primary school teachers who had knowledge of Romanian (Hablemitoğlu 1999, Anzerlioğlu 2006: 39, 47). These teachers built new schools and introduced Kemalist principles to the community first hand, similar to the work being done by diplomatic missions. In addition to sending missionary teachers, Turkey also provided local teachers among Outside Turks with training possibilities in Turkey on the new alphabet and Kemalist reforms. For instance in 1928, Turkish teachers from Razgard, Bulgaria, participated in a week-long training workshop in Turkey (Özdemir 1999: 185). Similarly, Turkey gave bursaries for children of Outside Turks so that they could be educated in Turkey. Hamdullah Suphi personally sent more than 400 children from Romania to İstanbul for education purposes (Hablemitoğlu 1999, Anzerlioğlu 2006: 38). Students from Cyprus, Bulgaria and Greece were also granted similar bursaries (Akgün 2006: 3, İsmail 2001a).

Nonetheless, Kemalist Turkey was more prone to funding media as these were seen "as easy and influential devices for spreading reformist and secular [Kemalist] ideas to the public" and "a more powerful weapon in any campaign against its opponents" (Köksal 2010: 207). In this vein, "the newspapers of the pro-Kemalists among the Turkish minorit[ies]" were heavily subsidised[11] and when considered necessary, newspapers were "forcefully encouraged" to print using the Latin alphabet (Boyar and Fleet 2008: 782). In the scope of this policy, for instance "the Turkish government provided Latin typeface to *Rehber* [newspaper] on the order of the Prime Minister" as early as 1928 in the case of Bulgaria (Ibid.). Similarly, in Cyprus, the pro-Kemalist paper *Söz* was sent Latin typefaces in 1929 (Keser 2007: 59).

In line with attempts at "tuning in" Outside Turks to the homeland, Turkey's diplomatic missions also began to celebrate Turkey's newly created national holidays. 1925 marks the first time Turkey's consulate in Cyprus organised celebrations for "Republic Day" (29 October) and Turkey's "National Sovereignty and Children's Day" (23 April) (İsmail 2001a). The Consul was also secretly providing schools and Turkish associations with Turkish flags to be used during these celebrations (Keser 2007: 58).

Furthermore, the diplomatic missions introduced the many enemies of the regime in Turkey to Outside Turks localities. In other words, the enemies of the state now became the enemies of the Outside Turks. These included the *Yüzellilikler*, who had fled to surrounding countries when the new regime led by Mustafa Kemal had denaturalised them, accusing them of being traitors who acted against the Anatolian government during the Liberation War (Erdeha 1998). Turkish government and the pro-Kemalist local Turkish community members worked in collaboration against *Yüzellilikler*'s presence in Greece, Bulgaria, Romania and Cyprus and made requests from the respective governments for the removal of "anti-Kemalist figures" from their countries (Boyar and Fleet 2008: 778–80, Öksüz 2001: 7, Demiryürek 2003: 2). Among the *Yüzellilikler* Sait Molla, one of the founders of the Friends of England Society (İngiliz Muhipler Cemiyeti), went first to Romania while Turkey's acting ambassador in Bucharest requested from Romanian officials that they force Sait to leave the country (Demiryürek 2003: 2). Sait Molla encountered a similar fate when he moved to Cyprus in May 1925 (Ibid.: 2). As Sait argued in his letters to British officials on the island, Turkey's consul in Cyprus was waging a propaganda war against him and calling him the "foe" of the Turkish nation and thus the Kemalist regime (Ibid.: 3). Such policies from Turkey were documented in the 1930 *Residence, Trade and Navigation Agreement* signed between Turkey and Greece when, as per the agreement, Greece agreed to deport 13 members of *Yüzellilikler* residing in the country (Öksüz 2001: 8).

Turkey's transformative involvements among the remnant Ottoman communities who spoke Turkish was also documented by secret service reports. In the example of Bulgaria, a secret report prepared in 1934 reveals that:

> Kemalist Turkey was ... wishing to spread chauvinistic nationalism among the approximately 600,000 Turkish Muslims in Bulgaria and aiming to create a Turkish minority which would be blindly loyal to Ankara and under Turkish control. Turkish newspapers published in Bulgaria and financially supported by the Turkish embassy, and Kemalist music and sport clubs were used to disseminate these ideas.
>
> (Boyar and Fleet 2005: 120)

Another report prepared in the same year by the Press Office of the Bulgarian Foreign Ministry stated that:

> Until recently Kemalist Turkey had been spreading propaganda in Bulgaria, Greece and Rumania in order to protect itself from reactionary Muslim Turkish circles in these countries, a Turkish policy which the Balkan states could ... tolerate.
>
> (Ibid.: 120)

The use of Kemalist propaganda in Turkish foreign policy was also noted by officials in Greece, as illustrated by the press reports on foreign espionage activities. As Boyar and Fleet report:

> Turkish espionage was wide spread, and was based in the Pireaus, Thessaloniki, Mitylene and Komotini, and controlled from İstanbul. Such propaganda activity was particularly active among the Turkish minority in Thrace whose nationalist spirit was kept aflame by propaganda material supplied to it from Turkey. Turkish newspapers published in Greece were spreading Kemalism and were striving to keep the Turkish minority immune from Greek influence.
>
> (2005: 120)

Turkey's policies were proving Bulgaria and Greece right in their claims about its involvements in their respective countries' affairs. To this end, in one instance Turkey sent "80 kilos of Turkish letters [typefaces]" for the use of The Bulgarian Turan Society though it "said [to the Society that] they will be sent to the embassy and be labelled as 'furniture'" (Boyar and Fleet 2008: 784). The secrecy shrouding Turkey's actions here gives a clue about its broader policies and concerns for "ensur[ing] that Muslims embraced the ideas of the new Turkish Republic" (Köksal 2010: 196)

In addition to Turkey's own state efforts, local community members joined efforts to socialise the community in Kemalist principles. In Bulgaria, for instance, "the Teachers' Union attempted to strengthen Turkish identity based on educational reforms, in line with Turkey's secular reforms" and decided to adopt Latin scripts in all Turkish schools throughout the country as early as July 1928 (Köksal 2010: 204). Additionally, newspapers such as *Halk Sesi, Rodop, Deliorman, Özdilek* were also involved in promoting Kemalist principals (Boyar and Fleet 2008: 777–84). A backlash followed however as pro-Islamic, pro-Ottoman and pro-Caliphate intellectuals among the Turkish-speaking community tried to "eliminate Kemalist influence" among the Muslim community (Köksal 2010: 206) through keeping "the Bulgarian Turks away from any Kemalist influence" (Boyar and Fleet 2008: 776). To them, the "adoption of the Latin script was synonymous with [the] acceptance of the new Kemalist approach" (Ibid.: 776). Therefore, to prevent Kemalist "indoctrination" of the community, they stood against Turkish schools and newspapers which adopted the Latin alphabet and started publishing a newspaper called *Medeniyet* (civilisation) using the Arabic script. They, moreover, initiated "a vigorous campaign for the re-introduction of the Arabic script in the schools which had begun teaching in the new alphabet, and from 1934 Bulgarian Turkish schools began to revert to the old script" (Ibid.: 777).

In Cyprus, however, "the legion of teachers" (*öğretmen ordusu*) allied with journalists to begin a campaign to introduce Latin alphabet and to wear western apparels as soon as Turkey had legislated on these issues. They also began using family names when it was introduced in Turkey in 1934, and made the call to prayer (*adhan*) in Turkish when the Kemalist regime had placed a ban on the call Arabic in 1932 (Keser 2007: 60–2, Özdemir 1999: 193, Nevzat 2005: 348, Bozkurt 1998). Moreover, both local teachers and *Kemal's teachers* went to even the most remote of places on the island to "educate Turkish Cypriots to become nationally aware, modern, progressive, and Kemalist persons" (Nesim 1989: 339). Among the pro-Kemalist papers, *Ses* made the so-called "Six Arrows"[12] its emblem and promoted them constantly (Akgün 2006: 5). Similarly, it persistently stood against the hijab (headscarves) and called women on the island to cast off this "vicious custom" (Ibid.: 9; also see Özdemir 1999: 182). Likewise, they welcomed circumscribing the religious judiciary and supported the "adaptation of the Kemalist Civil Law in Cyprus" (Akgün 2006: 10). Even here however, as in Bulgaria, there was a fierce anti-Kemalist resistance against the Latin alphabet, Kemalist clothing codes, secular education, reciting call to prayer in Turkish and even the use of *ethnic Turk* as a communal identity, all of which were routinely opposed.[13] Despite this resistance however, "Ankara's intimate concern ... [on] education, language, and culture solidified Turkish people's commitment to Turkey and facilitated the internalisation of the Atatürk's reforms in Cyprus" (Akgün 2006: 15). Thus soon "Kemalism became apparent in every aspect of life within the Turkish Cypriot community" (Xupolia 2011: 116).

In Romania, as Hamdullah Suphi notes in a 1934 report to the Ministry of Foreign Affairs of Turkey, these policies were more successful and "Turkish consciousness commenced to become grounded" among both the Christian Gagauz Turks and the Muslim Turks (Anzerlioğlu 2006: 45). Kemalist principles and the identity it espoused were shown acceptance and the new Turkish version of history, which viewed Anatolia as the "fatherland of the Turks", were firmly accepted. Many communities here worked closely with the diplomatic mission and Kemal's teachers. There was some resistance among Muslims who opposed the Kemalist reforms and who also "conducted a propaganda campaign against the adoption of the Latin alphabet" (Boyar and Fleet 2008: 781). Their effort yet was very ineffective.

As for Greece, it was both the teachers and the media which worked closely with Turkey's diplomatic mission to spread Kemalist principles. For instance, the newspaper *Inkilap* was heavily involved in propagating the idea that "learning the new alphabet is the first and the foremost mission of the modern Turk" and joined the Kemalist teachers in working to increase the use of Latin alphabet among the Turkish community (Öksüz 2001: 4). However, pro-Kemalist involvements was not always welcomed by religiously motivated anti-Kemalists and these there ultimately emerged hostility against anything related to Kemalism in Greece (Oran 1991: 297–8). Similar to what was happening in Bulgaria, the *Yüzellilikler* in Greece were also standing against the adoption of Kemalist norms, lining with the conservatives in the society and backing them (Onsunoğlu 2012, Öksüz 2001: 6–7). There then developed a struggle over control of education institutions and both sides attacked each other via the press. Despite these contestations, in the long run the Kemalists gained the upper hand and managed to take control of both the press and education.

In sum, despite instances of fierce resistances, due to continuous support from Turkey and its concern for spreading the Kemalist model of Turkishness to Outside Turks communities, this was mostly adopted in the Balkans too. Kemalism became visible in their use of language, ethnic representation, cultural practices, religious practices, self-identification, national celebrations, teacher training programmes, schooling and clothing.

This campaign by Turkey continued more or less with the same vigour even after the death of Kemal, hence, the "Kemalist state identity" continued to force governments to promote Kemalist visions of Turkish history, language and culture among the Outside Turks communities (Uzer 2010: 106, 148). Outside Turks, therefore, continued to be a cultural extension of the mainland during the Cold War era. The novel political experiences of these communities – exposed to communist regimes in the Balkans and the decolonisation move in Cyprus – did not change this. Various governments from Turkey did not consider socialism or decolonisation as direct threats to the existence of Turks outside Turkey as long as these communities were recognised as ethnically distinct and their rights were protected. In this sense, while Turkey was welcoming of the decision to legally recognise the ethnic rights of Turkish communities in those states, it was not particularly concerned with obstacles placed by those same states on religious practices. In a similar fashion, the governments in Turkey did not dwell on the rhetoric of "captive" Turk's coming from Pan-Turkists. This was the idea that Turkic and Turkish-speaking communities were living under oppressive Communist governments throughout Central Asia, the Caucasus and the Balkans and described as waiting for Turkey's help so that they can be liberated (Ayan 2011, Landau 1995: 148). Rather, Turkey's governments denounced the irredentist demands and the calls of both far-right nationalists and Pan-Turkists (Landau 1995: 187, 189). Therefore, Turkey's desire to intervene in Outside Turks communities was derived from its concern to promote their ethnic identity in countries they resided in and not from Pan-Turkist aspirations (Uzer 2010: 106, Karadeniz 2011: 215–40).

In Cyprus, due to Britain's inability to peacefully end its mandate and due to Greek Cypriots' aims of ending colonial rule and unifying with Greece, the Greek and Turkish Cypriots were initially engaged in political and later military confrontations. For the ethnic Turkish community this led to fervent nationalism, something which Kemalists used to take further control of the politics of this community (Beckingham 1957: 8, Xupolia 2011: 116). The Kemalist elites of the island, in this fashion, organised a counter-fight against the Greek Cypriots, yet, which in return gave them a chance to increase the nationalist appeals among the Turkish community through forcefully imposing nationalist and ethnic practices of "Turkishness". This fight was aided both politically and militarily – indeed supervised – by Turkey (Kızılyürek 2002: 337, Yiğit-Yüksel 2009: 177–80, Uzer 2010: 124).[14] To keep the community bounded and ethnically self-aware, these Kemalist political and military bodies, for instance, ran a *Citizen Speak Turkish* campaign, similar to the one prevalent in Turkey in 1930s, which encouraged people to speak in Turkish while "those who spoke Greek" were punished (Kızılyürek and Gautier-Kızılyürek 2004: 46). The Kemalist elite established a "Department for People's Education", which was in charge of homogenising the community in terms of language and of mobilising the community through language education "based on the same curriculum as that of Turkey" (Kızılyürek and Gautier Kızılyürek 2004: 46). Öz Türkçe (pure Turkish) was among the institutionalised Kemalist norms in the scope of which "[b]rand new Turkish names, often with nationalist connotations, were given to villages and towns where Turkish Cypriots lived" (Kızılyürek and Gautier Kızılyürek 2004: 47). This was not limited to place names, people's names and local businesses escutcheons (which were previously either Arabic/Persian or Greek) – they were all replaced with "pure" Turkish names (Kızılyürek 2002: 338, Hatay 2008: 149). They, moreover, introduced campaigns of economic nationalism which they called "from Turk to Turk"[15] which meant that the Turkish community's economic relations with Greeks was cut and followed by measures to cut all forms of relations between the two communities – including visits to Greek pubs and cafes (Kızılyürek 2002: 337). It was this same motive which led the Kemalist elite to create a brand new policy forcing mosques to call the adhan, or call to prayer, in Turkish rather than Arabic up until the 1970s, though it was changed to Arabic original in the 1950s in Turkey (Nevzat and Hatay 2009: 922, Beckingham, 1957: 83). All these imply an attempt by the nationalist secular elites to take control of the community and its representation long before Turkey's military intervention into the island.

Turkey's military intervention (that is, "invasion" according to Greeks and "peace operation" according to the Turks) in 1974 led eventually to the establishment of a de facto independent state in the northern part of the island in 1983, namely the Turkish Republic of North Cyprus (KKTC), something which progressed the Kemalist project massively. Accordingly, right after Turkey's military landed on the island in 1974, population exchanges began to take place and northern Cyprus was gradually homogenised (with Turks) (Uzer 2010: 135–6). Turkey's Kemalist education system was adopted in the KKTC and Islam was dropped from history books and from the names of schools (Killoran 1998: 187, Bizden 1997). Mustafa Kemal's name was given to many schools, stadiums, streets and his monuments were erected all over the new, internationally non-recognised but de-facto republic. Indeed, as a following move, "[a]ll geographical names [were] immediately [officially] changed into Turkish ones. The landscape was transformed into Turkish territory. Slogans like 'how happy to say I'm a Turk' and Turkish flags decorated the mountains and hills of north Cyprus" (Hatay 2008: 150). The national days of Turkey became official celebrations, Turkey's national anthem was adopted as the national anthem of the new Turkish state,[16] children in the schools started reciting *Our Pledge*,[17] and the Kemalist principles were made part of the constitution (Bizden 1997). For instance, the preamble to the KKTC Constitution stated that the republic will remain "faithful to the Principles of Atatürk" (KKTC Constitution). Article 59 also states that "the state shall carry out this duty [educational and training needs of the people] in accordance with the principles and reforms of Atatürk" (KKTC Constitution). Likewise, Article 71 states that "[t]he rules, programmes and activities of political parties shall not violate the ... principles of a democratic and secular Republic and the principles of Atatürk" (KKTC Constitution). Similarly, MPs and the president have to declare their commitment to Kemalist principles when taking the oath (Article 82 and Article 100) (KKTC Constitution). All these confirm a local scholars assertion on the issue that Turkish Cypriots "were often more successful in adopting Atatürk's reforms than their motherland itself" (Nevzat 2005: 346).

In Greece, the dispute between secular Kemalist nationalists and Islamist conservatives continued because the interwar period of contention was left unresolved and, secondly, because the transfer of Kemalist principle to Greece continued during the Cold War period as well. In the Democrat Party era in Turkey (1950–60), the anti-religious norms of Kemalism were somewhat softened. This had an influence on the existing contention between the pro-Kemalists and anti-Kemalists in Greece, similar to what happened in Cyprus in 1953. For instance, in the late 1940s and early 1950s pro-Kemalists propagated the idea of writing the Qur'an in Turkish letters (Latin script). As can be expected, this argument encountered fierce opposition from Islamically motivated part of the community and hence anti-Kemalist conservative Turks form Greece requested from the Presidency of Religious Affairs in Turkey (Diyanet) a "fatwa" (or religious opinion) on the merits of the Kemalist arguments being made in Greece. The fatwa given by Diyanet held that the Qur'an could not be written in the Turkish scripts and should remain in Arabic. This fatwa, an open religious and anti-Kemalist norm, was used by conservatives against pro-Kemalists in Greece in order for demonstrate the latter's infidelity and inconsistency with the motherland (Özdemir 1999: 198). However, this was far from being an adequate challenge to Kemalist dominance among the Turkish elite in Greece. This was because of the fact that the demands of Muslim conservative, such as changing the holidays from Sunday to Friday and the alphabet from Latin to Arabic scripts, had no chance of gaining a foothold among many in society (Ibid.).

Post-war political circumstances drove members of both parties to strive in their attempts to socialise the community into accepting their respective principles. The pro-Kemalist secular and nationalist groups within the community, overwhelmingly represented by teachers and journalists, continued to work for the cause of a secular Turkish nationalism, while the religiously motivated anti-Kemalist Turks continued to resist Kemalist institutional (associations, schools and newspapers) hegemony within the community. The publication of Turkish weekly papers, bulletins or journals in Turkish but with the use of Arabic scripts continued even until 1970s (*Hak Yol* 1948–52; *Peygamber Binası* 1957–66, *Isbat* 1971 onwards). This is a clear case of the continued contestation and contention between pro-Kemalists and conservatives regarding the dominant norms of the community (Popovic 1995: 351–3). In fact, the secular nationalist press was not silent, their publications – those that aimed to give a national character to the Muslim minority – were not only fighting against the "bigotry of the conservatives", but also provided society with secular and nationalist literary knowledge to increase a sense of nationalism. There were also some conservative journals who adopted the Latin scripts by 1950s onward, which suggests at least the partial triumph of secular Kemalist norms (Popovic 1995: 353).

As part of its Kemalist policy and its emphasis on *soydaş* (those of the same race), Turkey continued promoting the national development of the community during the Cold War era. In this fashion, Turkey continued sending teachers to teach in Turkish schools[18] despite Greece setting up "a special teacher-training centre for Turks ... in Thessaloniki [in 1968] to replace the teachers who had come from Turkey ... [and] to sever links between the minority and Turkey" (Poulton 1997: 86). Greece therefore could not succeeded in cutting Turkish community's ties with Turkey. Nonetheless, the developments in Cyprus and Turkey's military intervention had adverse and even destructive effects on Turks in Greece (Popovic 1995: 347, Özdemir 1999: 197). In response and as part of a deliberately repressive campaign, the Greek authorities replaced Turkish place names with Greek ones, the use of Turkish names was officially banned and the number of Turkish schools gradually declined; moreover, Turkish religious leaders and waqfs (charitable institutions) were exposed to official pressures, and the ethnic identity of Turks was denied legally and in official historiography (Küçükcan 1999: 61–2, Oran 1991: 121, Karadeniz 2011: 147–9, Poulton 1997: 86). These policies, however, were counter-productive and together with Turkey's continuous promotion of a Turkish national identity, ethnic Turks in Greece grabbed firmly to Kemalist principles meaning that their nationalist appeals were further reified. Turkey at this point built more intense and cooperative relations with the secular nationalist elites of the community and favoured the use of "Turk" not "Muslim" as a communal identification for the community, while the pro-Islamists were happy to continuing using "Muslim" as an identification.

In Bulgaria, by the 1950s and 1960s, the religiously conscious Turkish-speaking community that had existed in the 1930s had been transformed into an "ethnically conscious Turkish minority" (Höpken 1997: 61). The Communist regime in Bulgaria at the time was facilitative of this process and "officially supported the development of Turkish language and culture" (Eminov 1986: 506). In this sense, not forgetting the mass migration of Turkish people to Turkey in 1950–1, "[t]he number of Turkish schools increased dramatically, while periodicals and newspapers were published in all the main cities inhabited by Turks. Local Turkish literature began to emerge, along with the language and culture of the Turks in Bulgaria" (Karpat 1995: 733). Needless to say, the literature was in the new "purified" Turkish language and greatly influenced by Turkey's secular, Kemalist and socialist literary writings (Buttanrı 2005: 33–6). While promoting ethnicity, the Communist regime in Bulgaria was intolerant toward religion and prohibited religious practices and the teaching of the Qur'an in the 1960s and 1970s (Küçükcan 1999: 57, Bojkov 2004: 353). Turkey was silent towards the repressive Communist regime's moves and soon the regime's intolerance towards religiosity turned into an attempt to undermine ethnicity. Accordingly, Turkish education was banned and Turks were forced to assume Bulgarian names, their linguistic and cultural institutions were closed down and national festivals were banned. Only then did Turkey heavily criticise the Bulgarian government and began to assist the Turkish community to seek their rights in the international arena (Bulgarian Helsinki Committee 2003). Finally, when this intolerance resulted in the forceful mass exodus of some 340,000 people in 1989, Turkey welcomed these communities with open arms (Karpat 1995: 725).

In short, during the Kemalist era and through alternating Pan-Turkist calls, the Outside Turks have been dealt with via a nationalist policy agenda in that Turkey was concerned with tuning in these communities with the Kemalist developments in the "homeland". Accordingly, they were imagined as co-nationals (rather than co-religionists) who should to be moulded in line with Kemalist principles and norms. This was seen as crucial for the development of their national identity in their "home abroad". This Kemalist approach to Outside Turks communities continued until the late 1980s and resulted in the creation of ethnic Turkish communities in the Balkans and Cyprus with bold secular nationalist sentiments (other than religious) who firmly committed to Kemalist principles and imagination of history, language, culture and religion. Nonetheless, the gradual changes taking place in Turkey along post-Kemalist lines by the 1990s onwards and the following cultural and religious orientations forced Outside Turks alike to reconsider their identities, values, beliefs and cultures.

CHAPTER 3

POST-KEMALIST POLICY
TOWARDS THE OUTSIDE TURKS

The Post-Kemalist Turn of Turkey

'Post-Kemalist Turkey' has long been used to distinguish the periods
before and after the death of Kemal Atatürk in various fields of research
such as history, politics and even architecture (for instance see Feroze
1976, Kreiser 2002). The phrase, nonetheless, started denoting Turkey's
shift (or signs of shift) from the Kemalist path and creed by the 1990s
when Necmettin Erbakan's pro-Islamic government intended to open
more space for Islamic political voices in the country. In this sense,
Erbakan's pro-Islamic government was the first rigid political
manifestation of a post-Kemalist rule. Yet even before Erbakan, Turgut
Özal had planted the seeds necessary to transform Kemalist Turkey into
a post-Kemalist state. He did this via political means and through his
attempt to institutionalise neo-liberal and pro-Ottoman policies.
Without a doubt, the meanings that post-Kemalism connotes depend on
the actors introducing such practices. Therefore, Özal's and Erbakan's
post-Kemalisms were quite different; while the latter was an Islamic
attempt to replace secular Kemalism, the former was a liberal and
multiculturalism oriented one. Again, while Erbakan focused on the idea
of the global Muslim ummah, the Motherland Party of Özal had a strong
element of nationalism within the party. An unprecedented campaign to
dismantle Kemalism and Kemalist Turkey, however, has emerged only
with the ascent of the Justice and Development Party (JDP). It was
JDP's commitment to transform the country and its landslide electoral

victories in 2002, 2007 and 2011 which enabled them to do so (Şahin 2010: 169, Tüfekçi 2016a). JDP built its post-Kemalism chiefly on liberal and emancipatory values (backed by neo-liberal economic policies, a focus on discourses of Turkey's Ottoman legacy and EU-oriented political reforms). This further advanced the position Özal had taken, while softening the pro-Islamic posture associated with the JDP's predecessors.[1] It was within the scope of this shift that Turkey has fallen into disputes over the common values and boundaries of Turkish nation and national identity, and robust alternative conceptualisations of the basic building blocks of Turkish state and identity have surfaced. This is also the juncture where post-Kemalist Turkey mostly departed from the dominant Kemalist political frames in terms of state–society relations and in imagining societal links outside Turkey. The shift in approach to Outside Turks therefore has been had within the scope of this broader post-Kemalist turn in domestic politics.

To explain the post-Kemalist transformation of the country, a prominent researcher on Turkish politics, Soner Çağaptay, asserts that:

Kemalism appears to have lost its influence, not just symbolically but also politically ... The JDP, representing a brand of Islam-based social conservatism, has since replaced Turkey's former Kemalist ideology and secular elites. Turkey seems to be moving to a post-Kemalist era.

(Çağaptay 2012b)

In a similar manner, a leading liberal writer, Mustafa Akyol, argues that:

It would be fair to say that Turkey is now in a post-Kemalist phase, in which Kemalism is ceasing to be the dominant ideology, and is becoming one of the many competing ones.

(Akyol 2013)

Therefore, Kemalist codes have been replaced or at least changed by novel codes and patterns of practices which together constitute the post-Kemalist turn. This represents the loss of leverage of Kemalist norms against the post-Kemalist alternatives. Accordingly, for instance, Kemalism approves of a nation state based on single ethnic nation while post-Kemalism has brought an imagined multicultural legacy of the Ottoman Empire to the policy realm and within it, "the claim to cultural, ethnic, religious and language homogeneity los[t] its artificial substance ... [while the] heterogeneity admitted and decreed as a necessity" (Gürbey 2006: 157). Turkey thus re-invented the Ottoman state as offering a tolerant and inclusive framework, while also discovering cultural and ethnic diversity in its history, meaning that multicultural identities have become more concrete, non-Turkish and non-Muslim identities became more visible and reforms introduced to facilitate the practice of religions other than Islam, while also allowing the official use of languages other than Turkish (Kadıoğlu 2007). While Kemalism necessitates nationalism and resorts to ethnic conceptualisation of citizenship in both legal and practical levels; post-Kemalism, on the other hand, envisions a less "ethnic" and more post-national conceptualisation, "an understanding of national identity that is evolving from emphasizing homogeneity to recognizing diversity" (Kirişçi 2006: 194–5, Kirişçi 2009b). Therefore, in the scope of the post-Kemalist transformation of the country, the post-national qualities of Turkey have increased and in the words of Mehmet Altan,[2] the country gotten closer to becoming, "in sociological terms", normalised (Altan 2013).

This however should not be understood to mean that Turkey achieved a truly functioning democracy with regard to societal plurality, nor that Kemalist reflexes in policy making have been truly gotten rid of. A recent manifestation of this has been the war waged against the PKK in the country after the June 7 elections in 2015 and the rise to prominence of nationalist language and vocabulary – a quintessentially Kemalist method of dealing with ethno-political armed struggle. However, there are undeniably bold post-Kemalist practices which have long challenged, devalued and alternated the Kemalist socio-political frames and approaches, issues which I turn to below.

The post-Kemalist transformation of the country is generated by three interrelated and mostly divisive processes. The first process is Turgut Özal's trilogy of liberal reforms introduced and promoted in late 1980s and the early 1990s. The second process is the moving of political Islamists into the mainstream and their embracing emancipatory and multiculturalist discourses particularly by the time the JDP came to power. Last but not least, the third process is the experience of Europeanisation in the country whereby the post-national qualities of the country have increased thanks to the lifting of several legal and practical barriers pertaining to ethno-cultural rights.

Turgut Özal, the initial architect of change in post-1980 coup Turkish politics (Dağı 2010, Tüfekçi 2016a), came to power when the military rulers handed over power back to a civilian government in 1983. He was the main figure in Turkey's political scene until his death in 1993 (he was president of the country at the time). He built his political programme and ideological leaning on three liberties, namely freedom of expression, freedom of religion and conscience, and freedom of enterprise. He initiated a neo-liberal restructuring of the economy and other changes affecting society and politics. With regards to the economy, he gradually relaxed the state control and monopoly over enterprise, which allowed for new actors – religiously motivated and other bonded capital groups–to enter into the economy, some of which later came be known as the Anatolian Tigers.[3] Also included in this was the development of Islamic financial institutions[4] and the rise of popular religious orders investing in the economy[5] (Öniş 1997, Atasoy 2005). This entrance ultimately allowed these groups to gain considerable economic power and in turn paved the way for their claiming a powerful say in the media, education and politics (Yavuz 1998: 30). However, this should not lead us to think that it was only the religious groups which gained ground in the economy; military owned enterprises, such as OYAK, also gained massively from this process. In societal terms, new opportunity spaces were made available to hitherto deprived religious groups. This meant that, for instance, while "[t]he market share of Islamic journals and newspapers was only 7 per cent before 1980; by 1996, it had risen to 47 per cent, with 110 weekly and monthly Islamist journals in circulation" (Ibid.: 31). By the same token, the activities of some popular religious groups saw the establishment of private nurseries, primary schools, secondary schools, high-schools, university examination training centres and even universities in Turkey and abroad, which were mainly funded by the newly emergent Anatolian bourgeoisie and Islamic capital groups (Atasoy 2005: 156). In political a sense, Özal's reforms gave civil society a say in politics and a broader say over state identity and ideology, and the imagined "Ottoman experience"[6] was constantly recalled as a method to reach societal peace whereby Turkey's cultural, ethnic, religious and language heterogeneity were begun to be acknowledged and politically articulated. Such position however was restrained to certain intellectual and political circles, nationalism was still dominant among public and political domains. It was therefore too early for them to be conclusive in reshaping the state in the 1990s.

The second post-Kemalist transformation, which needs to be recalled here, is Islamist shift towards an embrace of liberal, emancipatory and multicultural discourses. The fact that religious groups were making use of new opportunity spaces which led to Kemalist building blocks of the state being challenged was however perceived as a threat to Kemalists from the very beginning. The degree of threat, as perceived by them, was multiplied when the pro-Islamist Welfare Party (WP) gained huge successes in the municipal and general elections, and thus began ruling the country in 1995. Such an openly Islamist government taking power of ostensibly Kemalist Turkey made the Kemalist bureaucratic elite very uncomfortable indeed. They therefore began accusing the WP of embarking on activities which threatened the state, including attempts to turn the country into an Islamic state by Islamising cultural spaces, seeking to change public holidays from Saturday and Sunday to Friday and Saturday, pushing the wearing of the headscarf, and establishing ties with radical Islamists locally and abroad (Yavuz 2009: 64). These alleged activities were soon made use of by the military and the Kemalist bureaucratic elite to topple the government in February 1997 (the so-called "February 28 coup"). The coup was followed by severe counter-measures which restricted the opportunity spaces for religiously-motivated actors, the suppression of political Islamists' economic and political activities, and the securitising of religious groups all in a bid to quash any questioning of the authority/validity of Kemalists and to strengthen the latter (Yavuz 2000).

This experience, however, taught the pro-Islamists a lesson in how they should deal with the Kemalist elite seeking to control the state. They diverted from an Islamist political agenda and embraced democracy and emancipatory discourses. Accordingly, after five years of political turmoil, in 2002, the Justice and Development Party (JDP) (a pro-Islamic party yet with a liberal agenda) took over the mission of the post-Kemalist transformation of the country. Having learnt from the WP experience, and despite organic ties with the former, the JDP distanced itself from assertive political Islamism which sought to give Islam a bigger presence and more visibility in the country. JDP, with a claim to being a successor to Özal's Motherland Party – rather than to WP – embraced conservative democracy as the basis for political manifestation and embarked on a genuine commitment to democratisation and liberalisation of the country with a strong reference to Ottoman multicultural legacy as a way to authenticate its emancipatory policies (Tüfekçi 2016a, Akdoğan 2003). There is no doubt that this emancipatory approach amplified the post-Kemalist turn inaugurated by Özal.

At this juncture, the third post-Kemalist transformation dynamic comes to the fore: Europeanisation. Turkey had long been in the pursuit of EU membership, which many considered a continuation of its Westernisation project. Some achievements during the 1990s, such as the granting of the much coveted Candidate Status at the Helsinki Summit of the EU in December 1999, are important though Turkey only achieved its "most significant and ambitious adjustment to European norms" with the JDP's coming to the power in 2002 (Müftüler-Bac 2005: 17, Tocci 2005: 73). The JDP, with its new ideological bent – that of conservative democracy and landslide electoral victories in 2002, 2007 and 2011, introduced unprecedented emancipatory reforms never before seen in the history of the country. To make ease this path, Turkey utilised two discourses: the EU membership goal and the imagined/invented match between the introduced reforms and the Ottoman civilisational legacy of multiculturalism.

In this regard, right after the November 2002 elections a new constitutional reform package was introduced on civil society allowing the use of languages other than Turkish in non-official correspondence (Grigoriadis 2009: 59, Erdenir 2012: 110). In a similar vein, imprisoned Kurdish MPs, who had been sentenced for reciting a parliamentary oath in Kurdish in 1991, were freed and the death penalty was abolished and replaced with life sentence. This last step was crucial because it meant that the imprisoned PKK leader Abdullah Öcalan had his sentence converted and he avoided the death penalty (Müftüler-Bac 2005: 24, 26). Through several other amendments such as "broadcasting of private TV and radio stations in minority languages and dialects became possible" at both the local and national level, the removal of punishments for "offences caused against Turkism", and learning minority languages and the establishment of relevant private institutions to teaching these languages were facilitated. Moreover, limitations on names given to infants were lifted, non-Muslim foundations' acquisition of immovable property was eased, and a new Law on Associations was ratified which meant that "[l]imitations on the establishment of associations on the basis of race, ethnicity, religion, sect, region or any other minority group were lifted" (Grigoriadis 2009: 140–2, Tocci 2005: 74). It was within the scope of such changes that the freedom to erect a place of worship, regardless of religion and belief, was recognised and a multi-religious committee was established in Antakya by the Diyanet to develop "harmonious relations" between Muslims, Christians and Jews (Grigoriadis 2009: 109).

These reforms also resulted in the state broadcasting institution (TRT) declaring its official aim to launch programmes in languages other than Turkish in June 2003. In May 2004 a local TV channel screened a movie in the Kurdish language with Turkish subtitles – a pioneering move which raised many eyebrows among Kemalists. Following this, in June 2004 TRT commenced broadcasting programmes in Bosnian, Arabic, Circassian and Kurdish (both in the Kırmanchi and Zaza dialects) though within limited broadcasting slots. In the same vein, radio and TV channel applications for broadcasting in Kurdish were approved and after 2005 nine began to operate. Private language schools for the teaching of minority languages were promoted and many opened by 2004 in Van, Batman, Urfa, Diyarbakır, Adana and İstanbul – all of which saw private schools beginning education and training between April and October 2004.[7] By the same token, in August 2005, Recep Tayyip Erdoğan,[8] in a historic move, admitted in his visit to Diyarbakır that Turkey had a "Kurdish problem" and that denying this has brought about nothing but harm to Turkey (Grigoriadis 2009: 152). To Erdoğan, the Kurdish problem should be handled "within the framework of Turkey's democratisation process" (Ibid.). This was the first time a government in Republican history had publicly declared the presence of such a problem. Considering the fact that "the existence of a Kurdish minority in Turkey was persistently denied and the use of Kurdish language [was] banned", this speech's real importance, as a profound move towards post-Kemalism and towards the consolidation of democracy in the country, becomes even more evident (Ibid.: 153).

The reforms mentioned above were chiefly based on the adoption of 261 new laws between 2003 and 2004. These enabled Turkey to start official negotiation talks for EU membership on 3 October 2005 (Müftüler-Bac 2005: 26–7). The reforms continued uninterrupted for many years. In this vein, TV stations and radio channels broadcasting in Kurdish and Armenian languages were established, the state television TRT founded channels broadcasting 24 hours a day in Kurdish and Arabic languages, the ban on speaking any languages other than Turkish during prison visits and the ban on prisoners' speaking Kurdish during their phone calls were all removed; moreover, running election campaigns and propagating in languages other than Turkish was allowed, denaturalised ethnic Kurds had their nationality rights returned, and the ban on the use of Kurdish forenames was lifted (Erdenir 2012: 114, *Time Türk* 7 November 2009; also see Taşpınar 2013a, b). Even the word *Kurdistan* started to be legitimately used as a forename (*Hürriyet* 13 July 2013).

Continuing with improvements in state–society relations, Erdoğan continuously called for investigations into Republican era crimes, such as the thousands of death sentences issued by the so-called Independence Courts (İstiklal Mahkemeleri, as it was then called) during mid-1920s or the mass killing of Kurds and Alevis in Dersim in 1938. The previously banned Cultural Association of the Union of Alevi and Bektahsi Institutions were also granted legal status and allowed to pursue its activities (Grigoriadis 2009: 109). Equally important, Erdoğan admitted that "Kurdistan" has been a legitimate geographical designator to refer to Southeastern Turkey and that derives from the fact that the region was called "Kurdistan" during the Ottoman era and throughout Islamic civilisational history (*Milliyet* 19 November 2013). Together with these changes many Kurdish or Armenian origin geographical place names, which were replaced by Turkish ones as part of the "Turkification" project during and after the Republican era were changed back to their original forms (*Radikal* 30 September 2013b).

In 2013 another democratisation package was introduced that allowed the opening up of private schools in languages other than Turkish. This was a follow up of previous amendments which had allowed the opening up of language teaching courses in 2003 and also the establishment of faculty departments focusing on minority languages and cultures in 2009; moreover, Kurdish and other minority languages could now be selected as elective courses in schools from 2012 (*Radikal* 30 September 2013b). In the same package, the ban on the use of the letters q, w and x was lifted in order to make possible the use of Latinised Kurdish (*Radikal* 30 September 2013a). Moreover, barriers imposed on wearing the hijab in public institutions were also removed and the name of "Nevşehir University" was changed to "Hacı Bektaş Veli University" in order to honour the Alevis. A Roma Language and Culture Institute was also planned to be established to support the ethnic and cultural survival of this group (*Radikal* 30 September 2013b). Last but not least, within the same reform package, the obligatory recitation of the nationalist oath "Our Pledge" in primary schools was abolished (*Radikal* 30 September 2013a).[9] The reason for this last move was to foster societal reconciliation and not to force non-Turkish ethnic groups to declare themselves "Turkish". The oath has been compulsory part of schooling life since 1933 (see Appendix 2; also see Appendix 3 for a similar text '*Mustafa Kemal Atatürk's Address to Turkish Youth*').

As seen, the most promising development in Turkey's post-Kemalist transformation came thanks to JDP rule and its successful use of European Union harmonisation process to achieve its aims. At this juncture, it should be borne in mind that the above-listed domestic changes should not be defined as externally imposed or a shallow political effort designed simply to meet the EU conditionality criteria.[10] As Tocci (2005), Müftüler-Bac (2005), Göksel and Güneş (2005), Aşık (2012) and Erdenir (2012: 114) demonstrate, this domestic change "occurred and is occurring not simply because it is imposed from the outside, but also because it interacts with domestic developments on the inside" (Tocci 2005: 79). This concern has been expressed by leaders of the JDP too, with Erdoğan arguing that "the European Union is a part of Turkey's civilisational project. However, we conducted these reforms to fulfil the democratic dreams of our own people. This was not just a requirement for a membership perspective" (quoted in Grigoriadis 2009: 180). The "civilisation" Erdoğan refers to bears certain characteristics of Ottoman multiculturalism and diversity discourses which are, it so happens, also in line with the democratisation mission defined by the EU. In this fashion, post-Kemalist Turkey has discursively taken the Western and Ottoman models as pace-makers simultaneously, with Europeanisation becoming a tool deployed to achieve rapprochement with both the liberal democratic values of the West and the multicultural values of the Ottoman Empire. The latter ultimately functions as a mean to authenticise the former.

Nonetheless, it is undeniable that some of the above-listed amendments have remained only on paper or the daily politics or the election environments made the political parties partially leave the reform agenda or liberal discourse, which has clearly been observable in particularly the JDP's political practices. Still, confirming Çağaptay (2012b) and Akyol (2013), it is impossible to deny that the Kemalist ideological basis of the Turkish republic has been shattered, that unprecedented post-Kemalist practices have emerged. A final example goes a long way in showing just how real and tangible the post-Kemalist transformation has been.

Ahmet Kaya, a famous Kurdish composer and singer, received a prestigious award of "Singer of the Year" by the popular Magazine Journalists Association in 1999. Upon receiving the award, he stated that "[since I am a Kurd,] I will sing a Kurdish song in my next album that I will release in the near future. I will also make a music video for this song. I know that there are brave television stations that will air this music video" (*Hurriyet Daily News*, 19 June 2012). Today, such a statement would not turn any heads or raise eyebrows, let alone elicit aggressive responses, since all the Kemalist-inspired bans prohibiting the use of Kurdish and other minority languages have been lifted. However, in the zeitgeist of the 1990s, Ahmet Kaya's statement sparked fury and the visceral hostility of many; as soon as he stated this onstage, he was exposed to physical attacks from the guests and knives and forks were thrown at him. Among the guests included celebrities who also reacted violently with verbal and physical assaults. Famous pop singer Serdar Ortaç was the leading figure here. Subsequent to throwing Ahmet Kaya out of the hall, these reactionary celebrities began collectively singing a nationalist march called "Tenth Year March". This incident and the subsequent denouncements, media attacks and "a prison sentence as a result of false media coverage about him" forced Ahmet Kaya to flee to France, where he died and was buried in 2000 (*Today's Zaman*, 28 October 2013).

In 2012, 13 years after this unfortunate incident, the Magazine Journalists Association bestowed a special award in memory of Ahmet Kaya (*Today's Zaman*, 18 June 2012). In 2013, Ahmet Kaya was announced the winner of the Presidential Grand Awards in Culture and Arts – an official recognition of his contributions to Turkey in the field of music. The award was announced on Kaya's birthday – 28 October – two months earlier than the date it is usually announced, as an official apology and honour (*Today's Zaman*, 28 October 2013). Finally and most interestingly, Serdar Ortaç, the lead protester against Ahmet Kaya in the infamous 1999 incident, apologised publicly and expressed his deep regret on 20 November 2013 and admitted that "in those days even saying 'hello' in Kurdish was kind of prohibited, whenever I see myself in those [video] recordings [of the incident] I loathe myself" (*Radikal*, 20 November 2013).

This example is representative and best exemplifies what I mean by post-Kemalist change.

Before concluding, a final point deserves mention regarding the post-Kemalism debate. The implications of post-Kemalist transformation have been seen also in the breaking of the Kemalist bureaucratic/military tutelage over civilian politics in the country. Although this change is a ground-breaking development in Turkey's domestic politics, it is yet not principally related to Turkey's approach to Outside Turks nor to state–society relations. Within the scope of the removal of the military's control over the state bodies, military members in State Security Courts, Higher Education Board (YÖK), Information and Communication Technologies Authority and Censure Board (RTUK) were removed (Müftüler-Bac 2005: 26, Grigoriadis 2009: 84, Erdenir 2012: 110). The number of the civilian members in the military-dominated National Security Council (MGK) was increased and the Secretary General of the Council was made to be a civilian thereafter (Tocci 2005: 74). As part of opening the security sector to more civilian engagement, the military was brought under strict judicial control of the Court of Accounts and was made more accountable to Parliament (Bardakçi 2013: 412–13, Erdenir 2012: 115). With the following constitutional amendments, civilian trials in the military courts during times of peace were ended and the trial of military officers in civilian courts was made possible (Aşık 2012: 149). The amendments also opened legal ways to trial the coup-committers; trials on 1980 and 28 February coups were made possible in this regard.

Nonetheless, although the imprisoned military officers were released, the cases later dropped and politically denounced, the Ergenekon and Balyoz cases where the means through which the military – long considered by many to be the saviour of the Turkish state and guardian of the Kemalist regime and "revolutions" – was neutralised and made accountable to democratic processes. With the Ergenekon and Balyoz trials, a former chief of general staff, former force commanders, retired and incumbent generals/colonels, political party leaders and executives, MPs, journalists and lawyers were given aggravated and consecutive life sentences while many others were sentenced to lengthy imprisonment on charges of plotting to overthrow the civilian government (*Today's Zaman* 5 August 2013, *Hurriyet Daily News* 18 October 2013). This was unimaginable under a Kemalist conception of civil–military relations. Moreover, during the trial process, despite vocal Kemalist calls for the military to interfere in the trial, the chiefs of general staff remained impartial "on issues passed to the jurisdiction" (Taraf 21 October 2013). This attitude is "in stark contrast with Turkey's former chiefs of general staff [prior to the JDP rule], who habitually expressed their opinions on political matters, even those not related to the military or its officers" (*Today's Zaman* 21 October 2013). As a result of these changes, in today's Turkey, the resignation of a general does not cause a stir while the military's even minor attempts to interfere in daily politics comes in for heavy criticism by civilian politicians and public opinion. Therefore, although the trials were politically motivated, these cases facilitated the ending of the military's de facto control over civilian politics.

To conclude, in the course of Turkey's post-Kemalist turn, the key Kemalist building blocks of the country have been shattered and to an extent dismantled. In terms of lifting the legal and practical barriers on the use of ethno-cultural rights, some of which admittedly remained only on paper, we see that the post-national qualities of the country have increased. Moreover, along with its post-Kemalist turn, Turkey also discovered its own cultural and ethnic diversity. It is at this juncture that understandings of "national identity" evolved from one which emphasised ethnic homogeneity to recognising ethnic diversity – the influence of which has also been seen in Turkey's post-Kemalist approach to Outside Turks.

Post-Kemalist Approach to Outside Turks

In line with the above-reviewed post-Kemalist turn in Turkey after the 1980s, it is clear that the way Turkey has come to think of Outside Turks also begun to change. The aspiration shifted towards considering these communities as "fellow believers" (co-religionists) rather than merely "fellow nationals" (co-nationals) representing a ground-breaking post-

Kemalist turn (Üstel 1996: 64). However, their localities were still a cultural extension of the mainland and they were approached concomitant to the motive of moulding the Turkish-speaking Outside Turks communities, however, this time with post-Kemalist Turkey. This, however, does not mean that Outside Turks' ethnic Turkishness was ruled out completely – they were still co-nationals. Indeed, Prime Minister Mesut Yılmaz confirmed as much in a 1989 speech when he argued that "Turks living outside Turkey are as Turk as the Turks living inside Turkey" (Aydın 1995: 60; Karadeniz 2011: 268, Tüfekçi 2016b). The idea of "looking after them" continued to be considered as a "sacred national responsibility" as Meral Akşener, Minister of Interior from the Nationalist Movement Party (NMP) had remarked in 1997 (Meral Akşener 1997: 142–3). This consideration occurred concomitant to the rediscovery of the Turkic world and the revival of Pan-Turkist ideology whereby Turkish identity was envisaged as an international and cross-border identification on which inter-state and inter-communal relations could be built (Yanık 2006: 5). The efforts made towards developing a common Turkish alphabet, the organisation of state-sponsored Turkology conferences with expert participants from the Turkic states, the establishment of the TRT Eurasia media channel to foster a sense of "brotherhood" among the Turkic communities are just some of the state-led moves made in this direction (Börklü 1999: 279–84, Tüfekçi 2016b, Burris 2007).

Despite Pan-Turkic inclinations however, Turkey's political decision makers were more prone toward "neo-Ottomanist" tendencies and begun to distance the official state position from Kemalist nationalist project of building the "Kemalist-Self" outside Turkey in favour of an Ottoman conception of nation, geography and Turkishness (Üstel 1996: 63, Çetinsaya 1999). In this sense, the Ottoman–Islamic sources of Turkish nationhood have been revived and became "more assertive and effective in conditioning and shaping the state's policies and the society's perceptions of 'self'" (Yavuz 1998: 22). Accordingly, religion has become imagined as a firm component of Turkish identity and a complementary bond between Outside Turks and Turkey (Bulut 2004). Therefore, the new nationalist mission was not to imagine the greater Turkic nation in purely ethnic terms, but rather along cultural and religious lines. Framing the relationship between Turkey and Outside Turks along religious lines has been considered as indisputably consistent, because "at the end of the day, the Outside Turks were as well among the components of the Islamic world" (Üstel 1996: 64). As a result, the new 'Turkish' geography was no longer limited to the Turkic space; it now covered "the Muslim Turkic world from the Adriatic Sea to the Great Wall of China" and the territories "from the mid of Europe to the Pacific Ocean, from Adriatic to China, [and] from Siberia to [Saudi] Arabia and India" (Öge 2009: 59).

In the making of this new cognitive map and in Pan-Turkism gaining religious qualities and tendencies, religious organisations and a new Anatolian bourgeoisie began to engage with newly independent Muslim and Turkic states of Central Asia and the former Ottoman territories in the Balkans (Üstel 1996: 64). In this newly imagined world, Turkey was a kin state not only to the ethnic Turkish communities, but also to Muslim-majority communities, which consequently blurred the difference between ethnic Turks and Muslim communities and thus promoted the idea of *ethnic plurality* as part of the concept of 'Outside Turks' (Karadeniz 2011: 275, Laciner 2001: 292).

This new conception of ethnic plurality became more solid by the early 1990s when a bloody war erupted in the former Yugoslavia and the Muslim population there became exposed to massacres and ethnic cleansing. It was in this crisis that Turkey for the "first time in Republican Turkish history ... considered the protection of Muslims outside its borders as an integral duty of its foreign policy" (Yavuz 1998: 37). The same was the case in supporting the Chechen liberation struggle against Russia. Moreover, by opening its borders to the ethnic Turks from Bulgaria in 1989 and to ethnic Kurds in Iraq in 1991 also affirmed the development of this new ethnic plurality model. Accordingly, Turkey received both the Muslim Kurds of Iraq and Muslim Turks of Bulgaria with open arms during turmoil and when the time came to send them back to their homes, an equal stance was taken towards them. During debates regarding the status of refugees, while ultra-nationalists advocated the expulsion of Kurdish refugees from Turkey, Necmettin Erbakan, the Prime Minister and the leader of the pro-Islamic Welfare Party retorted that Turkey should also therefore "expel the Bulgarian Turks back to their 'homeland'" (Gangloff 2001: 92).

As a consequence of this framing of relations along religious lines, the Turkish Cooperation and Coordination Agency (TIKA) – the institution built to deal with ethnic Turkish communities – was deployed with a responsibility towards Muslim communities more generally (Üstel 1996: 64). To this end, the Presidency for Religious Affairs (Diyanet) and the Turkish Radio and Television Corporation (TRT) were deployed with an international mission of dealing with the affairs of Muslim communities, leading to NGOs and religious groups finding enough room to contribute to Turkey's policy towards the Outside Turks.

Accordingly, TIKA-run projects such as rebuilding the Old Bridge in Mostar and the Et'hem Bey Mosque in Tirana or translating Hacı Bektaş-ı Veli's books into Albanian which underscored attempts to promote the cultural and religious bonds between Turkey and kin communities (Öge 2009: 83).

Diyanet, on the other hand, began acting on a truly global scale and began establishing official links with Muslim communities in the Balkans and Turkic communities in Central Asia based on the idea of shared religious identity. In tandem with this, the long ignored religious identity of Outside Turks and general religious issues in favour of cherishing their national identity was also given up and religous issues slowly began to become overseen by Diyanet. Additionally, in order to protect a common religious identity, which would come to be called "Turkish Islam", the Diyanet explicitly competed with Iran and Saudi Arabia and hence promoted its own understanding of Islam throughout the former Ottoman territories (Bulut 2004: 8). Moreover, Diyanet initiated the establishment of the Eurasian Islamic Council and start of the Eurasian Islamic Meetings in 1995 which was attended by religious leaders from all Turkic and Muslim communities in Central Asia and the Balkans to discuss their common concerns such as "Wahhabism" (Karadeniz 2011: 256, Öktem 2012: 42, Korkut 2010: 125).

The Ministry of State in charge of Outside Turks, the first institutional body specifically established to develop and enhance relations between Turkey and the Turkic republics and kin communities, was also used as part of a bid to regulate Muslim affairs (Karadeniz 2011: 251). For instance, when Adullah Gül of the Welfare Party was appointed as the minister of this institution in 1996, he stated that the ministry was in charge of "enhanc[ing] the economic, commercial, industrial, educational, health, social and cultural relationship between [Turkey] and Muslim communities and states, and the co-nationals living in the Balkans, with whom we share common cultural bonds" (quoted in Öge 2009: 54). Without a doubt, the reference to 'cultural bonds' refers here to religion.

Last but not least, the Great Student Exchange Project (Büyük Öğrenci Projesi), launched in 1992 via a Nationalist Movement Party (NMP) initiative, was designed to foster relations with Turkic communities and this too involved religious framing. Although it was a purely nationalistic initiative, it is clear that this project featured many hundreds of students who were also registered to imam-hatip schools or theology faculties in Turkey. Along with ethnic Turks, students from the former Ottoman territories were also brought to Turkey in the scope of this policy (Börklü 1999: 283).

The 1990s generated several post-Kemalist practices regarding the Outside Turks with reference to Ottoman and Islamic bonds. These practices have further been developed by the JDP governments in the 2000s.

Turkey's policy towards Outside Turks in the 2000s, in the main, bears non-nationalist sentiments, concomitant to the anti-nationalism project of the JDP government in power at the time. In domestic politics the JDP highlighted the ethnic plurality of the country. In this sense, JDP officials have constantly abhorred nationalism and many times stated that it was nationalism which had ruined the historically and religiously built bonds between Kurds and Turks (see *Hürriyet* 18 February 2013). Indeed, lifting legal and practical bans on the use of ethnic and cultural manifestations were partly a reflection of these ideas. In tandem with this, in foreign policy, nationalism came to be seen as the trigger for the break in ties between Turkey and Muslim majority countries and communites around the world (*Hürriyet* 17 September 2012, Aslan 2013: 28). Nationalism is considered a threat also to the historically built religio-cultural bonds between Turkey and the former Ottoman communities. This anti-nationalist stance led to an attempt to frame relations between Turkey and the Ottoman remnant communities in a religious, not ethnic, sense. This had an inevitable impact on the way Turkey comprehended Outside Turks and the way in which the JDP developed its policies.

Nevertheless, one can hardly argue that Turkey completely ruled out the idea of Turkic ties and myths. Accordingly, Turkology projects have continued to be conducted (*Avrasya Bülteni* July 2006: 1–5). Nevruz continued to be celebrated as one of the "Turkish" (Turkic) national festivals (Öge 2009: 133). The nationalist Pan-Turkic myths such as that of "Ergenekon" continues to be referred to in official publications in explain the roots of the Turkic nation (Ibid.: 134). In the same way, financial and technical funding for a highway project in Mongolia resulted in it being called *"Bilge Kağan Highway"*, which refers to one of the antient Turkic state leaders. Other such initiatives include protection given to *Tonyukuk* Scriptures in Mongolia, documents which shed lights on pre-Islamic Turkic history; or the idea that Turkish presence in Kosovo dates back to the time of Avars, Pechenegs and Kumans (ancient Turkic clans) in official publications all of which indicate the functioning of nationalist framing (*Avrasya Bülteni* October 2003: 6, Avrasya Bülteni June 2006: 9, Reşat Doğru 2008: 314, Beşir Atalay 2007: 232, Bekir Bozdağ 2012, *TIKA Faaliyet Raporu* 2008: 8, Uysal 2004).

This represents the continuity of attempt at a nationalist framing of Outside Turks and the Turkic world, yet religious framing has, in the past decade or so, began to overwhelm nationalist leanings and inclinations. Post-Kemalist considerations, in this sense, have led to an attempt to religiously and culturally frame the relationship between Turkey and Outside Turks communities. By the time of JDP rule, for instance, diplomatic convoys to Outside Turks localities have aspired to and developed interests in things like visiting mosques, Islamic religious authorities, imam-hatip or religious schools, Sufi tekkes (dervish lodges), and in joining prayers and religious congregations with local people. Interestingly, for the last couple of years Turkish state officials in charge of Outside Turks appear in the Outside Turks localities during religious feasts. For instance, Bekir Bozdağ[11] and Kemal Yurtnaç[12] visited Bulgaria in 2013 during the holy month of Ramadan and celebrated the Eid-ul Fitr celebrations (Ramadan Bajram) with the local Muslim Turkish community there (*YTB News* August 2013). They fasted with the local people, performed Eid-ul Fitr prayers with them, distributed Qur'an and roseries after the Eid prayer as gifts; they also visited the head of the Islamic authority, and visited an Imam-Hatip school in Ruschuk (Ibid.). During 2012 Eid-ul Fitr celebrations, Bekir Bozdağ visited Western Thrace (Greece). His visit began during the Friday prayer, continued with visits to local religious authorities and the Western Thrace Imam-Hatip Alumni Association, and ended with the performance of "teravih" (night) prayer (Yavuz 2012: 68–9). As can be seen, the "Muslimness" of the Turks has been experienced, performed and promoted from the firsthand.

Nonetheless, in addition to individual level involvements of ministers or senior bureaucrats, there are institutions specifically in charge of Outside Turks affairs, something which reveals more about Turkey's post-Kemalist approach to Outside Turks communities. These institutions include the YTB, TIKA, Diyanet and Yunus Emre Institute. Religious groups also play a role in this policy.

The Presidency for Turks Abroad and Related Communities (YTB), the contemporary institution in charge with Outside Turks, was founded in 2010 with the aim of enhancing the relations with Turkish citizens abroad, and with kin and related communities. YTB embraced the motto of "wherever there is a citizen, kin or related community, we are there" (Yurtnaç 2012: 10).[13] Here, whilst the *citizens* live mainly in Europe, for the *kin and related communites*, the YTB President Yurtnaç draws a broader circle and argues that they reside in "the Balkans, Eastern Europe, the Caucasus, Central Asia, the Middle East, and Africa" (Ibid.). Nonetheless, despite this plurality of addressee, YTB has devoted much of its efforts to fostering bonds with citizens abroad and two prominent endeavours in its policies towards these communities have focused on religion and religious identity: Islamophobia and the placement of foster children of Turkish-descent with non-Turkish and non-Muslim foster-parents in Europe.

From the very beginning, the government officials including Abdullah Gül,[14] Recep Tayyip Erdoğan, Bekir Bozdağ and Kemal Yurtnaç have continiously stressed that YTB has a great mission in the fight against Islamophobia that threatens not only Turkish people but also other "brotherly" communities in Europe (Altınok 2012: 4). This mission was set according to the findings of a survey "conducted with 3500 Outside Turks members throughout Europe" by the YTB (Altınok 2013b: 12). As the survey reveals, the most worrying issues for Turks living in Europe were racist attacks and Islamophobia (Ibid.). Thus the YTB was encouraged by Gül and Erdoğan to work closely with the Turkish and other Islamic NGOs established in Europe in the fight against Islamophobia, to guarantee the protection/defence of religious freedoms and sacred values (Altınok 2013a: 9, Altınok 2012: 4). Second, YTB tries to prevent the placement of foster children of Turkish descent with non-Turkish and non-Muslim foster-parents in Europe. YTB advocates that, as argued by Gül too, these children need to be placed with Turkish foster parents and, if not, Muslim foster parents otherwise this "would come to mean changing the religion of the children which is unacceptable" (Altınok 2012: 7). Bekir Bozdağ similarly assessed that "these children are virtually being Christianised. We are facing a tremendous tragedy, an assimilation" (*T24* 5 November 2012). It was under such circumstances that YTB's mission was promoted as "protecting Hasan from being Hans"[15] and helping Turkish people to gain their rights that would enable them to manifest their religion and protect their religious identity (Altınok 2013b: 15).

The activities of YTB thus confirm Üstel's contention (1996: 64) that Turkish people outside Turkey have been rediscovered as "Muslims" and are being dealt with accordingly. Secondly, it is assumed that anything that affects Turkish people also effects other Muslim populations. Thirdly, Islamic identity and Islamic internationalist consciousness in Turkey began to become conclusive in policy choices and hence Muslim communities have been included into the sphere of activity of the institutions built to deal with Outside Turks communities (Atmaca 2012: 78–81).

The other tasks YTB runs in this regard have included the Great Student Exchange Project. The project is historically designed to bring students from Outside Turks communities to Turkey. With YTB's involvement in this project, the content, extent, scope and methods have changed massively. The project was renamed as *Türkiye Scholarship* and its scope has been vastly extended.[16] In the old system, the ethnic Turkish members of Outside Turks were given contingent and additional placements. However, with this new programme, Outside Turks' privileges were lifted and they were equated with other communities. The transformation of the student exchange programme has occurred steadily. This first meant increasing the number of countries which could benefit from this scholarship programme. This was five in 1992 and gradually rose to 57 until 2008 (*Avrasya Bülteni* June 2006: 16). Beneficiary countries were initially those with whom Turkey has "ethnic unity". However, this has gradually shifted to countries with whom Turkey has "cultural unity". Today, there is no single Muslim and/or Turkic populated country which is left outside the target audience. The states built on the former Ottoman Empire territories are also well represented as beneficiary countries. Therefore, the programme lost its pure ethnic connotation and the ethnic Turks members of Outside Turks became equal with their Muslim counterparts in the eyes of Turkey.

Similar to YTB, by the time the JDP came to power "TIKA extended its sphere of influence beyond the geographies of the Turkic states towards entire Muslim world" (Karadeniz 2011: 254). In the first ten years, TIKA's main sphere of activity was restricted to the post-Soviet republics and most of the projects were conducted here (*Türk Dünyası Bülteni* 2002: 2). As soon as the JDP came to power, TIKA began to act in new regions and opened offices, for instance, in Ethiopia (2004), Kosovo (2004), Macedonia (2005), Palestine (2005), Afghanistan (2006) and Sudan (2006) (*Avrasya Bülteni* February 2005: 3–5, *Avrasya Bülteni* October 2005: 3, *TIKA Faaliyet Raporu* 2006: 5). Considering that Afghanistan, Bosnia-Herzegovina, Palestine and Lebonan were the top four countries in terms of TIKA funding in 2009, we can see just how far the policy focus has shifted in seven years (*TIKA Faaliyet Raporu* 2009: 4–16). By the same token, since nine out of top ten countries receiving the most funding in 2010 were Muslim-populated countries, this also confirms this shift (*TIKA Faaliyet Raporu* 2010: 9). Today, TIKA runs projects in more than 100 countries and has coordinatorships in 33 countries, many of which are mainly economically under-developed Muslim states (Bekir Bozdağ 2012).

TIKA also expanded the types of functions it performs. For instance, TIKA was assigned in 2008 with the task of "coordinating the protection of [Turkey's] cultural heritage abroad" as a testimony to the change in the priorities of TIKA (Bekir Bozdağ 2012, *TIKA Dünyası* December 2012: 22–6). Here the "cultural heritage" refers to both the Ottoman and Turkish–Islamic legacies, just with Davutoğlu arguing that these constitute the foundations of the "cultural memory" upon which relations could be rebuilt between the "brother communities" set apart by national boundaries and nation states (*TIKA Faaliyet Raporu* 2009: 19). Restorations projects in Afghanistan, Macedonia, Kosovo, Bosnia-Herzegovina, Serbia, Bulgaria, Crimea, Lebanon, Syria, Ethiopia, Montenegro, Kazakhstan and Turkmenistan were part of this post-Kemalist concern with Ottoman and Turkish–Islamic issues (see *Avrasya Bülteni* July 2003: 1, *Avrasya Bülteni* January–February 2006: 22, *Avrasya Bülteni* February 2008: 19, *Avrasya Bülteni* August 2009: 18,

Avrasya Bülteni September 2010: 4–7, *TIKA Faaliyet Raporu* 2009: 53, *TIKA Dünyası* December 2012: 27, *Arti90* April 2012: 91, Beşir Atalay 2006, 2007).

The protection of cultural heritage, however, went well beyond taking care of historical artefacts and took the shape of protecting the vulnerable Muslim communities throughout the aforementioned countries (*TIKA Dünyası* June 2012: 21). TIKA's presence in Somali and Sudan; the humanitarian mobilisation towards Muslim communities effected by war or natural disasters in Syria and Indonesia; and TIKA's cooperation with the Islamic Development Bank in assisting the reconstruction of Afghanistan and in enhancing the capabilities of the Muslim minorities in Ukraine, Macedonia, Serbia and Montenegro all point to this (see Beylur 2012: 77, *TIKA Faaliyet Raporu* 2007: 130, *Avrasya Bülteni* July 2006: 11–12, *Diyanet Faaliyet Raporu* 2011: 45). Therefore, the idea of bearing a historical responsibility towards the vulnerable Muslim communities became a core impulse for TIKA.

Another important organisation is Diyanet. This upholds post-Kemalist responsibilities too by providing religious services, trainings and education "to citizens and co-nationals, [and] kin communities resided in 40 states" (Bekir Bozdağ 2012). In terms of the religious education activities, for instance, Diyanet brought 318 students (248 for bachelor degrees, 43 for Masters, 27 for PhD students) from "Kosovo, Bulgaria, Russia, Albania, Turkish Republic of North Cyprus, Macedonia and Bulgaria" to study at theology faculties in Turkey during the 2011–12 educational year. In the same year 188 students – many of whom were from Africa – were registered to the Kayseri Imam-hatip School (Ibid.). Similarly, in 2012–13, 360 students were registered to theology faculties and 324 to imam hatip schools in Kayseri, Istanbul and Konya (Bekir Bozdağ 2012; Mehmet Aydın 2006: 172–87; *Diyanet Faaliyet Raporu* 2006: 52–3). Moreover, Diyanet also "gives direct support for building, refurbishing and the maintenance of sites such as mosques, histrorical artefacts, schools, theology faculties, social spaces and cultural centres" (Bekir Bozdağ 2012). In this sense, for instance, Diyanet "built theology faculties in Kazakhistan, Kyrgyzstan, Azerbaijan; Theology College and Islamic Advanced Studies Institute in Romania and Bulgaria; high school in Azerbaijan; Pedagogy school in Romania; ... imam-hatip schools in Bulgaria" and contributed to the restoration of "Ottoman Turkish historical artifacts" in Rhodes Islands, Bosnia-Herzegovina and Kosovo (Bekir Bozdağ 2012, Mehmet Aydın 2006: 174–93).

Another mission Diyanet upholds is "break[ing] the influence the Salafist and Wahhabist associations have been posing"; hence it provides assistance and support for the protection of the Turkish–Islamic cultural heritage and cultural memory particularly in the Balkans (Karadeniz 2011: 254). Acts of this kind have been done due to a belief (often believed but rarely expressed) that "Turkish Islam is different from and superior to Arab-infused Islam" (White 2013: 101). This idea is not only dominant among the pro-Islamic circles in Turkey but even the Kemalist seculars show approval of it. Onur Öymen, a notable Kemalist and former vice-president of Republican People's Party (RPP), articulated in a parliamentary speech in 2005 that "after the war ... [our] cultural heritage in Kosovo was blasted ... by the Saudi Wahhabi Aid Agency", the agency that took the responsibility to restore the damaged Ottoman artefacts and buildings (Onur Öymen 2005: 246). As Öymen puts forward, "the examinations show that during the restoration works the idea of restoring the Ottoman artifacts to its original condition was left aside and these historical buildings were re-erected according to Wahhabi culture, and some Ottoman artifacts were simply blasted, the graveyards were blasted, the mosques were blasted ... we should not allow a Wahhabi institution of Saudi Arabia ... to blast our cultural heritage in there [Kosovo]" (Ibid.: 246–8).

Turkey has had concern and a concrete agenda to deal with so-called Wahhabism as early as the early 1990s. At a Eurasian Islamic Meetings, the former president of the Diyanet Mehmet Nuri Yılmaz stated that "there are some streams, some movements mass propagating such as Bahaism, Kadiyanism, Ahmedijja, Moonism, Wahhabism ... [throughout the Turkic and former Ottoman lands] we have to take measures regarding this" (*Eurasian Islamic Meeting Report* 1998: 3). In the 2000 Eurasian Islamic Meetings, Mehmet Nuri Yılmaz also argued with reference to the founding father of "Salafism", that "today it is impossible to implement the Badawi Arab lifestyle based economic ideas Ahmet bin Hanbel put forth a thousand years ago to the Anatolian people or to the people of any place on earth" (*Eurasian Islamic Meeting Report* 2000: 3). Therefore, "Salafism" or other forms of practices not consistent with those practised in Turkey are denounced. In such denunciation, the emergence of the so-called "Wahhabis" as a reactionary stream to Ottoman-era religious practices plays a critical role here. Accordingly, the founder of the Wahhabi school of thought, Muhammad Ibn Abd al-Wahhab (1703–37), after his visits to other parts of the Ottoman Empire in the mid-eighteenth century, came up with the idea that Islam should be purified from deviations and blamed the Ottomans of making the Muslims deviated from Islam's original teachings (Tibi 1990: 20–1). Here, some see a schism between orthodox and heterodox practices of Islam. The challenge of the Wahhab's ideas to Ottoman Islam forced the Diyanet to take clearer stand against what is later called "Wahhabism". The Diyanet's approach, however, did not stop in denounciation; it championed, encouraged and incentivised the renewal of an Ottoman/Turkish practice of Islam. Accordingly, in 1995 Diyanet launched a project to build Ottoman architectural style mosques throughout the Turkic world and the former Ottoman hinterland (*Eurasian Islamic Meeting Report* 1995: 54). In a similar vein, Diyanet institutionalised certain religious practices in those places abroad where Turkish citizens, ethnic Turks or kin communities lived. The most popular of these is the celebration of the Holy Birth Week, a week invented by Diyanet in the early 1990s to celebrate the birth of the Prophet Muhammed based on Gregorian calendar rather than the Islamic Calendar (Bulaç 2012, *Diyanet Faaliyet Raporu* 2011: 44, *Diyanet Faaliyet Raporu* 2012: 37–46; for a biased yet relevant research see Toprak 2008: 142–4).

With the coming to power of the JDP, another actor in the Outside Turks policy also gained complete freedom to plan and organise, set up institutions and operate both nationally and internationally. These were the various religious groups from Turkey which came to engage in the Balkans. In such an atmosphere, the number of religious groups operating in the localities where ethnic Turks and kin communities were settled accordingly increased. Previously, only a number of groups were capable of running operations and delivering services; today, however, almost every religious group has associations and schools abroad. In Kosovo, for instance, historically only the Gülen movement was active, though today the Süleymancıs, Menzil, İskenderpaşa and Erenköy (Osman Nuri Topbaş) groups all have institutions and conduct activities in this country. In their operations abroad, despite their differences in terms of certain religious rituals or beliefs, these groups convey a single message – the necessity of the performance of "Turkish/Ottoman way of Islam", thus recalling the Ottoman past in the Turkic and Outside Turks localities (Bulut 2004: 9, Bulut 2006). They even cooperate with Turkish diplomatic missions in this regard (*TIKA Faaliyet Raporu* 2008: 76–82, *TIKA Faaliyet Raporu* 2010: 7, *TIKA Faaliyet Raporu* 2011: 22, Abdullah Gül 10 December 2009).

In sum, the post-Kemalist comprehension of Outside Turks communities has focused on an Ottoman–Islamic conception of nationhood, geography and Turkishness. The new mission, therefore, became to imagine the Turkish nation and Outside Turks in cultural and religious lines, rather than in purely ethnic lines. In this fashion, firstly, religious identity was considered as indisputably consistent as a basis in maintaining relations with Outside Turks communities. Secondly, Turkey is imagined as a kin state not only to the ethnic Turkish communities, but also to the Muslim communities living particularly within the former Ottoman domains. Consequently, while the ethnic emphasis is downgraded, safeguarding the practice of Muslim identity, history and culture became a priority concern in the Outside Turks policy agenda. Therefore, the transformative motive became to recall religio-cultural identities, contrary to the Kemalist comprehension of transforming religious communities to ethnic ones.

CHAPTER 4

OVERSEAS IMPLICATIONS OF DOMESTIC NORMS

The above chapters reviewed the post-Kemalist transformation in Turkey and in Turkey's approach to "Outside Turks" communities. Since the main enquiry this book seeks to address is the impact that post-Kemalist Turkey has had on these communities, the question of how such an impact could be measured remains unanswered. This chapter, therefore, demonstrates how norms can be employed as a foreign policy analysis tool in examining and exploring the processes by which domestic changes have overseas influences and implications. The chapter initially reviews the role of norms and norm-guided practices in domestic change and foreign policy, and ultimately presents a foreign policy analysis framework capable of explaining all processes involved in the formation and conduct of a domestically initiated foreign policy with overseas constitutive influences.

The Role of Norms in Foreign Policy

Norms became a subject of enquiry in the fields of sociology, economics and anthropology as a means to examine the behaviour governing social settings long ago. In the field of International Relations, on the other hand, norm-based analysis could be found only during the late Cold War era. This is because of the prevalence of a positivist methodological tendency during this era, which intellectually disabled IR scholarship from benefitting from ideational enquiries. Even when this was not entirely the case, norms were still approached as material determinants of actor behaviour. Nonetheless, the constructivist challenges had soon come up with severe and powerful critiques to the positivist position in IR and there blossomed thereafter robust challenges (Onuf 1989, Kratochwil 1991, Wendt 1992). Accordingly, ideational factors such as identity, knowledge, beliefs, norms, values and culture are beginning to be considered as notions with influence on policy choices via the effect of defining the manner in which they can organise action for actors. Yet, among many ideational factors, norms, along with identity, have been employed most in constructivist theory development in offering explanations for international politics, transnational politics, regional politics, domestic politics and foreign policy. In due course IR has seen the development of several propositions regarding definitions of norms and the role they play in politics. However, the definition (or role) a study chooses is intimately tied to theoretical/paradigmatic preferences. For instance, positivist and constructivist studies have different approaches to ideational settings and suggest differing conclusions on their roles. Moreover, even within constructivism, mainstream and critical constructivist streams approach norms differently. Subscription to a definition thus matters a lot.

Since norms are theorised with reference to agency and agents' actions, in the IR norms literature, all proposed definitions, in one way or another, subscribe to a *logic of action*. In other words, norms have been principally utilised to make sense of the actions of agency, therefore; the roles attributed to norms differ in each *logic of action* theorisation. In this sense, in IR norms literature there are four dominant logics of action considerations: namely, *logic of consequentialism*, *logic of appropriateness*, *logic of arguing* or *logic of contestedness*. All these logics offer different roles for norms and suggest different definitions; they are also embraced by different schools of thought in IR. Realist, Neo-realist and Neo-liberal schools, for instance, subscribe to a logic of consequentialism, while the mainstream constructivist school to a logic of appropriateness. The logic of arguing and the logic of contestedness, on the other hand, are embraced by critical and post-modern constructivist schools respectively.

The earliest definitions of norms in the IR literature hold the *logic of consequentialism* and reflect a positivist slant which tends to treat norms as rules governing behaviour. For Stephen Krasner, for instance, norms are "standards of behaviour defined in terms of rights and obligations" (Krasner 1983: 2). Robert Axelrod puts this differently though with similar assumptions underpinning his thought: "a norm exists in a given social setting to the extent that individuals usually act in a certain way and are often punished when seen not to be acting in this way" (Axelrod 1986: 1097). Within such studies, norms are depicted as the *causes* of certain types of behaviours "which can be ascertained analogously to that of Newtonian laws governing the collision of two bodies" (Kratochwil and Ruggie 1986: 768). In fact, this is the conventional positivist epistemology "that treats norms as 'causes'" and constrains the role of norms to "moulding decisions" (Kratochwil 1991: 5–4). This means that if a norm is present the outcome is predetermined. Additionally, according to this, norms operate within an exogenously given social setting and in non-normative manners. In this, it is considered that "norms are about *behaviour*, not directly about ideas" and represent "a *legitimate* behavioural claim" (Florini 1996: 364–5, italics original). Taking this definition leads us to argue that the role of norms in foreign policy is to determine the behaviours of states in the international arena and that violating a norm incites punishment. Therefore, norms are imagined as predetermining the behaviour and constraining it via a punishment mechanism. Here, norms are treated as rules making states obliged to act in certain ways.

The *logic of appropriateness*, secondly, is the most common position embraced by mainstream constructivists. Differing from the logic of consequentialism, the logic of appropriateness treats norms as ideational settings constructed through social processes. In other words, norms are not pre-given and nor are the interests. As this logic suggests, norms give messages to agents about appropriate behaviour. In this fashion, Audie Klotz, in her pioneering study argued that norms are "shared (thus social) understandings of standards for behaviour" (1995: 14). Through adopting Frederick Kratochwil's definition of the regulative and constitutive character of norms (Kratochwil 1991: 26) and conducting an empirical examination on the global diffusion of the norm of racial equality, Klotz came up with the argument that "[i] norms constrain states' behaviour through reputation and group membership, and that [ii] norms constitute states' definitions of their own identities and interests" (1995: 166). For her, norms play two basic roles in policy making; regulating behaviour through setting standards for conduct and, second, constructing actor identities and interests.

Peter Katzenstein similarly suggests that norms possess regulative and constitutive characters and there are regulative and constitutive norms. The regulative norms "define standards of appropriate behaviour that shape interests and help coordinate the behaviour of political actors" while constitutive norms "express actor identities that also define interest and thus shape behaviour" (Katzenstein 1996b: 18). Norms, therefore, do not specify "the ends of action"; rather, they offer ways to organise action (Ibid.: 19). Constitutive and regulative characters are closely tied and norms might embody both (Katzenstein 1996b: 19, Katzenstein 1996a: 5). In light of this, Katzenstein comes up with the following definition: Norms are "collective expectations for the proper behaviour of actors with a given identity" (1996a: 5, also see Jepperson *et al.* 1996: 54). Klotz and Katzenstein thus both resort to the same categorisation with regard to the norm characteristics, yet Katzenstein's definition also takes into account the identity of the agents.

In their highly influential work, Finnemore and Sikkink (1998) endorse Katzenstein's definition while placing more emphasis on the regulative character of norms. To them, it is the "prescriptive quality of . . . 'oughtness' that sets norms apart from other kinds of rules" (Finnemore and Sikkink 1998: 891). The oughtness argument suggest in general that "'norms do not necessarily identify actual behaviour; rather they identify notions of what appropriate behaviour ought to be" (Bernstain 2000: 467). Therefore, appropriateness is the main motivational factor for norm compliance and do not determine action. Yet, this argument confines the role norms to forcing actors to conformity through generating disapproval or stigma (Ibid.: 892).

Annika Björkdahl, in her detailed analysis on norms, further diminishes the behavioural determinacy (positivist tendency) by arguing that "when defining norms one must separate norm existence and strength from actual behavioural changes" (2002: 15).[1] Therefore, the change in behaviour is not the cause norms generate, nor are norms consequential. This thus goes beyond Katzenstein's initial position that suggested norms do not determine the end of action. It is now known that norms do not determine the end of action and that they do not even have the qualities to cause actual behavioural change. More so than this, as Björkdahl suggests "norms must be defined separate from the issue of *enforcement* and *compliance"* (2002: 15, italics added). Accordingly, Björkdahl offers the following definition of norms: "Norms are intersubjective understandings that constitute actors' interests and identities, and create expectations as well as prescribe what appropriate behaviour ought to be" (Ibid.: 21).

In short, Klotz, Katzenstein and Björkdahl all follow by and large the logic of appropriateness and in their accounts the role of norms in foreign policy is that norms offer ways to organise action, structure realms of possibilities, establish the boundaries for foreign policy deliberation and execution, identify notions of what appropriate behaviour ought to be (collective expectations), and provide the inspiration and motivation for foreign policy. In other words, norms guide, legitimise, motivate and limit foreign policy behaviours without predetermining both the action and conclusion. Nonetheless, the identity-constituting role of norms remains less researched.

Amy Gurowitz makes some points to overcome this dearth in the literature. She ascertains two core roles for identity. The first is what she calls the *purposive role* within which "identity is the primary source of plans for action; it defines not only means but also goals" (Gurowitz 2006: 311). In the second *justificatory role*, identity "provide[s] the basis on which action can be rationalized" (Ibid.). In this sense it is the identity that "shapes how governments will weigh and interpret various courses of action, or sometimes whether they will consider another course of action as possible" (Ibid.). Since the identity a state has is shaped by both domestic and international environments, state identity has dual control over actions (Ibid.). However, this does not mean that identities predetermine the actions or outcomes with Gurowitz arguing that "identities shape responses to material and social factors, but they do not determine the precise form that responses will take" (Ibid.: 312). In this way, the concomitancy between the role of norms and of identities in state conduct under the logic of appropriateness is evident. Nonetheless, it is vital to place emphasis on the notion that state identity "is something greater than the opinions of the current government; both state and non-state actors operate within the structure and constraints of state identity" (Ibid.: 311).

Critical constructivists, while sharing the regulative and constitutive character of norms and normative rationality's part in action with mainstream constructivists, place more emphasis on probing "symbolic systems that govern actors' discourses" (Katzenstein *et al.* 1998: 677). Therefore, for critical constructivists, actors are in search of communicative consensus about shared understandings; argumentative rationality thus prevails over normative rationality in the functioning of norms. It is due to this that, as Risse holds, when norms are contested or when actors are uncertain about their interests and identities the logic of appropriateness does not apply, and action becomes driven by the deliberation endeavours of actors about what the true conduct is (Risse 2000: 6–7). Risse thus introduces a third mode of social action: *logic of truth seeking or arguing.*

This logic invokes the idea that actors are in search for communicative consensus about shared understandings and "no longer hold fixed interests during their communicative interaction but are open to persuasion, challenges and counter challenges geared toward reaching a reasoned consensus" (Ibid.: 33). Therefore, actor "interests, preferences, and the perceptions of the situation are no longer fixed, but subject to discursive challenges" (Ibid.: 7). Consequently, a norm guides actor behaviour after actors undertake the processes of argumentation, deliberation, persuasion and other practices to develop an understanding of the situation and norms (Risse *et al.* 1999: 14). Once the consensus is reached behaviour becomes guided by intersubjectively shared norms (also see Kratochwil 1991, Kratochwil and Ruggie 1986).

Post-modern constructivists, however, suggest that logic of arguing introduces a communicative interaction process while still embracing many of the assumptions of appropriateness logic.[2] From this logic, it is learned that the appropriateness is constructed by argumentative processes, thus the state or quality of appropriateness is not given. Moreover, with regard to the contested character of norms, the logic of arguing successfully directs attention to communicative processes leading to this contestation. Nonetheless, besides the contestation upon the meaning of norms, the arguing logic is interested more in contestation upon the validity of norms.

At this juncture, it is post-modern constructivists who debate the contestedness of the meaning of the norms via recourse to linguistic approaches. Post-modern constructivists, while recognising the constructed nature of norms, epistemologically differ from the rest of the constructivists and argue that "there is no firm foundation for any knowledge" (Katzenstein *et al.* 1998: 677). Hence, they point the attention of the scholarship to the "instability of all symbolic and political orders" (Ibid.). To post-modernist constructivists, daily language (that is day-to-day practices) and the linguistic processes (interaction, interpretation and contestation) represent or present the "cognitive and political processes of destabilization" (Ibid.). Therefore, meaning, validity and facticity of norms are not stable.

The meanings of norms are not stable and static; they are subject to constant renegotiation and interpretation. Renegotiation and interpretation, however, are not driven by normative or argumentative rationality. It is, on the contrary, the cultural practices that define the ends and the means of interpretation and negotiation (Wiener 2007b: 3–5). In terms of the validity of norms, it is assumed in the logic of contestedness that since norms "evolve through interaction in context. Norms are therefore contested by default" (Ibid.: 6). Therefore, "while norms may be considered as valid and just under conditions of interaction in one cultural context, that perception cannot be generalized" and "normative validity cannot be assumed as stable" in all cultural contexts (Wiener 2007a: 55). Norm facticity, similarly, is not assumed to be secure. In the logic of contestedness, it is the norm facticity that structures behaviour and in return behaviour, as a social practice, exerts influence on the meaning and validity of norms (Ibid.). However, if the norm facticity is taken as stable then the role of norms becomes confined to guiding just as in the logic of appropriateness. However, in the logic of contestedness, the facticity is similarly contested (Ibid.: 64).

Therefore, according to post-modern constructivists, the meaning, validity and facticity of norms are altogether contested and hence the role norms play depends "on the specific contextual conditions" (Wiener and Puetter 2009: 15). At this point, these "contextual conditions" (interpretation, contestation, argumentation and negotiation) create different contexts within which the meaning-in-use of norms changes depending on the experience and enacted behaviour (Ibid.: 9). Therefore, when norms are contested their role in the *conduct* of the behaviour becomes contextual and depends on cultural validation, and vice versa.

In conclusion, all constructivist logics, in one way or another, embody some commonalities, even though their degrees vary; they do not totally deny each other's conclusions and there are certain points where all logics may merge. In this sense, for instance, the logic of contestedness is imbued with concepts from the logic of appropriateness, while the logic of arguing shares some assumptions regarding the role of norms with the logic of appropriateness and vice versa.

Accordingly, on the basis of overlapping roles casted to norms, norms spark ideational transformations, create cognitive frames, shape intersubjective understandings and meanings, reconstitute and mould conceptual categories, regulate (without defining the ends) and guide behaviour (discursive, cognitive and behavioural), generate habits of interpretation, constitute – verifying and disputing – identity without restraining behaviour (constitutive character). In the empirical section of the research, therefore, these roles will be employed and their validity will be tested.

Domestic Norms, Norm Change and Foreign Policy

As the above review illustrates, norms matter and are influential in policy choices. Subsequently, regardless of the way it changes, a change in the character of norms or the replacement of a dominant norm with another may be said to impact policy choices and thus force a shift in policy direction – something which is also deemed a highly possible scenario. This is because it has been acknowledged within the norms literature that "unsettled norms ... tend to have less impact on state action", while "settled norms are [more] influential on the behaviour of states" (Björkdahl 2002: 19–20). In this sense, when a settled norm is replaced with another settled norm or unsettled (competing) norms get closer to become settled through institutionalisation, policy changes are very likely.

In the literature, norm change has been extensively studied by international norms scholarship. The international norms literature approached norm change in two ways. In the first instance, an international norm becomes replaced by another norm and this norm change requires or invokes a change in actor behaviour. For instance, as Finnemore (1996) informs, with the part replacement of the norm of sovereign equity and non-interference with the norm of humanitarian intervention, state sovereignty became contested and international society conducted multilateral interventions to such as Iraq, Cambodia, Somalia, Bosnia or Kosovo (see Dağ 2016). In the second instance, due to the implementation of international policies toward some countries, the dominant domestic norm becomes replaced with the internationally recognised norm. Audie Klotz's (1995) work on the dislocation of the apartheid regime in South Africa due to the replacement of the apartheid norms with global norm of racial equality, stands as a concrete example. As Klotz suggests, international pressures (sanctions, enforcement and isolation) and "the global diffusion of a norm of racial equality" forced the South African government to replace the domestic norm that was legitimising the minority rule in the country (1995: 4, 195). Consequently, since South Africa was socialised into a global norm, the government abolished the apartheid regime (Ibid.: 165). This norm change, consequently, had an inevitable impact on the domestic and foreign policy choices, interests and identity of South Africa.

Nonetheless, the story that the domestic norms scholars tell is different in scope and content. With norm change, domestic norms literature refers to the emergence of a new dominant norm or one emergent norm gaining dominance over others via the institutionalisation in the domestic realm. In this sense, the analyses offered by domestic norm scholars resort to the idea of norms change in making sense of the shifts in foreign policy practices and to understanding the ways in which shifts in foreign policy are related to domestic changes.

For instance, Robert G. Herman argues that it was domestic norm change in the Soviet Union that "made the transformation of superpower relations possible" and hence "paved the way for the end of the Cold War" (1996: 272, 300). In that way, it is argued that during the Mikhail Gorbachev era "Soviet international policy was the product of cognitive evolution and policy entrepreneurship by networks of Western-oriented in-system reformers coincident with the coming to power of a leadership [refers to Gorbachev here] committed to change" (Ibid.: 273). It was, therefore, the dominancy of the norm of New Thinking that sparked the cognitive evolution of the intellectual and policy-making circles and eventual policy changes.

Similarly, according to Peter Katzenstein (1993), it was a change in the dominant norm in Japan and Germany by the end of WWII that enabled Japan and Germany to pursue non-violent (antimilitarist) national and international security policies. This corresponds to the decline of militarist norms in both countries since 1945. Having borne in mind that those two states were key in the development of WWII, Katzenstein explains the changing patterns of behaviour through addressing the changes in domestic norms. He also holds however that "norms themselves are not the sole determinants of the interests that shape actors' political choices and political outcomes ... [the] structural conditions ... [alike] shape interests, choices, and outcomes" (1993: 288). As for Japan, Katzenstein shows that the dominance of norms guiding Japan's security policy fluctuated after World War II. However, this was a long process and antimilitarist norms did not excessively influence the definition of Japan's policies in the early 1950s because of the contestation within the bureaucracy (1996b: 199). It was only with the redefinition of Japan's collective identity in economic terms by the end of 1950s and early 1960s that we begin to see the norm of antimilitarism gaining leverage and beginning to guide and inspire Japan's national and international security policies (Ibid.: 200–1). To this end, as norm changes remake policy choices, its stability and dominance leads to continuity in policy conduct and, as we see today in contemporary Japan, the antimilitarist norms are still dominant.

In another example, Anne-Marie Burley (1993) argues that the norms of the New Deal which have directed attention to liberal social welfare and institutional design programmes in the domestic realm have also had an impact on the foreign policy of post-WWII United States. Moreover, this shift in domestic politics had eventually led to the establishment of liberal international institutions at the international level due to United States led initiatives. Consequently, the norms of New Deal became internationally consequential after gaining a high degree of validity in domestic politics (Burley 1993).

These examples confirm Finnemore's suggestion that "changing norms may change state interests and create new interests ... [consequently] new or changed norms enable new or different behaviours" (1996a: 158). Therefore, new norms become dominant and policy orientation changes according to the teachings of the new dominant norm. This does not mean that the previously dominant norm vanishes from existence, it only loses leverage yet may still continue posing influence on policy choices. Thus, norm dominancy fluctuates. Confirming this Jeffrey Checkel holds that "within a polity one can have several different levels of norms" (1999: 106). In tandem with this, Legro argues that "different norms can have competing or even contradictory imperatives" (1997: 33), meaning that some norms become more influential and more dominant in strength than others. In a norm change thereby what is changing is the dominancy among norms, whereas behaviour continues to be guided with multiple socially constructed interests, identities and norms. This however does not simply mean that certain norms are selected and influence policies while others fall completely (Risse-Kappen 1994: 187). I rather put forth that there are multiple norms at play during the making of policies; however the dominant norm is more likely to generate policy implications. To sum up, norm change motivates shifts in policy choices. In this sense, although the occurrence of norm change differs, both domestic and internationally imposed norm changes are followed by policy shifts through one norm's gain of dominancy over others, which confirms that "what is true of domestic norms holds also for international norms", and vice versa (Katzenstein 1993: 269).

Norm-guided Behaviours and Foreign Policy Conduct

I established above that norms hold a guiding and constitutive role in relation to actor behaviour and that once actor behaviour is guided, this behaviour or action is called "norm-guided behaviours".[3] Here, while the guiding role of norms corresponds to the foreign policy formation, norm-guided behaviour matches up to the conduct of a foreign policy act. This is because once behaviour becomes guided by a norm, it means that a "norm is translated into a policy" (Park and Vetterlein 2010: 5). Nonetheless since norms do not determine the ends of the action and only refer to the appropriate means, a norm-guided behaviour is different to rule-guided behaviour[4] or merely materially motivated behaviours.[5] One, therefore, needs to ask what kind of functions does a norm-guided behaviour/policy upholds or perform? Put differently, "what role do norms play in the conduct of foreign policy?"[6] (Björkdahl 2002: 22). To understand the functions of norm-driven foreign policy, a satisfactory response needs to be given to these questions and probations. Concomitantly, in order to further clarify the difference between norm-guided, rule-guided or non-guided behaviour, the functions of norm-guided behaviour and the role of norms in behaviour guiding have to be explored.

As noted above, in the IR norms literature the norm-guided actions of actors (both state and non-state actors) are assigned with five different but closely interrelated functions: (i) norm-guided behaviour is a meaningful action and denotes the intentions of the conductor; (ii) norm-guided behaviour invokes the identity of the policy conductor;

(iii) norm-guided behaviour conveys/transmits the norm; (iv) norm-guided behaviour urges the endorsement of the norm by the target actor/s; and (v) norm-guided behaviour leads target agents to internalise new roles, identities and interests, therefore, it has a constitutive function. It is indeed obvious that there are overlaps between the role of norms and the functions of norm-guided behaviours.

The first function that norm-guided behaviour is allocated with is that it is a meaningful action for both the conductor and the target (Jepperson et al. 1996: 54 and Kratochwil 1991: 11). The meaning of the action reflects the teachings of the norm and denotes the intentions of the conductor on the one hand. On the other, it reflects the result of cultural validation regarding the norm. In this sense, the meaning given to the action by the conductor and the target would differ, as the target community/agent interprets the action according to its own historical and cultural context. Nonetheless, a norm-driven foreign policy as a guided-action is a meaningful act for both parties, even for the third parties and this feature of norm-guided action is justified in the literature since "in the absence of norms, exercises of power or actions would be devoid of meaning" (Hopf 1998: 173).

The second function of the norm-guided action is that it invokes the identity of the policy conductor. This role has been conceptualised in several ways. In the first instance, it is argued that norm-guided behaviours make similar behavioural claims on dissimilar actors, those who conduct similar behaviours are considered to be holding the same identity or a membership to the same group (Kowert and Legro 1996: 465, Finnemore 1996b: 342). This is even more relevant to international norms. In another instance, it is suggested by Ted Hopf that norm-guided behaviours have constitutive function because "constitutive norms define an identity by specifying the actions" which causes "[o]thers to recognize that identity and respond to it appropriately" (1998: 173). In this case, the norm-guided foreign policy becomes a representative of state/collective identity, which is invoked by the action and perceived by the receiver agent. Therefore, once a norm starts guiding behaviour, concomitantly, the constructed collective identity accompanies the behaviour and becomes indicated and enacted by the conduct of the action (see Katzenstein 1996a, b).

Following this, non-action is also valued as an identity-invoking action. It has been acknowledged that not acting in certain ways or the reluctance in acting, due to the normative concerns, reflect the identity of the actor. For instance, Germany and Japan's disinclination and unwillingness to "resort to the use of military force" in both national and international relations are argued to be stemming from the historically constructed domestic norm of antimilitarism (Berger 1996: 318). Here the behaviour of non-acting in military terms suggests that Germany and Japan hold non-violent state identities.

Accordingly, the second function of norm-guided behaviours is to indicate actor identity. This function of norms would be more solid if the behaviour is guided by an identity norm (or a constitutive norm in Katzensteinian sense) because "[collective] identity norms make much more powerful claims on behaviour than do the causal beliefs and schemata" (Herman 1996: 285).

The third function of norm-guided behaviour is to convey a norm. Annie Klotz presents a self-evident example of norm conveyance by norm-guided behaviour. She explains that in South Africa it was both domestic and international pressures that ended the racist apartheid regime in 1994. As soon as the norm of racial equality became embraced globally, its teachings were translated into sanction policies against South Africa. These sanction policies forced South Africa to adhere to the norm of racial equality. This could be seen as a norm-guided behaviour whereby sanctions worked to force the target community to show endorsement to the norm of racial equality. It is seen here that a norm-guided behaviour conveys the norm and contains the qualities of convincing the target community to embrace the norm that guides it.

In a similar vein, Robert Herman argues that with adherence to the norm of New Thinking in the USSR, "Gorbachev actively encouraged Warsaw Pact governments to emulate Moscow in introducing greater liberalisation in economic and political life" (1996: 305). Here, again, norm-guided foreign policy was transmitting the norm to new realms and asking for the endorsement of these norms. Besides, there are also discursive practices within foreign policy (or *as* foreign policy) which also serve as mechanisms through which an international norm enters into a domestic arena (Cortell and Davis 2000: 76). Thus discourses, as discursive practices and as norm-guided foreign policy practices, convey norms into new domestic fields and request validation and adherence (Ibid.: 76–7).

Regarding the fourth function of norms, it is seen in the empirical evidences produced by Burley (1993), Klotz (1995) and Herman (1996) that the transmitting of a norm and the urging of endorsement go hand in hand during the conduct of a norm-guided action. Socialisation of the target community/actor into a norm therefore stands as a self-evident proof of such function, as it involves both the diffusion of a norm and the urging of endorsement to it (Finnemore and Sikkink 1998). In a clearer example, Thomas Risse formulates the function of norm-guided behaviour as the translation of international norms into domestic practices in the target community (2000: 28–9). To Risse, norm-guided behaviour functions as a kind of transmission belt between the norm-setter community and the target community. Therefore, norm-guided behaviour both (i) conveys the norm and (ii) aims at increasing the endorsement to it (Risse 2000: 28).

Christine Ingebritsen, similarly, demonstrates that Scandinavian states are in many ways "norm-builders" who act in international politics as norm entrepreneurs and hence their foreign policy aims to disseminate regionally and domestically constructed norms (2002). Among these norms, sustainable development, conflict resolution, and aid provisions are well-known. As Ingebritsen argues the small states in Scandinavia have "consistently and actively sought to influence more powerful states in establishing and strengthening global norms of cooperation" (2002: 1). Therefore, norm entrepreneurship comes to the fore here as a norm-guided acting and its envisaged role overlaps with and confirms the functions of the norm-guided action offered in the literature: transmitting the norm and seeking to increase adherence to it.

As for the final function of the norms, at this point it is possible to confidently argue that the functions of norm-guided behaviour exert influence on the target actor because norm-guided behaviours lead target agents to internalise new roles, identities and interests (Checkel 2005: 801). In the literature, this character of norms has been valued as a constitutive quality. To Checkel, "norms coming down to a [new] domestic arena has constitutive effects" by which the norm-guided behaviour request adherence to the norm and the roles and identities attached to it (1999: 85). This quality of norm-guided behaviour results in the occurrence of a response by the target either in the form of adherence, rejection or something in-between, which constitutes the impact generated by the conduct of the norm-guided behaviour.

This constitutive character analytically facilitates the formulation of a measurement tool to disclose the influence a norm-guided foreign policy exerts.

In conclusion, as has been demonstrated so far, understanding the role of norms in foreign policy is vital to making sense of how a conduct becomes generated. However, this alone would be deficient in comprehending the implications and impact of norm-guided behaviours or policies. Therefore, enquiring into the functions of norm-guided behaviour is of fundamental importance. As listed above, norm-guided foreign policy holds five functions: gives meaning to action, invokes identity, conveys the norm, urges the endorsement of norm, and lastly it exerts constitutive effect. As can be seen, the functions of norm-guided foreign policy and the roles of norms in foreign policy are mutually inclusive. They affirm and complement each other. In this manner, portraying the role of norms in foreign policy formation is telling only the first half of the story of the foreign policy process. It is also necessary to tell the second part of the story: that is the conduct of the foreign policy. Only after explaining the influences of norm-guided behaviour on the target community/state, can the consequences of norm-change in the norm-emergent community be made sense of. Therefore, considering the purposes held by this research, it is academically noteworthy and essential to illustrate the functions of norm-guided behaviour, which renders possible the tracing of the implications and influences of the conduct of norm-driven policies. These roles and functions are relevant also in formulating the framework of the research, which I deal with below.

The Framework: Overseas Implications of Domestic Norms

Having been informed by the above review, this section presents a norm-informed foreign policy analysis framework for exploring the overseas implications and influences of domestic norms or norm changes. To respond to questions, which involve analyses on several levels, the framework needs to be holistically formulated. In this sense, the framework needs to explain the domestic norm change in the scope of which new norms emerge and gain dominance over old ones. Moreover, it needs to be capable of disclosing the domestic norms and foreign policy conduct relationship in the scope of which domestic norm-guided foreign policy is conducted. The framework, finally, should be able to disclose the implications of the norm-guided foreign policy in a new domestic locality abroad. The roles of norms and the functions of norm-guided behaviours do indeed provide a firm ground to stick to in conducting research; however, they are alone far from presenting a structured framework. This research needs a well-structured framework to analytically, systematically and scientifically set out the course and present the findings.

The norm's life cycle model

Within the study of norms in IR, the "norm's life cycle model" of Finnemore and Sikkink (1998) that analyses norm survival can provide the required structure on which to build this present research project. Accordingly, the model formulates and values norm survival as a three-stage process as illustrated in Figure 4.1, namely norm emergence, norm cascade, norm internalisation. As will be shown below, each stage within the model matches well with the stages the foreign policy scrutiny this study conducts; namely foreign policy formation, conduct and implications.

The first stage represents the emergence and the gaining of mass acceptance of a norm in the international arena. Both state and non-state actors are involved and play imperative role in the creation of norms as "norm entrepreneurs and the organizational platforms from which entrepreneurs act" (Finnemore and Sikkink 1998: 896). Norms are built by entrepreneurs as the language and the cognitive frames that signify and evoke the essentiality of a norm are constructed by them (Ibid.: 897). Therefore, the process is run by entrepreneurs on the basis of persuasion and promoting ideational commitment (Ibid.: 898). In order

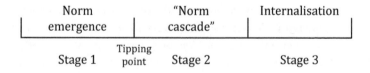

Figure 4.1   The norm's life cycle model. Source: Finnemore and Sikkink (1998) "International Norm Dynamics and Political Change", *International Organization*, Vol. 52, No. 4, p. 896.

to proceed with the persuasion process, norm entrepreneurs use the media tools along with organisational platforms such as NGOs. Through determining the inappropriate modes of behaviour and through moulding public discourses, organisational networks facilitate the dissemination and institutionalisation of norms. The institutionalisation of a norm and later the construction of a relevant identity are necessary for a norm to transcend the *tipping point* – that is, the point after which the second stage commences.

The second stage of norm survival is characterised by actors' attempts to socialise[7] others to become norm followers. State and non-state actors altogether "act as agents of socialization by pressuring targeted actors to adopt new policies" that are compatible with the standards set by the norm (Ibid.: 902). Nonetheless, what makes a targeted group adhere to a norm is their concern for complying with the identity as a member of a larger group (such as the international society if the target is a state). Finnemore and Sikkink come to this conclusion with reference to the argument that a membership to a particular social category that signifies and evokes a particular identity requires compliance to certain norms (Ibid.). This process thus involves the utilisation of some motivational factors such as legitimation, conformity and esteem along with identity and peer-pressure to secure norm-conformance (Ibid.: 903).

The third stage is related to norm internalisation and described to be the "far end of the norm cascade", in other words, the time when a norm gains a taken-for-granted quality by the target community/state (Ibid.: 895). The internalisation is not an instant process; the socialisation of the targeted community should be entirely completed for this quality to be gained. Therefore, internalisation depends on the resolution of the contention and inconsistency between the externally coming norm and internally existing one and on the externally coming norms' prevailing over the existing one's during socialisation.

As can be seen, the demarcation of the stages corresponds neatly to the phases of my enquiry in this research. Accordingly, the emergence stage is the phase which I seek to understand domestic norm emergence by which new norms emerge, gain dominance over the old ones and influence foreign policy choices. The cascade stage corresponds to the phase where I try to disclose the domestic norms and foreign policy relationship in the scope of which domestic norm-guided foreign policy is conducted. Finally, the internalisation stage corresponds to the phase where I try to disclose the implications of the norm-guided foreign policy in a new domestic locality abroad. Therefore, although the norm's life cycle model is designed to explore international norms and looks at the norm processes mostly at the inter-state level, its formulation and stage demarcation perfectly matches with the aims of this research and stands out as a well-structured model that can be utilised as a framework to analyse domestic norms and their overseas implications. Still, to make sure that this is suitable for a domestic norm analysis, the model should be elaborated more fully.

Elaborated norm's life cycle model for the analysis of domestic norms

This section illustrates how the norm's life cycle, a model to analyse international norm influence, becomes applicable to examining and exploring the overseas implications and impacts of domestic norm change. I, therefore, elaborate the mechanisms, processes and interactions operating within the demarcated stages (norm emergence, norm cascade, internalisation) and illustrate how and through which dynamics the model would work in the analysis of domestic norms and foreign policy interrelationship. As for the empirical side of my research I present a conceptual framework for the analysis of the post-Kemalist norms concerning Outside Turks and the causal mechanisms stemming from them in foreign policy conduct.

Stage 1- Norm Emergence

This study values norm emergence as a domestically occurring process of historical, social and political interaction, construction and institutionalisation. This should not invoke the sense that norm emergence in general is confined to the domestic processes. International, transnational or regional processes and mechanisms are also exemplified intensely in the literature as the creators or builders of norms (see Finnemore 1996a). Nonetheless, in the literature there also exists a common understanding that "[m]any international norms began as domestic norms and become international through the efforts of entrepreneurs of various kinds" (Finnemore and Sikkink 1998: 893, Björkdahl 2002: 18, Kier 1996). Still, one may think that the norm's life cycle model focuses its attention on the international norms and thus domestic norms could not be dealt with via recourse to this model. Nevertheless, Finnemore and Sikkink (1998) acknowledge in their study that most of the time international norms first emerge domestically. They demonstrate that although norm emergence takes place domestically, the *norm cascade* makes domestic norms international ones (Ibid.: 902–4). Christine Ingebritsen exemplifies this in her study on the domestic construction of global norms such as the norms of eco-politics, conflict resolution and aid provisions with reference to the unique domestic structures of Scandinavian states (2002: 13).

Nonetheless, since the norm scholarship focuses its attention chiefly on international norms, the mechanisms and dynamics of domestic norm emergence remains under-researched. Moreover, since norms are present in different forms in different societies, cultures, institutions or states, the emergence of domestic norms become contextual. Therefore, scholars have come to qualify norm emergence differently.

Elizabeth Kier, for instance, underscores the role of culture, more specifically the bureaucratic organisational culture, in the emergence of the norms that defined France's defensive military policy against Nazi Germany (1996: 204). Similarly, Alastair Iain Johnson resorts to historically transmitted strategic culture in explaining the ideational roots of China's endorsement of realpolitik behaviour during the Maoist period (1996: 257–60). Berger, in a similar vein and in using the example of Japan and Germany's reluctance to using military force in the post-WWII period, draws attention to the historicity and cultural–institutional accounts of the emergence of domestic norms (1996: 318). Robert G. Herman, having subscribed to the relevance of cultural–institutional context, alternatively, places emphasis on the collective ideational constructs, cognitive evolution and policy entrepreneurship in domestic norm emergence (1996: 273). As the leading figure in formulating the domestic norm construction, Peter Katzenstein (1996a), also adds to this debate by integrating institutionalisation and norm-compatible identity construction to the norm emergence process, along with admitting the constitutive role of socio-political processes, cultural–institutional context, history and cognitive evolution in domestic norm emergence following the previous studies. Therefore – and based on these propositions – domestic norm emergence becomes a domestically appearing process of historical, social and political interaction, construction, and institutionalisation. Thus, the following mechanisms are suggested to be active during norm emergence: (i) historical and cultural evolution (ii) social and cognitive construction (iii) social and political institutionalisation (iv) identity construction.

This reformulation of the first stage of the norm's life cycle does not cast aside the mechanisms Finnemore and Sikkink (1998) offered. Indeed, the constructive role norm entrepreneurs, organisational platforms, and argumentation play in norm emergence is acknowledged throughout the mechanisms and it is still the norm entrepreneurs and organisational platforms that act as the core agents in norm construction and promotion.

Historical and cultural evolution

In this mechanism, the historical and cultural contingencies norms possess are addressed and it is admitted that norms are "made and unmade in history" (Katzenstein 1996b: 2). Yet, "history itself is not the creator of norms, political processes makes and unmakes norms" and they "crystallize at critical historical junctures result[ing] from political conflict and change" (Ibid.: 38). In this sense, it is not "the push-and-pulls of daily politics" but history and earth breaking events that "give norms both importance and endurance" (Ibid.: 3). Thus, the changing and evolving character of norms are relevant to critical historical junctures besides every day politics, as opposed to Wiener's (2007a) argument on the ultimate necessity of daily politics. Culture, as referred to by all studies listed above, nonetheless, is in charge of providing the cognitive frames to interpret the historical events through which norms are constructed and evolved (Katzenstein 1996b: 3). The strategic culture or institutional culture thus represents the context in which norms' presence and functioning could be traced.

Social, communicative and cognitive construction

The construction process is subject to the direct involvement of human or institutional agency as suggested by Finnemore and Sikkink (1998); therefore, the role of entrepreneurs becomes imperative here. Altogether the social, communicative and cognitive construction processes are carried out by entrepreneurs. The idea of social construction suggests that we not consider norms as something "out there" and pre-given. As social facts, domestic norms are constructed through domestic social processes; hence they are socially constructed and interactively construed through communicative and cognitive processes. Norm emergence therefore is also a communicative process and norms communicatively emerge in various ways, sometimes "spontaneously evolving, as social practice; consciously promoted, as political strategies to further specific interests; deliberately negotiated, as a mechanism for conflict management; or as a combination, mixing these three types" (Katzenstein 1996a: 21). In this sense, societal or political types of communication become necessary as individuals, societies and institutions (including Finnemore and Sikkink's entrepreneurs and organisational platforms) are altogether involved in the construction process (Katzenstein 1996b: 41–2). Therefore, mass media and public opinion, all communicative by-products, can be regarded as communicative platforms through which norms are made and remade, and political realities are produced and gain acceptance (Ibid.: 38–9). The contestation upon the meaning of norms thus derives from these continuous and communicative-bounded constructions as Weiner (2007a) argues. Finally, cognitive engagement is fundamental for both norm construction and deconstruction and for norm entrepreneurs. This is because cognitive framing is a means of interpretation, reinterpretation and persuasion in constructing social realities and intersubjective understandings. Norm entrepreneurs, therefore, construct cognitive frames that vitalise norms in order to make the acceptance of the norm grounded and widespread. Or, on the other hand, cognition itself causes norm dissolution. Eastern European socialism constitutes a concrete example of this. In Eastern Europe, for instance "masses were no longer willing to believe and die for [socialism], and leaders no longer believed and killed for it" and consequently it was erased from existence (1996b: 5).

Social and political institutionalisation

Institutionalisation is the phase within which an ideational social setting or an intersubjectively shared idea gains the quality of influencing behaviour. As Katzenstein states, "[n]orms do not float freely in political space. They acquire particular importance when they crystallise, through institutionalization" (1996b: 21). Thus, institutionalised norms express collectively held preferences, values and ideas more evidently and recognisably. However, for some norms, institutionalisation does not come in a straightforward manner because institutionalisation is hard to achieve for all norms, particularly for the political ones. Yet, since several other constitutive processes are at play throughout the emergence process such as cognitive evolution and reframing, norms can impact actor behaviour with or without institutionalisation. This is the reason why Finnemore and Sikkink argue that institutionalisation "is not a necessary condition" and not an absolute must for the emergence of a functioning norm (1998: 900). Nonetheless, this does not change the fact that institutionalisation enhances norms' longevity and capacity to pose impact.

At this point, how institutionalisation occurs should be probed. To Finnemore and Sikkink (1998) the institutionalisation comes when the critical mass of actors embraces the norm and its prescriptive quality. Yet since "in international level the institutionalization ... is in the monopoly of small group of people and institutions ... the institutionalization of norms in international level is not dense as much as the one in national level" as Katzenstein informs (1996b: 20). In a domestic context, however, the institutional context provides a meaningful institutionalisation to norms. For instance, constitutions, national education curricula, laws, procedures, government institutions, security forces, universities and others are mechanisms for norm institutionalisation (Katzenstein 1996b: 33, Boekle *et al.* 2002). Moreover, in domestic politics, the press and visual media serve as organisational platforms through which norms become institutionalised (Finnemore and Sikkink 1998: 899). Media makes social communication possible and determines and gives shape to the course of cognitive evolution and communicative construction of social facts, values and norms through which the emergence process reaches the institutionalisation stage (Katzenstein 1996b: 22).

Identity Politics (Tipping Point)
Finnemore and Sikkink argue that there is a *tipping point* "at which a critical mass of relevant state actors adopt the [international] norm" (1998: 895). By transcending this point, a new stage begins in norm survival which is norm cascade, and new mechanisms and actors enter into the scene. In domestic norms, nonetheless, the tipping point represents the threshold beyond which a domestic norm becomes an international one. Therefore, domestic norms need to get translated into foreign policy to transcend the tipping point. Mass public endorsement

to norms might prompt such acts. However, as Boekle *et al.* demonstrate, it is the construction of identity that eventually generates a norm-induced foreign policy act (2002: 123). This is because, to them, identity is constructed by domestic norms hence identity politics is also a norm-guided policy act (Ibid.).

How, then, does identity become constructed by norms? The literature has generally conveyed the idea of a straightforward correlation between norm institutionalisation and identity construction. According to this, norm institutionalisation is argued to have identity-constructing capabilities. This character of norms has been championed chiefly by Katzenstein (see 1996a: 24–5, 1996b: 18–9). In this view, "institutionalized norms ... embody the qualities that define actor identities and the standards of conduct that actors seek to uphold" (Katzenstein 1996b: 18). Here, Katzenstein addresses the regulatory/guiding and constitutive characters and roles of norms. To Katzenstein, these two roles are "closely linked" (Ibid.: 19) and while the regulative role defines the standards of appropriate behaviour, the constitutive character "express[es] actor identities that also define interest" (Ibid.: 18). He, moreover, holds that "such identities are often expressed in and moulded by state institutions" (Ibid.: 29).

Therefore, the correlation between foreign policy, norms and identity with regard to life cycle of norms is that identity construction and identity politics in foreign policy represent the "tipping point" by which "an emergent norm" reaches "a threshold [thus gains mobility] and move towards the second stage" (Finnemore and Sikkink 1998: 900). Upon the identity politics and foreign policy relationship, it should be made clear that institutional subscription to an identity is key in internationalising norms and identity "is something greater than the opinions of the current government [and] both state and non-state actors operate within the structure and constraints of state identity" (Gurowitz 2006: 311). This is consistent with the ascribed roles entrepreneurs play throughout the process of norm survival.

Stage 2: Norm Cascade

Drawing from Katzenstein's accounts of domestic norms, I now hold that domestic and foreign policies become intertwined due to the fact that identity politics begins to prevail over other foreign policy choices.[8] Katzenstein explains this by giving the example of a non-violent identity, which was constructed via the domestic norm of "anti-militarism" – this is best exemplified in the example of the identity which came to explain Japan's decision to opt out of United Nations' resolutions on military peacemaking operations (1996b: 150–1). Although, the Katzensteinian norm analysis perfectly accounts for explaining foreign policy change (or stability), elucidation of the international mobility of a norm and *foreign policy*'s prominent agency role in this would require concentrating on the international dimension of norm survival. Finnemore and Sikkink's model does exactly this and suggests that after the tipping point has been reached, "international and transnational norm influences become more important than domestic politics for effecting norm change", which means that new dynamics are at play at this stage in terms of both the international mobilisation of norms and their cross-border influence (1998: 902). Thus, the "cascade stage" (as it is called by Finnemore and Sikkink) comes to the fore as part of the smooth continuum of the norm-emergence stage.

In Finnemore and Sikkink's (1998) formulation, the second stage of the norm's life cycle – *norm cascade* – is characterised by attempts by agents to socialise others to become norm followers. The motivation here is to secure conformance through socialisation and involves direct involvement of "[n]etworks of norm entrepreneurs and international organizations" along with the states "as agents of socialization" (Finnemore and Sikkink 1998: 902). Socialisation,[9] in Finnemore and Sikkink's (1998) accounts, functions as the core and all-encompassing mechanism at this stage. Nonetheless, Checkel informs by way of a response to the question of "how norms actually reach the domestic arena" of the target community, that prior to socialisation a diffusion mechanism is at play (1997: 476, 1999: 86). The diffusion refers to the international mobility of a norm held via foreign policy on the one hand and, on the other, it implies the adopter population's attention and involvement in the transmission process (transnational relations). The socialisation, therefore, commences only by the successful diffusion of a norm into the target locality. This is also admitted by Finnemore and Sikkink, yet they argue that socialisation involves diffusion.

Diffusion

As Finnemore and Sikkink suggest, norm diffusion is not a contagion process or a passive course of actions that come about without direct interference; instead it involves active engagement of agency (1998: 902). This is because norms are not free-floating entities – their mobility is provided by agents. The agency here, as suggested by Checkel (1999), is constituted by norm-setter and norm-taker entrepreneurs. Concomitantly, there are present two distinct entrepreneur driven internationalising dynamics within the diffusion mechanism: norm mobility through foreign policy and social learning through transnational relations. Norm mobility is sparked by the entrepreneurs in the norm-setter community, while the social learning refers to the transfer of the norms by the local elites of the norm-taking community through learning. Nonetheless, both processes of the norm diffusion depend critically on social and cultural characteristics and identities of the norm-setting and norm-taking communities (Checkel 1999: 86, Cortell and Davis 2000). This is because diffusion is provided by agents with a certain identity and with identity politics' determining of where the norms diffuse.

In this sense, state identity and the role of identity in shaping the state's foreign policy is one of the core determinants of triumphant international mobilisation. As Amy Gurowitz establishes, norm mobilisation is mediated by "a state's international identity ... and by how secure or insecure the state is at a given time about that identity" (2006: 307). This is how and why diffusion of norms differs from one country to another (Ibid.: 306–11). In addition to identity, as shown above, agency too is of primary importance for norm mobilisation and governments take the lead in this. As the prime agent, governments perform the much of the norm-driven acts and convey the norms internationally – however, their actions are constrained and motivated or mediated according to their identities (Risse-Kappen 1995: 18). Within the structure and constraints of state identity, however, along with governments, non-state actors can operate as norm entrepreneurs – something which means they are also becoming involved in giving the norm international mobility (Gurowitz 2006: 311). In this fashion, in addition to governments, NGOs, diplomatic missions, state institutions, religious groups, transnational ties or even individuals may have a role in norm mobilisation through performing norm-driven actions. In short, the mobilisation dynamic corresponds to the norm entrepreneurs' (thus foreign policy's) conveyor role via its performing of norm-driven actions that connect two separate political units through norm transmission.

The social learning dynamic, on the other hand, is a transnational kind of social practice engaged by local elites in a norm-taking community and constitutes the second path to the question of how norms reach the domestic arena. Social learning is a process whereby a norm catches the attention of domestic elites and sparks discussions and debates (Checkel 2001: 561–4). Therefore, it is a communicative process prompting the learning of the new interests and identities, and leading to discursive and practical behavioural changes (Checkel 1997: 477, Checkel 2001: 561). The social characteristic and cultural match of the norm-taking elites therefore increase the possibility of smooth and rapid diffusion (Checkel 1999: 87). As an affirmation of this, Meyer and Strang inform us that the "cultural match between global norms and domestic practice will be key in determining the pattern and degree of diffusion" (1993: 503–4, cited in Checkel 1999: 87).

Socialisation

A clear-cut separation or demarcation of the mechanisms is impractical considering that the social interactions are taking place in a processual web of relations within a mechanism and expecting a linear or sequential set of action is thus futile. In this vein, it can be argued that social learning is a mechanism for socialisation too because learning among many other functions facilitates norm compliance. It is known that local agents "learn through socialization" (Harrison 2004: 528) or are taught new values and interests during socialisation (see Checkel 1999: 87, Finnemore 1993), thus learning comes to be a necessary dynamic within the socialisation mechanism as well. Nonetheless, my appraisal of social learning is that it is a transnational diffusive mechanism that heralds successful socialisation.

This research, following Finnemore and Sikkink (1998), values socialisation as the mutual effort of agents in both norm-setting and norm target communities, and a distinctive mechanism within the norm cascade stage that commences thanks to the successful diffusion of a norm into the norm-adopting domestic arena.

For Finnemore and Sikkink, socialisation corresponds to the efforts aimed at persuasion of the target community (or state) to change their behaviour through adhering to the promoted norm (1998: 903–4). Socialisation comes therefore to be a firm *process* (not an outcome[10]) whereby agents strive to persuade others to comply with a norm

(Ibid.: 902). In Finnemore and Sikkink's formulation, three methods shine out for successful socialisation: peer-pressure, identity and motivational factors such as legitimation, conformity or esteem – all of which address a worry of avoiding "disapproval aroused by norm violation" (Ibid.: 904). Consequently, the actors' representation of themselves as a particular identity-holder or as a member of an *international* society motivates them in favour of norm conformance, which ends up with socialisation.

Concomitantly, in Jeffrey Checkel's accounts, three dynamics operate in the socialisation of a target community/state into certain norms: namely, strategic calculation, role playing and normative suasion (1999: 805). Strategic calculation suggests that it is the careful calculation that governs norm compliance, the sole operation of which bears no possibility to talk about socialisation (Ibid.: 809). To Checkel, this dynamic is relevant only to show the change in the logic of action when a social process commences via the diffusion of norms (Ibid.). Role playing, on the other hand, represents the change in the logic and "involves non-calculative behavioural adaptation" (Ibid.: 810). Target agents adapt roles because it is appropriate to do so. Identity plays a constructive role here because holding an identity is strictly tied to adapting relevant roles. The role-playing agents may comply with norms in a non-reflective manner, meaning that there is no negotiation about the meaning of norms though the interests the role playing brings are of main concern. In the normative suasion, finally, agents engage in persuasion to convince each other via communicative means (Ibid.: 812).

There is also the assumption here that the two accounts given above confine the role of norms to behavioural compliance. However, socialisation is first and foremost a normative and ideational process and leads to the acceptance of new intersubjective meanings and frames. The processes depicted by Checkel (1999) and (partly) Finnemore and Sikkink (1998) may therefore lack the social and ideational content when rationality is considered. Moreover, since, in the end, socialised communities internalise certain mind-sets and identities, any analysis devoid of social content would not account fully for this process. Accordingly, during socialisation it is the "socio-cultural rather than the material context that is critical to motivating [actor] behaviour" (Harrison 2004: 525). In this fashion, a community or state becomes socialised to a norm via the utilisation mainly of culture (cultural match) and identity thus socialisation is more an ideational and normative notion than a strategic calculation based process. Nonetheless, leaving aside the target's position on rationality and calculation relating to conformance, there exists a consensus that along with cultural match, communicative processes such as persuasion or argumentation are the dynamics for socialisation (Finnemore and Sikkink 1998, Risse *et al.* 1999, Checkel 1999, Wiener 2007a, b). Furthermore, having admitted the role of persuasion/argumentation and cultural match in socialisation, Wiener (2007a) suggests that the reification of the norm in the target domestic setting facilitates socialisation and that this happens through the institutionalisation of the relevant norm.

The communicative processes are necessary for a triumphant socialisation because the socialisation is not a monolithic or unilateral process in which an outsider agency socialises a community into a norm without communicating or interaction (for a similar explanation, see Boekle *et al.* 2002: 110). Complementarily, re-institutionalisation of a norm in the target domestic locality, in addition to reifying the norm, provides relevant platforms in which argumentation take place (Wiener 2007a: 55). This is the reason why Checkel values institutions as both the promoters *and* the sites of socialisation (2005: 806–7). In this respect, re-institutionalised norms' meaning is subject to negotiation and renegotiation between norm setters and norm takers (Wiener 2007a: 55). Therefore, one cannot assume the occurrence of an *agreement* as soon as a norm cascades. Nonetheless, the institutionalisation does not confine involvements to local agency; the foreign agents (diplomatic mission, state institutions, civil initiatives, individuals among others) may also be involved in institutionalisation.

To sum up, socialisation requires the active engagement of agency and involves normative, ideational and material endeavours and discussions to persuade a community to adopt a norm. Socialisation mechanisms thus aim to secure the grounds for norm compliance and to bring the cascade stage to completion. It should also be borne in mind that, although Boekle *et al.* (2002: 110) hold that the effect of norms can be seen to appear in the socialisation mechanism, its actual impacts are expected to appear in the internalisation process according to the framework formulated by Finnemore and Sikkink (1998). Last, but certainly not least, norm-induced acts are necessary as well for socialisation, as they have functions such as transmitting norms and urging endorsement to them.

Stage 3: Norm Internalisation

The final stage of the elaborated norm's life cycle is "norm internalisation" and the enquiry turns to the degree of internalisation of the norm in the target domestic sphere. Finnemore and Sikkink value the internalisation as the "far end of the norm cascade" thus of the process of socialisation (1998: 895). To them, on the far edge of the internalisation a norm retains a taken-for-granted status though this does not happen for every norm. By the same token, Risse and Sikkink argue that "[t]he goal of socialization is for actors to internalize norms" thus securing the ground for norm compliance (Risse and Sikkink 1999: 11). Similarly, Checkel suggests that internalisation is the end point of socialisation (2005: 805). He further holds that the instrumental rationality that governs the behaviour during the socialisation ceases to function with the internalisation of the norm. The rational calculations become replaced by the "taken-for-grantedness" after the internalisation (Ibid.: 804). Not every norm can be qualified as totally internalised, therefore the degrees of the internalisation vary.[11]

In relation to this, internalisation is not an instant process; it depends on the resolution of the contention and inconsistency between the external norms and internally existing norms; in other words, the question is whether the former can prevail over the latter. Therefore, in this process, the degree of norm internalisation varies and some may remain non-internalised. This is a result of what Weiner calls "norm validation" (2007b: 5). Paying attention to different levels of internalisation would provide the contentions and contestations regarding the local reflections on or resonations of the norms. Furthermore, the consideration of varying degrees of internalisation also enables the measuring and revealing of the implications and influences that a norm poses in the target locality. If the norm is fully internalised, then norm-compliance will be firm and the impact will be easily discernible. This is so also in cases of full rejection of the norm. However, the practical impact would be unexpected and unpredictable if a norm is modified or localised in order to reach the best match between the externally coming norm and domestic cultural context during the negotiations/argumentation phase. Moreover, it is also likely that some parts of the community may internalise the norm while others may not. This may lead to contestation, reaction and resistance to norms within the community all of which gives us scope to trace the impacts.

Consequently, which mechanisms the internalisation stage operates through is the next issue to deal with. The mechanisms of norm cascade, such as socialisation or institutionalisation continue to function during internalisation (Risse *et al.* 1999: 5, Park and Vetterlein 2010, Cortell and Davis 2000). This shows that norm cascade and internalisation appear to be mostly interlaced and the mechanisms operating within the cascade stage continue rendering influence on the internalisation of norms. In addition to these mechanisms, Finnemore and Sikkink (1998) pay particular attention to the role local agencies plays in internalisation. As they suggest, local professionals and organisations "serve as powerful and pervasive agents working to internalize norms among members" (1998: 905). Therefore, in addition to the aforementioned mechanisms, norm entrepreneurs continue to play a role in internalisation. In short, communicative processes, institutionalisation, cultural validation, socialisation and norm entrepreneurs are the mechanisms by which internalisation occurs and the result of attempts at norm internalisation is revealed. At this juncture, the result of the attempts varies, in tandem with the degrees of internalisation of a norm. Broadly speaking, if the norm could not been fully internalised, alternatives are either it is modified to fit the local context or rejected depending on the degree of contestation, reactions and resistances. Either result leaves a trail of influence which can be discerned.

Contestation/rejection refers to a state of affairs in which resistance to the socialisation continues (Acharya 2004: 254). In the scope of the contestation, partly or en masse, a community either does not "seriously consider or discuss whether to conform" or feels that its identity or culture is at stake due to the alien norms' constitutive influences (Finnemore and Sikkink 1998: 904). Once a community gets exposed to the constitutive processes of the functioning of norms, the result is not always the adoption of a new identity and the contention may lead to enhancement of existing identities. Thus, the culture and identity may sharpen and crystallise, and the resistance becomes more solid. In this case, contention or even conflict between newly incoming norms and existing ones would lead the community to completely reject the former.

Nonetheless, at this very juncture, it is localisation that offers a way for contention to be resolved in the new locality. Localisation, thus, is a degree of internalisation in which "norm-takers build congruence between transnational norms ... and local beliefs and practices"

(Acharya 2004: 241). Therefore, in the scope of the localisation, "local agents reconstruct foreign norms to ensure the norms fit with the agents' cognitive priors and identities" (Ibid.: 239). With this process, foreign norms become exposed to the active reconstruction by local agents through discourse, framing, grafting and cultural selection (Ibid.: 239–45). To this end, localisation is neither the wholesale acceptance nor complete rejection of foreign norms; instead it is the mechanism to settle the "normative contestation" (Ibid.: 239). In this way, localisation comes to mean validation, reinterpretation, modification or even the reconstruction of norms in the target domestic realm by local actors through bringing prior culture, belief, cognitive frames or norms on to the scene, something which confirms the work of Wiener (2007a: 2).

In short, almost all mechanisms that have a role in the cascade process continue to function in the internalisation stage. Moreover, internalisation is not a secured/guaranteed end and the degree of internalisation varies with each result invoking different reflections and resonation in relation to the functioning and influence of the new norm.

Conclusion

In this chapter, I have shown the ways in which norms can be employed as a foreign policy analysis tool in examining and exploring the overseas influences of domestic rearrangements. Throughout the chapter, I examined the role of norms and the norm-guided behaviours which led me to a framework in which the emergence of domestic norms, their translation into foreign policy, their international mobilisation, the entrepreneurs' attempt for socialising the target community into such norms, and finally the local responses to the socialisation attempts are elaborated with relation to one another. In the scope of the elaboration, through incorporating Katzenstein's (1996a, b) accounts of domestic norm analysis, the model, which is originally designed to study international norms, became an apt means for analysing domestic norms and their overseas influence. Defining the identity politics as the core mechanism at play in the phase of tipping point facilitated demonstrating the stage where norms translate into foreign policy practice. Moreover, the dominance of identity politics during the cascade stage makes tracing the lifespan of norms and the relevant communicative processes easier. In this way, one can be sure about whether a norm has gained international mobility, transcended over the national borders, and been delivered to a new domestic locality in abroad. Separating international mobilisation and socialisation mechanisms enabled the unveiling and demonstrating of the practices of diffusion and socialisation more accurately. The integration of the idea of "localisation" to the internalisation stage further rendered possible the revealing of the functioning communicative processes – such as argumentation and contestation, and the proposing of alternative forms and varying degrees of norm internalisation.

Moreover, I not only modified the model according to current debates regarding the mechanisms and dynamics of norm processes, but also made the model embody reflections from different logics of actions. The elaboration work I did therefore brings together the findings of the logic of appropriateness, the logic of arguing and, to a limited extent, the logic of contestedness scholarship. Accordingly, communicative processes are boldly highlighted throughout the development of this framework, something which is informed by Peter Katzenstein's account of communicative construction of norms.[12] I also introduced the cultural validation prepositions of Risse (2000) and Wiener (2007a, b), which makes the model more capable of observing the argumentation taking place thus the possible impacts that domestic norms generate abroad.

All these have shown that the model is well suited for foreign policy research. Below is the revised and elaborated foreign policy analysis model the above discussions have led me to.

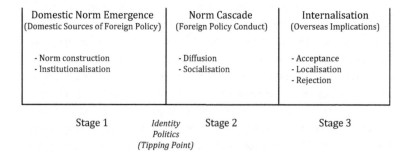

Domestic Norm Emergence (Domestic Sources of Foreign Policy)	Norm Cascade (Foreign Policy Conduct)	Internalisation (Overseas Implications)
- Norm construction - Institutionalisation	- Diffusion - Socialisation	- Acceptance - Localisation - Rejection

Stage 1   *Identity*   Stage 2   Stage 3
                 Politics
                 (Tipping Point)

Figure 4.2 A foreign policy framework for analysing overseas implications of domestic norms [Elaborated norm's life cycle model].

Whether this elaboration carries explanatory capabilities will be dealt with in the concluding chapter, after applying the model to an analysis of post-Kemalist norms and the influence of these on the ethnic Turkish community in Kosovo. The first stage of the model will deal with the emergence of post-Kemalist norms concerning Outside Turks, how they gained dominance and their translation into foreign policy acts. The second stage will demonstrate norm entrepreneurs' practices of diffusing post-Kemalist norms into Kosovo and of socialising the ethnic Turkish community into such norms. The internalisation section, consequently, will unveil contestation directed towards post-Kemalist norms and the degree to which their internalisation within the ethnic Turkish community has occurred. This will also allow me to analyse the implications of post-Kemalist domestic norms for the Outside Turks community in Kosovo.

CHAPTER 5

OUTSIDE TURKS LOCALITY IN KOSOVO – MAKING OF KOSOVAR TURKS

The state of being at home "abroad" began to be experienced by Turkish-speaking communities in Kosovo as early as 1913 as the Ottoman Empire suffered a huge loss in the Balkan Wars. Until the establishment of the Kingdom of Serbs, Croats and Slovenes in 1918 (changed to "the Kingdom of Yugoslavia" in 1929), the Turkish-speaking community lived under the rule of the Kingdom of Serbia. Their initial reaction to living separate from the "homeland" was to immigrate to Ottoman territories en masse. WWI did not change this pattern much, neither did the establishment of the new kingdom in 1918. The mass immigration of Turkish-speaking communities to Turkey continued until the early 1960s. Nonetheless, those who did not choose to leave remained in Kosovo as a religious minority. The idea of being a religious minority rather than a national one was a promoted and a preferable status at both the societal and political levels for the Yugoslav states (Banac 1984: 298). Indeed, the Turkish-speaking community in Kosovo chose to act as a confessional group rather than an ethnic one (Lampe 1996). Their political organisations were highly reflective of this. This can be evidenced, for instance, in the case the Cemiyet,[1] a political party founded by Albanian and Turkish-speaking Muslim communities in Macedonia and Kosovo that was concerned primarily with defending the confessional identity and rights of the Muslim community (Tabak 2011: 6). This is clear from the party's programme published in 1921. The key concerns of the organisation, as reflected in the programme, were autonomy in religious affairs, autonomy in religious education, the maintenance of the Sharia (Islamic) courts, and again attempts by the state to impose recitations of Orthodox Christian prayer and verses in state schools (Hrabak 2003: 81). This early political awakening was therefore along religious lines.

There is also some suggestion however that Kosovo's Turkish-speaking community was following events in Turkey closely. For instance, Altay Suroy Recepoğlu, a judge and member of Kosovo's Constitutional Court, reports in one of his books that the Turkish-speaking community partly adopted the Latinised Turkish alphabet as early as 1929 (Recepoğlu 2007: 46). Another instance that reveals an awareness of ethnicity for this group was Pan-Turkist ideals held by some members of the Kosovar Turkish community. Indeed Landau informs us that some members of the community who previously worked closely with the Young Turks (an Ottoman-era political movement) also launched appeals for the unity of all Turks as early as the 1930s (Landau 1995: 83). In a final example, Süreyya Yusuf – a pioneering figure in Kosovar Turkish literature – reports that as of 1937 the Turkish community had developed a national consciousness thanks to literature coming from Turkey (Yusuf 1976: 6). Among the most notable books he notes were Nazım Hikmet's poems and play writings (Ibid.). Despite the above developments, in 1951 the Turkish-speaking community officially became recognised and referred to in official state discourse as the "ethnic Turkish community".

In 1951, socialist Yugoslavia officially recognised the existence of ethnic Turkish community in Kosovo and granted it communal rights such as primary and secondary school education, broadcasting and publishing rights – all in the Turkish language; what more is, it gave ethnic representation at municipal level (Recepoğlu 2006: 11, Derviş 2010: 169). It must be noted that Yugoslavia was ruled by a single party during the socialist period (1945–89) and all other political parties were banned. The Turkish community, in this sense, did not involve itself directly in politics yet it adapted well to the socialist regime. The inclusive policies of Tito were facilitative and encouraging in this sense. Due to Yugoslavia's more progressive policies from 1951 onwards, the ethnic Turkish community achieved success in three areas – all of which were used in the service of promoting their ethnic identity; namely education, cultural activism and media.

Since there was no Turkish-language teaching available to this community prior to 1951 (when the right was recognised) the community desperately needed Turkish instructors for their new schools. People were thus encouraged to pursue a career in education. Initially, Turkish instructors from Macedonia were brought and those with secondary school diploma were sent to Macedonia for teacher training (Interview LE2, Yusuf 1976: 6–7, Topsakal and Koro 2007: 80).[2] This was possible because the Turkish-speaking community in Eastern Macedonia had already been granted Turkish instruction seven years before those communities in Western Macedonia and Kosovo. Nonetheless, after education began, it was seen as of utmost important for the survival of Turks in Kosovo. In order to keep Turkish education functioning, they urged community members to send their children to Turkish-language schools. This not only increased the number of educated members of the community, but also enabled the community to become more involved in cultural and community activism – a means to ensure their ethnic survival in Kosovo.

Within the scope these newly recognised ethnic rights, national communities in Yugoslavia were allowed to establish associations which would run cultural and artistic activities. Regardless of the size of the community in question, they had the right to open one association in each city (Recepoğlu 2007: 8–9). In this respect, in two places with the largest number of ethnic Turkish residents at the time – that is, Prizren and Pristina – two cultural associations were established, namely the Doğru Yol Culture and Art Association and the Gerçek Culture and Art Association in 1951. These associations increased community involvement in arts, literature and folklore – all of which were to express the presence of ethnic Turks in the country and to maintain their ethnic survival (Interview LE7). With regards to the art, theatre and other types of performances in Prizren have been traditionally mostly taken up by the Turkish community when compared to others; this is because the small Turkish community saw these as a mean of expressing their identity and preserving their community (Interview LE3). Folkloric activities, on the other hand, were also intense and provided a platform to perform dances from Turkey (Interview LE9). The community was also actively involved in literature and produced a huge collection of writings in Turkish (Çelik 2008). Accordingly, the *Tan* newspaper, founded in 1968, served as the platform for such ethnic literary activities.[3] This paper also took on efforts aimed at the "purification" of Turkish language (*öztürkçecilik*), a step further than other Turkish communities abroad by inventing novel vocabularies. They even suggested that these new words should be adopted by Language Council in Turkey, which oversees official Turkish language (Türk Dil Kurumu-TDK) (Interview LE20). Therefore, all their efforts in artistic, cultural and literary realms overlapped with the aims of the leaders of the community, that is, to ensure the survival of an ethnic community (Interview LE5, Interview LE7).

Along with these initiatives, Turks were highly integrated into the Communist system and were overwhelmingly secular. For instance, in historical monographs listing ethnic Turkish teachers in Kosovo since 1951, which also included their photographs, I found none of the female teachers wearing a headscarf (Türk Öğretmenler Derneği 1996, Hüdaverdi 2001, Safçı and Koro 2008). Likewise, none of the members of the ethnic Turkish community sent their children to madrasas (religious schools) during the communist period. Therefore, not a single ethnic Turk was trained as an imam except for those who were educated prior to 1951 (Interview LE20, Interview LE33). A religiously identified community therefore was transformed into a secular ethno-national community under a socialist state in a relatively short period of time.

The transformation of the Kosovar Turkish-speaking Muslim community into ethnic Turkish community has its own peculiar characteristics. The Turkish-speaking community, in this sense, learned their "Turkishness" almost entirely on their own, rather than through a socialisation process involving Turkey. This does not mean that Turkey ignored the community; on the contrary, it provided the schools with textbooks and education materials as well as teachers or training courses in Turkey which included a visit to Anıtkabir (Atatürk's Monument) (Aşıkferki 1996: 191). However, Kosovo remained outside of Turkey's direct sphere of influence. Accordingly, due to the socialist government's tolerance towards them, the community learned what it means to be Turkish and how to follow Kemal (Atatürk) from more socialist-oriented Kemalists of Turkey (Interview LE1). In other words, this community relied on people and papers such as Fazıl Hüsnü Dağlarca, Yaşar Nabi Nayır, Nazım Hikmet, Aziz Nesin, *Varlık* magazine, *Cumhuriyet* newspaper and Cem Yayınları (Interview LE35, Recepoğlu 2006: 56–7). Dağlarca's famous saying "Türkçem benim ses bayrağım" ("Turkish is my national flag") became the motto for literary production in the community during this time. The community had close relations with Dağlarca, Nayır and Nesin at a personal level too and these authors/poets often visited Yugoslavia (Bâkiler 2010: 22–7, Baymak 1987: 132–46, Interview LE20). These figures inspired the ethnic Turkish community and were closely followed by the community in their own project of building their national-self. The literary branch of the Doğru Yol Association, for instance, was named as the *Nazim Hikmet Literary Branch*. Following the example of pro-Kemalist socialists, almost all Turkish poets in Kosovo also wrote poems in honour of Atatürk, his glories, and his contributions to the Turkish nation (Yusuf 1976: 99, Hafız 1989: 55–207, Baymak 2013: 189–232).

With this in mind, the 1990s inherited from the socialist era a community with attachment to Turkish nationalism and Atatürk and a deep devotion to secularism. This, in many ways, is comparable to Turkey's Republican Party and its members.[4] The Turkish-speaking, religiously conscious community of the 1940s, therefore, was during the communist era rebuilt to become a secular nationalist community. The dissolution of Yugoslavia was to affect the community in profound ways.

During the socialist era, the community did not engage politically and therefore lacked experience in this domain. Literary and artistic performances became their way to express their cultural and ethnic presence in the state. Nonetheless, decades of cultural activism in the cultural and social spheres helped them later in their political struggles during the turbulent 1990s despite their lack of political experience. When Slobodan Milošević in Yugoslavia abolished the autonomous status of Kosovo (and Vojvodina), the Albanian population collectively protested this decision and withdrew from state institutions and state education bodies. Albanians expected a similar reaction from the Turkish community, though this was not forthcoming. This is because, firstly, the Turkish community did not have enough funding to support and therefore be able to afford a separate education system (or "parallel education" as it was referred to in the 1990s). Secondly, to withdraw from state-sponsored education meant to remain without education facilities completely. Education had always been the most important tool to ensure the ethnic survival of the Turkish community and they felt that they could risk losing it. They therefore continued sending their children to state schools. This was the first vital decision taken and supported through collective political activism among the ethnic Turkish community in Kosovo. This was followed with the establishment of the first political party, the Turkish Democratic Party (TDP), though it never participated in elections under Serbian rule. The party was established so as to create a platform to promote ethnic rights, to give the community a single voice, and to establish direct relations with Turkey (Interview SVN1). Inclusion into the Great Student Exchange project in Turkey was one result of the TDP's activism (Interview SVN1).

Inclusion in electoral politics began only after the international community intervened in Kosovo in 1999 and ousted Serbia. The Turkish community re-established the TDP as the KDTP (Democratic Turkish Party of Kosovo). Its first aim was to give the Turkish community a voice in the country now awash with international organisations (the UN had formal authority in the form of the UNMIK mission), the interim Kosovo government, and local authorities. The initial struggle concentrated on the status of the Turkish language (Interview LE9, Interview LE4). Before Serbia's departure, the Turkish language had equal status with other minority languages in the country. This status was initially ignored by the United Nations interim administration (UNMIK) authorities in the early days of their rule in 2001. However, it eventually gained legal equality with other languages after the Turkish political party boycotted the first elections in late 2001. Today, Turkish is an official language in areas where the Turkish population constitutes 5 per cent of the total population and is an *official language in use* in areas where the Turkish population constitutes 3 per cent of the total population (Recepoğlu 2005). Nonetheless, the Turkish community still complains about the unwillingness of Albanian authorities to abide by these rules (Interview LE17). However, the size of the political representation of the community at the parliamentary and municipal level is helping to solve such problems. Despite constituting 1.1 per cent of the total population (18,738 people) according to the 2011 census, Turkish representation in Parliament between 2008 and 2013 looked like this: one minister (Ministry of Public Administration), three vice ministers (Ministry of Health, ministry of Trade and Industry and Ministry of Local Administration), and three MPs (out of 120).

Moreover, the KDTP was a coalition partner of the ruling party and is also one of the best represented communities in the country (between 2008 and 2013). Without a doubt this resulted from Turkey's strong backing for this community and its general close concern for events in Kosovo.

Accordingly, right after the NATO intervention in 1999, Turkey sent military troops to Kosovo to contribute to the peace-building mission (Kosovo Force-KFOR). Turkish troops (Türk Taburu or Tabur) were deployed and its military camps set up mostly in areas where the ethnic Turkish community resided: Prizren, Mamusha and Dragos. Turkey aimed to maintain close contact with the ethnic Turkish community in Kosovo. The establishment of Turkish Coordination Offices in Pristina and Prizren and a monitoring office in Mamusha facilitated this (Altunya 2003: 134). However, Turkey's military presence was not only significant for ethnic Turks. The warm welcome shown to the Turkish troops when they arrived in Prizren on 4 July 1999 by thousands of people from all ethnic backgrounds who had lined the streets shows that not only ethnic Turks but also the Albanians, Bosnians and Gorans were happy with Turkey's military presence in Kosovo[5] (*Sabah* 5 July 1999, Interview LE4). It was in line with this that from the very beginning of its mission the Turkish troops or "Türk Taburu" has had a say in inter-ethnic relations among Muslim communities in Kosovo. Nonetheless, Tabur has dealt mainly with protecting, publicly supporting and financially backing the Turkish community[6] (Abazi 2008: 4). In addition to Tabur, with the coming to power of the JDP, Diyanet, TIKA and Yunus Emre Institute have built permanent offices in Kosovo and Turkey has gained direct access to the Turkish community, both in relation to its affairs with the Kosovo state and other communities in the country. Nonetheless, the Turkish community does not consider themselves as a diaspora community in the country. Kosovo, therefore, is not a "host state" to them; ethnic Turks in Kosovo feel that they are one of the native communities and constituent elements of the Kosovar state; indeed, one of the stars in the Kosovar flag is there to signify their presence in the country (Interview LE1, LE2, LE4, LE8, LE9, LE11, LE12).

Nonetheless, despite Turkey's presence in Kosovo in the form of several official institutions and despite the constitutional guarantees to them, not everything in the garden was rosy for the ethnic Turkish community. In addition to problems regarding the use of Turkish language, at the societal level too, and particularly among Albanian nationalist circles, there has long been strong sense of hostility towards the presence of ethnic Turks in Kosovo centring mainly on the claim that members of the ethnic Turkish community are in reality "Turkified Albanians". Since the ethnic Turkish community refused to join Albanian political machinations during the 1990s as Albanians withdrew from state schools, once the war ended and Albanians came to occupy the entire state apparatus as a reward for their victory, this denial again resurfaced, meaning that in extreme, yet rare, cases the Turkish community was warned not to speak Turkish in public (Interview LE12). This policy of denial increased together with Albanian nation-building efforts in the post-independence (2008) era (Interview SVN2). Nonetheless, it is impossible to talk about an ethnic conflict between Turks and Albanians in Kosovo, as the societal level relations are so intense and inter-ethnic marriages are so common. Tensions may be said to remain beneath the surface but restricted mostly in the political sphere.

The Turkish community have produced a huge amount of literature in the Turkish language and have embarked on long-established cultural activism projects precisely for the reasons detailed above. In this sense, they separate sharply their Islamic and ethnic identities as a means of ensuring ethnic survival. They believe that religion is utilised by Albanians to assimilate ethnic Turks. Accordingly, anything that addresses the Islamic ties between Albanians and Turks and the necessity of taking Islam as a basis for building relations causes fierce reactions among members of the community. They therefore underline and try to reify the differences between themselves and Albanians, rather than to emphasise commonalities, as an ethnic survival strategy and a strategy to refute the Albanian nationalist claims of the non-presence of Turks in Kosovo.

Before concluding this chapter, there is an issue emanating from defining the Turkish-speaking community in Kosovo on an ethnic basis that needs to be dealt with. As has been underlined above, the Turkish community has given utmost importance to practising their ethnicity in their literary writings, cultural events, education and the media. Practising Turkishness therefore has been a way to protect their identity and to sustain a sense of belonging to a distinct ethnic community in Kosovo. This tendency confirms what Fredric Barth argued long ago regarding ethnic categories: ethnicity is a product of inter-group interaction – it is a result of practices of (self)classification/categorisation (Barth 1969: 9–38). Rogers Brubaker's (1996) definition of ethnicity as a "practical category" is also illustrative here. Accordingly, having considered that the ethnic Turkish community has long been involved in performing Turkishness via all possible means, my use of ethnicity as a practical category is a valid one. An example of an ethnicity performative act, for example, includes voting for the ethnic Turkish party and sending children to Turkish-language schools; these are compulsory practices which must be performed in order to be considered an "ethnic Turk".[7] In short, the Turkish-speaking community in Kosovo performs Turkishness as an ethnic category and thus allows me to refer to them as the "ethnic Turkish community".

CHAPTER 6

EMERGENCE OF POST-KEMALIST NORMS CONCERNING OUTSIDE TURKS

Introduction

The post-Kemalist transformation of Turkey was shown to have emerged thanks to the novel emancipatory and atavist discourses in the country that have given previously deprived groups adequate room in the economic and sociopolitical spheres. This was followed by the weakening of Kemalist tutelage and the removal of the obstructions towards the use of ethnocultural rights, which eventually increased the post-national qualities of the country. Therefore, hypothetically at least, the emergences of post-Kemalist practices and the norms guiding them have been prompted by the same processes. At this point, several questions arise regarding the presence of post-Kemalist norms. In this sense, while post-Kemalist practices are indisputably present, as shown in Chapter 3, one still needs to be certain about the presence of post-Kemalist norms and the question remains, how can this be done? Another question may be why do post-Kemalist practices need to be guided by any norm in the first place? In a similar vein, if we are sure about the existence of post-Kemalist norms, then, what do these norms entail? How many individual norms exist under the umbrella of post-Kemalist norms? Moreover, how do they interact with one another or what do they share in common? Finally, which particular post-Kemalist norms are influential when the Outside Turks are considered?

These questions should be satisfactorily answered in order to be certain about the presence of post-Kemalist norms that hypothetically governed Turkey's policy towards the Outside Turks and eventually had a constitutive influence on Outside Turks communities. Answering these is also a prerequisite for presenting the emergence of the post-Kemalist norms concerning Outside Turks, with which I deal with in this chapter.

Any research on norms has to overcome certain methodological problems relating to the measuring of norms. This is simply the case because of the fact that one cannot, empirically speaking, presume to be certain about the presence of norms as "there is only indirect evidence of the existence of a norm" (Björkdahl 2002: 12). Therefore, in claiming the presence of norms, behavioural, discursive and representative practices altogether carry importance and may invoke the presence of norms. Among them, particularly the discursive practices carry particular significance and could be very much guiding because such discursive acts leave trails of communication to be traced (Florini 1996: 364–5, Finnemore and Sikkink 1998: 892). This communication mainly includes discourses of legitimising (justifying) or denouncing an action. Adopting this approach would confirm that this is what is seen in post-Kemalist practices, the justifications of which have been based on the crises of Kemalism and on issues such as the Kurdish question and the re-invented Ottoman legacy. Therefore, post-Kemalist patterns of behaviour and discourses would reveal the presence of post-Kemalist norms. This constitutes the initial step in norm identification though there are also other indicators.

Accordingly, the theory also suggests that norms operate as a beneath-the-surface element or mechanism, that makes a particular practice meaningful (Kratochwil 1991: 11; Jepperson et al. 1996: 54). In other words, "in the absence of norms, exercises of power or actions would be devoid of meaning" (Hopf 1998: 173). Therefore, to be able to talk about the post-Kemalist form of practices, I accept that these *meaningful* practices are driven by, or induced with, norms that teach the need to go beyond Kemalism. Therefore, the norms which involve post-Kemalist teachings are what I call post-Kemalist norms.

Another indicator of norm presence is the institutionalisation of certain practices (Katzenstein 1996b). Accordingly, institutionalisation of a norm "creates, across different segments of state and society, a degree of stability and uniformity which otherwise might be lacking" (Ibid.: 21). In this respect, having witnessed outstanding levels of commitment to involvement with Muslim and ethnic Turkish communities abroad, couple with the establishment of new institutions or recalibration of older ones to fit new post-Kemalist roles, one can confidently argue that there are salient post-Kemalist norms.

I argued in explaining the Kemalist Turkification of the Turkish-speaking communities outside Turkey that this process was run via the adoption of Kemalist norms by these communities. Here, Kemalist norms refer to a set of principles which became institutionalised in the Republican Era with the aim of transforming state–society and inter-communal relations to fit the new nationalist mould. Accordingly, the "Turkish" society at home and abroad were "legitimately" socialised into these norms. In a similar manner, post-Kemalist norms address principles gradually institutionalised as a remedy to the crises faced by Kemalism via suggesting and envisioning a new multicultural form of state-society and inter-communal relations – both inside and outside the country. The latter refers to communities historically tied to Turkey with religion, culture, language or ethnicity. In this sense, post-Kemalist norms are the anti-thesis of the nationalist norms moulded in and promoted by Kemalist Turkey. In foreign policy, for instance, the temporary 'zero-problems with neighbours' policy introduced by Ahmet Davutoğlu was a sort of antidote to the prevelant idea among politicians and the military which imagined Turkey as a country surrounded by its enemies (also known as the Sèvres Syndrome). In domestic politics, the new multiculturalism has resulted in the lifting of restrictions on use of Kurdish and other minority languages and paved the ways for the restoration of the destruction wrought on inter-communal relations in the country by Kemalism. Indeed, this has replaced the suppressive Kemalist-inspired nation-building policies. Therefore, in brief, while Kemalist norms suggest a nationalist, homogenous, societally and ideologically exclusive country and set of actions; post-Kemalist norms stimulate a multicultural, anti-nationalist, atavist (Ottoman nostalgia), diverse, pluralist and mostly Muslim-identity-driven actions. The post-Kemalist norms thus envision Turkey as a societally, culturally and ideologically inclusive country with a specific set of actions in the domestic and foreign spheres guided by these listed principles.

For a norm to simultaneously embody all these teachings is not practically possible. Therefore, I suggest the presence of multiple norms under the umbrella of "post-Kemalist norms" which share the principle of the necessity of going beyond the historically determined and exclusivist Kemalist state-society framework of relations for the sake of peaceful co-existence in political, societal, religious and even economic issues. Giving a list of all post-Kemalist norms requires conducting separate research in several fields. However, the examples given below (which are derived from the post-Kemalist practices listed in Chapter 3) reveal the post-Kemalist norms with implications in Outside Turks localities.

In domestic politics, for instance, the norm of ethnic non-discrimination is a noticeable shift and something that is evident in the given rights to Kurdish people in the country. In the local and national elections since 2014, for example, not only do pro-PKK parties (such as the Kurdish Peoples' Democratic Party, HDP) or Islamist Kurdish ones (such as the Free Cause Party, Hüda-Par) use Kurdish in their campaigns, but also the JDP (*Hürriyet* 27 December 2014). This was unimaginable before. In religious affairs, similarly, the norm of "non-discrimination" towards religious minorities had already been institutionalised on paper by the mid-2000s due in part to the EU accession process. As soon as the norm was institutionalised the Ministry of National Education was entrusted with a task of reviewing school textbooks and eliminating prejudical sections against non-Muslim minority groups and also redrafting the religious textbooks "to address the concerns of Christian minorities" (Toktaş and Aras 2009: 712). Moreover, the Directorate of Religious Foundations, which had historically only subsidised the country's mosques was now put in charge of paying the bills of the places of worship which included those of minority groups (Ibid.). Recently, an Armenian church, used as a cinema for many years, was given back to the Armenian community to be used as a church. Moreover, for the first time in Republican history, as announced by Ahmet Davutoğlu, a church would be built in Yesilköy, İstanbul, for the Syriac community (*Radikal* 2 January 2015). These examples could be extended.

In tandem with this broad post-Kemalist turn, the Kemalist mindset in relations with the Outside Turks was also replaced. As the post-Kemalist policy practices of the 1990s and the 2000s (which were in detail explained in Chapter 3) suggest there has emerged in Turkey at least four robust post-Kemalist norms concerning Outside Turks.

First and the foremost, over the course of the last two to three decades the Ottoman Empire and culture have become reference points for institutional, cultural, historical, political and even in artistic expressions in Turkey. In other words, this has been reflected in popular culture, fashion and architecture and to the very formulation of political solutions to on-going ethno-religious problems in the country. Indeed, the Ottomans became a point of reference and justification in managing inter-ethnic and inter-religious relations, in reimagining both the co-national and kin communities abroad, and in developing relevant policies towards Outside Turks communities. Accordingly, both in domestic and foreign policy imaginations, the idea of Ottoman (or *Ottomania* as White 2013 calls it) has gradually become a prominent cognitive frame, which constitutes the first influential post-Kemalist norm when comprehending Outside Turks.

Secondly, in the last two decades, the idea of ethnicity has lost its weight in policy making as the main reference; there rather emerged a de-ethnicised tendency on defining the broader Turkish nation. Outside Turks, accordingly, have been recoded as "fellow believers" and represents a ground-breaking post-Kemalist turn; hence the "Muslimness" of the Outside Turks has been given more consideration. Common history, culture and faith became more concrete determinants in building ties rather than ethnicity. This much was argued with the idea that Turkey is a kin state not only to the ethnic Turkish communities, but also to the Muslim communities throughout the former Ottoman hinterland. Consequently, this blurred the differences between ethnic Turks and Muslim communities in the eyes of Turkey. With this process, the Ottoman–Islamic sources of Turkish nationhood were retrieved and ethno-nationalist references were minimised. Turkishness is now used frequently devoid of ethnic connotation. This was due to the functioning of the norm of *de-ethnicised nationhood* and/or de-ethnicised Turkishness.

Thirdly, post-Kemalist practices regarding the authenticity of the "Turkish way of practising Islam" reveal that from the post-1980s onwards, the state bodies and religious groups have championed and promoted a certain way of performing Islam both within and outside of Turkey. This manifests itself, for instance, in the reaction of religious groups, political parties and governments approaches to the so-called threat of "Wahhabism". This is also related to activities among Outside Turks communities, and to the Ottoman and Turkish Islamic cultural heritage abroad. Diyanet and many religious groups thus share a concern for conveying a "Turkish way of practising Islam" to Outside Turks localities. Therefore, the third post-Kemalist norm manifests itself in the form of *Turkish Islam*.

Lastly, in post-1980 Turkey we see that cross-border concerns extended beyond a focus entirely on ethnic kinship and slowly begin to see the emergence of a religiously based and ummah-oriented sense of solidarity. State-level concerns for Bosnian and Albanian Muslims, Iraqi Kurds and Palestinians, and the sense of Islamic solidarity shown by NGOs from Turkey and people during the humanitarian crises in Muslim countries of South East Asia, the Caucasus, Balkans and Africa indicate that the idea of ummah has been revitalised. This coincides with geographical rediscovery of the ummah. Accordingly, seeing that this internationalist concern for Muslim communities has been institutionalised and run by the institutions initially built to deal with Outside Turks, I argue that Outside Turks have now gained the quality of becoming an umbrella concept which covers a broad set of communities under a common category of Muslimness. This is the reason why, the source of solidarity between Turkey and ethnic Turks has, to some extent, become focused more on a sense of Muslim identity and constituted by an *Islamic internationalist* concern.

In short, in the post-1980 period we see that post-Kemalist practices and the ways in which the Outside Turks are comprehended are guided by four powerful and dominant post-Kemalist norms; namely *Ottomania*, *de-ethnicised nationhood, Turkish Islam* and *Islamic Internationalism*. These are the most relevant post-Kemalist norms in our discussion of Outside Turks. These norms suggest and envision a multi-cultural society both inside and outside Turkey, as for the latter this is particularly relevant to communities which have been historically tied to Turkey via religion, culture, language or ethnicity. The teachings of these four norms may overlap, yet they also have distinguishing characteristics.[1] Some of these norms were unsettled during the 1990s and had limited impact (see Björkdahl 2002: 19–20). However, as is clear now, by the time the JDP came to power, these post-Kemalist norms had gained salience, become more influential, and eventually replaced many of the previously held Kemalist norms. Moreover, it should be noted that it is highly likely that there exist other norms guiding Turkey's policy towards the Outside Turks, yet these four are the most powerful ones which were identified via the methods suggested by the literature. Without a doubt, the analysis below is revealing about the presence of such norms and their salience.

The Emergence of "Ottomania"

Contemporary political and cultural life in Turkey has witnessed a trend towards viewing "the Ottoman heritage as a more inclusive framework" and a cure to the crises of Kemalism in the country (Şahin 2010: 177). Well beyond the political patterns and discourses the trend encompasses "mass interest in everything Ottoman" (*Tokyay* 17 October 2011). From formulation of political solutions to the ethno-religious problems in Turkey, to popular culture, fashion and architecture, the idea of *Ottomania* has gradually become a prominent cognitive frame. Today, in a commercial dimension too, "Ottoman history books, Ottoman-styled jewellery, museum exhibitions ... calligraphy" and also television series, cookery and decoration have become very popular (Ibid.). Tulip, an indispensable symbol in Ottoman–Islamic calligraphy, not only decorates parks and gardens in the city centres but also appears on logos of major global companies such as Turkish Airlines, and even featured in the logos of Turkey's 2020 Olympics bid, Turkey's G20 presidency in 2015 and the Borsa Istanbul (Stock Exchange) (Tataroglu 10 April 2013). The point here is that Ottoman visual and spatial aesthetics have gained considerable dominance in the country (Walton 2010). Morever, the "Ottoman Islamic golden age" is now celebrated through annual festivals which are organised by municipalities and ministries on, for instance, Tulip, Ottoman Empire's establishment or Istanbul's Conquest (Onar 2009: 235, *Haber7* 5 April 2008). This "Ottomania" introduces the Ottoman Empire as a "culture of living" which was historically treated as nothing but an out-dated form of state organisation (*Tokyay* 17 October 2011).

This Ottomania trend has also become dominant in discourses about the reformulation of state–society relations. It has been a heavily endorsed idea that Ottoman heritage provides Turkey with an inclusive framework "to resolve internal socio-cultural tensions that resulted from cultural diversity" (Çolak 2006: 587, Şahin 2010: 177). In this sense, it is believed that "the Ottoman past can provide the society with a strong reference for identifying its different components, such as Kurdish people or non-Muslims" (*Tokyay* 17 October 2011). Accordingly, reforms centred on resolving the Kurdish problem in terms of the EU accession process have been justified to the public via references to an imagined Ottoman experience of inter-community relations. Moreover, in foreign policy, a reinvented Ottoman legacy is used to justify a deep sense of responsibility towards neighbouring regions and the imagined "Ottoman model of dealing with cultural diversity" has been promoted as an effective solution to inter-ethnic and inter-religious tensions in post-conflict states in the Balkans (*Tokyay* 17 October 2011, Çolak 2006: 587).

The practices evoking the presence of an Ottomanist concern or taking Ottoman experience as a reference to produce solutions to contemporary problems dates back to the early 1990s (Yavuz 1998, Onar 2009, Çolak 2006, Şahin 2010, Çalış 1996, Çalış 2001).[2] In domestic politics, Turgut Özal in collaboration with growing pro-Islamist Anatolian bourgeoisie and oppressed Kurdish elites, championed pluralistic and inclusive forms of state–society relations very early on. He aimed to reformulate the "Turkish" collective memory and Kemalist nationalist and secular "social contract" in the country in line with reinvented Ottoman multicultural experiences. Via the fostering of an Ottoman collective memory, Özal endeavoured to open room for "a more pluralist understanding of political and cultural belonging" wherein Islamists, Kurds and even non-Muslims could be equally embraced and a more pluralistic "social contract" could be achieved (Onar 2009: 233). Therefore, "(neo)Ottomanists rejected the ethnic version of Turkish nationalism and reinterpreted Turkish identity on the basis of regional and religious grounds (multi-ethnic and multireligious bases) and cosmopolitan [multinational] liberal values" (Çolak 2006: 592–3). Ottoman heritage, therefore, was argued, could provide this inclusive framework. Despite this re-invention of the Ottoman Empire as a tolerant and inclusive model, the salience of the Kemalist frames in the 1990s did not allow this to generate substantial policy implications.

In foreign policy, the manifestation of the Ottomania was mainly seen in the increase of ties Turkey made with communities throughout former Ottoman territories. During the 1990s, Turkey behaved as the successor of the Ottoman Empire and endeavoured to protect Ottoman (and Turkish Islamic) heritage. The motive for this was the idea of protecting the remnants of the Ottoman Empire – i.e. those Muslims (including Albanians, Bosnian, Pomak or Gypsies) who were being killed for "being Turk" as Yugoslavia was breaking up (Bulut 2004: 3). Here, the importance of Serbian nationalist policy, which called all Muslims in the Balkans "Turks", was constitutive and led to the dominance of this understanding among people in Turkey: "Turk means Muslim and Muslim means Ottoman, vice versa" (Çalış 2001: 129). This coupled with the influence of the "Turkish Islamic Synthesis" which had gained prominence in Turkey by 1980s served to make "the Ottoman state as the 'glorious' achievement of the Muslim Turks" (Yavuz 1998: 23).[3] However, it was also this same nationalist outlook which enabled ardent secularists such as President Süleyman Demirel (1993–2000) or the Parliamentary President Hikmet Çetin (1997–9) to confidently announce Turkey's responsibility towards – and cultural unity with – the Balkans (Akıllı 2013: 70).

The idea of "(neo)Ottomanism" was also referenced heavily during the Erbakan's time in charge (1995–7). In offering solutions to Turkey's internal political crises, for the Welfare Party the *millet* system of the Ottoman Empire, which suggests framing a community in religious lines (hence a common identification for both ethnic Turks and Kurds) was "more just, humane, and superior to the monism of the secular nation-state" (Çolak 2006: 597). Therefore, the Ottoman *millet* system was proposed to be "a panacea to resolve Turkey's ethnic problem" (Ibid.). In foreign policy, Ottoman atavism was also traceable in the Welfare Party's policies due to their declared nostalgia for the "glory days" of the Ottoman Empire. Erbakan passionately articulated the creation of "[a] Greater Turkey just as the Ottomans did" (Yavuz 1998: 23).

Building on this tradition of recalling the Ottoman Empire, an imagined Ottoman model has been vigorously promoted by the JDP governments in both domestic and foreign policies. In domestic politics, multiculturalism or multi-ethnic coexistence were promoted as Ottoman norms and values; they were not merely Western values and Turkey's embrace of these was, as the government argued, merely the adoption of the Ottoman model (and not necessarily Western model) (Şahin 2010: vi). This derives from the idea that "the cultural and political legacy of the Ottoman Empire makes Turkey both Western and Islamic geographically and culturally" (Ibid.: 187). The discursive parallel set by the JDP leaders between "Ottoman references to justice, freedom and ... treatment of religious minorities" and the EU harmonisation process shows this well (Ibid.: 185). Unlike Özal and Erbakan, the JDP managed to put this Ottomanist rhetoric into practice while also complying with European norms and standards (Çağaptay 2012b).

In foreign policy, similar to Özal, the JDP embarked on symbolic acts of peace and harmony with countries in the former Ottoman domain in an attempt to replicate the Ottoman legacy. The doctrines of "strategic depth" and "zero problems with neighbours" – both of which come from Ahmet Davutoğlu – both called for an active "re-engagement" with the Middle East, the Balkans and the Caucasus. These were key frames in Turkey's reintegration with the former Ottoman domains (Çağaptay 2009, Taşpınar 2008, Şahin 2010). In the scope of such reintegration, Turkey, for instance, played a reconciliatory role in the trilateral meetings between Bosnia-Herzegovina, Serbia and Croatia, and Davutoğlu called in Sarajevo to "create a new multicultural co-existence"[4] in post-conflict Balkans cities and countries (Knaus 2010). Moreover, the way in which Ahmet Davutoğlu framed the cities of Aleppo and Antep, Batumi and Artvin, and Skopje and Edirne as twin cities sharing the same culture, civilisation and destiny against the idea of national borders should also be seen in this light (Davutoğlu 2010a).[5] Despite the breaking of relations with some of the neighbouring countries by and after the Syrian civil war and Arab Spring and the failure in the sustaining the zero-problem-with-neighbour due to the same process after 2012, Turkey's continuously opening of TIKA offices, promoting of projects with the aim of fostering historical and cultural links, and restoring of Ottoman heritage in the former Ottoman territories before and after the Arab Spring demonstrate that the idea of Ottoman has become salient and Turkey integrated itself with the former Ottoman domains.

All of these historically inspired and political acts of recalling the Ottomans have been run through what can be described as the entrepreneurial involvement of pro-Islamist or conservative elites, politicians and capital groups in Turkey. Therefore, the norm of *Ottomania* carries imprints of pro-Islamic concerns and serves pro-Islamists' political and societal agendas. To this end, processes on the ground were shaped by the deconstruction of the dominant Kemalist frames in domestic and foreign policies, and of opening more room in political circles to the alternative Ottomanist discourse(s).

The commercialisation of Ottoman as a "meta-value" that manifests itself in TV series or movies is also important. The romanticisation of the Ottomans through novels, the common subscription in architecture to Ottoman aesthetic tastes and also the adoption in the visual arts of Ottoman symbols such as the tulip or the sultan's signature (*tughra*) is also part of this. I should also mention the rigorous efforts to restore Ottoman artefacts both at home and abroad as evidence of this massive interest in everything Ottoman. In many ways, therefore, this reveals the discursive and representational communications relevant to the construction of Ottomania as a norm. Anthropologist Jenny White notes this and argues that:

> Ottomania ... has now infected all society, pious and secular alike. Some participate in an "Ottoman" national identity by purchasing genuine antiques for their homes and modern art with Ottoman references.
>
> (White 2013: 183)

Nonetheless, the functioning of processes and entrepreneurial endeavours related to the above, revealed itself more firmly in Ottoman-inspired debates regarding citizenship and nationality. The "entrepreneurs of (neo)Ottomanism" such as Özal and proponents of the Second Republic,[6] have rejected the ethnic definition of the nation and suggested a redefinition along non-territorial and religious grounds[7] (Çolak 2006: 592–3). Along with this, they supported the idea that the state should be transformed to suit the cultural and ethnic plurality of the country (Altan 2013). These entrepreneurs have been heavily inspired by a reinvented Ottoman model of dealing with diversity. In the JDP era too, pro-Ottoman entrepreneurs continued modelling "[the] nation on the historical, flexibly bounded and multidenominational Ottoman Empire, rather than solely on a defence of the present boundaries of the nation-state and a Central Asian bloodline" (White 2013: 96). The JDP-era entrepreneurs have, however, covered more ground when compared to the Özal era. This could be seen in Abdullah Gül's cognitive reframing of Turkish citizenship, something which can be seen in his speech that:

> in history, Ottoman and Seljuk Empires were both known as Turkic states. Yet there is no such thing as the "entire citizens of

the Ottoman Empire were Turks" ... [in the Republican era] we forced people to declare themselves as Turks even to the ones who said "I am not a Turk, I am a Kurd, I am a man of this land". These are our mistakes ... If we act in an imperialistic flexibility and confidence [like the Ottomans did] ... we will see that many of these problems are artificial.

(*Ensonhaber*, 3 April 2013, *Haberartiturk*, 3 April 2013)

As a continuation of the cognitive reframing along Ottomanist lines, the JDP's democratic opening was also awash with the idea that they were taking the Ottoman as a model. Via the introduction of ethnic and religious minority rights and freedoms, the JDP recalled a "1920 Spirit" – a notion representing the efforts of the multicultural and multi-ethnic Anatolian people to build a common home from the ashes of the Ottoman Empire in the first parliament of Turkey in 1920 (*Akşam* 16 November 2013). Restoring language rights, returning geographical names to their historical origins or opening schools with education in the mother tongue of the local community, similar to the *mekteb-i sultani*'s of the Ottoman times, are all moves designed to get closer to this spirit (White 2013: 13, *Radikal* 30 September 2013). Along with this, the JDP made excessive use of the memory of the Ottoman *millet* system and endeavoured to integrate "Jews and Christians within the nation" (White 2013: 12, Grigoriadis 2007). A clear indication of the functioning of the *millet* model was seen during Eurovision 2012 when Can Bonomo, a Turkish Jewish singer represented Turkey. Despite some unrest among nationalist circles, his participation was warmly welcomed by the public with a reference to the Ottoman era co-existence.

It is fair to argue that the norm of Ottomania has been institutionalised at the societal and cultural levels along with domestic and foreign policies. The societal institutionalisation of Ottomania manifested itself in architectural aesthetics, visual corporate identity designs, commemorations, the commercial domain, literature and even in cookery. The idea of the Ottomans as a "culture of living" has been well embedded into society (*Tokyay* 17 October 2011). In domestic politics, Ottoman-inspired "democratic openings", Ottoman-inspired reframing of nationality debates and institutional nostalgia also show Ottomania's institutionalisation. In foreign policy, TIKA's upholding of hundreds of project to re-erect Ottoman cultural heritage abroad, or

Ahmet Davutoğlu's framing of Ottoman history as a primary reference source in dealing with the problems in former Ottoman domains also reveal its institutionalisation. Its translation into foreign policy acts was, therefore, within the scope of this institutionalisation and its post-Kemalist identity implications.

With regards to post-Kemalist identities, it should be noted that Turkey has multiple identities and can barely be wholly defined with a single identity (Warning and Kardaş 2011: 125). Within this post-Kemalist turn, therefore, there appeared several alternative state identities in competition with traditional Kemalist identity. These post-Kemalist identities involve, for instance, Islamic, Pan-Turkic–Eurasian and Ottoman identities which have all surfaced as alternatives and occasionally competing identities in terms of the post-1980 post-Kemalist transformation of the country (see Demirtaş-Coşkun 2008: 33, Akıllı 2013: 5, Tüfekçi 2012: 101). All these identities have also affected foreign policy practices in post-1980s Turkey (Demirtaş-Coşkun 2008: 33–9). Confirming what theory suggests, norms have constitutive influences on identity and identities contribute to the construction of norms; post-Kemalist norms and post-Kemalist identities have a mutually constitutive relationship (Katzenstein 1996b: 18–29, Herman 1996: 285, Risse et al. 1999: 10). In this respect, post-Kemalist norms concerning Outside Turks have contributed to the construction of relevant identities and such identities contributed to Turkey's post-Kemalist approach to Outside Turks. This is seen in the emergence of the norm of Ottomania and Ottoman identity. The Ottoman state identity, which is primarily involved in the internationally mobilisation of the norm of Ottomania, emerged concomitant to the ground-breaking changes in former Ottoman hinterland in the early 1990s; it has also stood out as the "other" of the Kemalist Western-centric identity (Çalış 2001: 17). Post-Kemalist acts of backing Muslim communities in the Balkans throughout the 1990s and of re-erecting Ottoman cultural heritage in former Ottoman domains in the 2000s have been driven by the norm of Ottomania and have also contributed to the institutionalisation of the Ottoman identity.

In conclusion, Ottomania has emerged as a norm in post-1980 Turkey with implications on domestic politics, foreign policy as well as social and cultural domains. Pro-Islamist political and economic elites and liberal intellectual circles were the main actors working for its emergence. Ottomania enjoys a certain degree of atavism and champions the Pax-Ottomana as a "just order" and is also inspired by this. The teachings of the Ottomania norm are based on the Ottoman model which includes, for instance, Ottoman multiculturalism and an identity which is not territorial bound (that is multinational) and pluralism. Ottomania takes these teachings as *should-be-embraced* principles in Turkey and abroad as necessary when dealing with the problems created by the nation state structure and nationalism. Its teachings thus overlap to a certain degree with de-ethnicised nationhood and partly with the idea of Islamic Internationalism.

The Emergence of "De-ethnicised Nationhood"

A part of the post-Kemalist turn, particularly during the JDP era, there has been a decline of nationalism in policy making. This is a contested state of affairs and does not lead to the conclusion that nationalism, as an ideology, has been wiped out completely. On the contrary, nationalist discourse has risen dramatically during times of crises and nationalist discourse among political parties is an undeniable reality. However, there are developments which point towards an increasingly anti-nationalist tendency and policy pattern, at least with the JDP government, during the last decade and a half. It is no coincidence that these changes were in tandem with the Europeanisation and economic–political liberalisation of the country, but also the discourses around Ottoman–Islamic conceptions of Turkish nationhood.

The construction of de-ethnicised nationhood is concomitant to the construction of Ottomania and is thus rooted in multi-ethnic (neo)Ottomanist discourses of the 1990s that have been promoted by pro-Islamic capital/political networks and some liberal circles. The first challenge here was to reinterpret the narrowly defined Turkish identity through an elaboration of "Ottoman heritage as a more inclusive framework" (Şahin 2010: 177). In this sense, the 1990s was definitely pivotal in terms of public articulations of this "redefinition"; however, anti-nationalist considerations of Turkish nationhood were only institutionally operationalised during the JDP era. The JDP not only "developed" but also "implemented an unorthodox alternative definition of Turkishness and the nation" which "appears to be less boundary, and less blood-driven than that held by Kemalist nationalists" (White 2013: 96). Recep Tayyip Erdoğan's very common utterance "the Turkish nation refers to a citizenship not a race" became a routine manifestation of this (*Sabah* 21 January 2013). Similarly, Erdoğan's rephrasing of Atatürk's famous dictum that 'in history this land was Turkish, therefore, it is Turkish in the present time and will remain Turkish forever" to "[t]his homeland is that of the Kurds', the Turks', the Laz's, the Circassian's, the Zaza's, Romans' and Arabs', it is all of ours" was also driven by the same consideration (Ibid.). Indeed, it was this "Turkish postimperial sensibility" that also affected foreign policy and its decision to open its "borders to Arab states, [to make] alliances globally, and pursue economic interests without concern for the ethnic identity of its interlocutors or the role they played in Republican history (with former enemies Greece and Armenia, for instance)" (White 2013: 9, 19, 96).

Moreover, the developments touched on below all suggest the ways in which – institutionally speaking – anti-nationalism and de-ethnicised nationhood have been supported during the JDP era: the Kurdish problem and the legitimate use of *Kurdistan* as a geographical designator of the Southeastern Turkey are admitted by the Prime Minister; geographical names' turn to their historical Kurdish or Armenian originals in East and Southeast Anatolia are allowed; the limitations on the Kurdish names given to infants are lifted; opening TV channels in minority languages are allowed; obligatory recitation of nationalist oath Our Pledge in schools is removed (see Appendix 2); Atatürk's "happy is the one who says I am Turk" saying is mostly removed from streets, state buildings, mausoleums or schools and replaced with his "peace at home, peace in the world" saying; and the "Turkish flag" has commenced to be often used as the "flag of Turkey" in order to reduce the ethnic connotation of the phrase (*Hürriyet* 6 November 2013, *Zaman* 7 November 2013, *Zaman* 26 October 2013, *Akşam* 26 March 2013, *Milliyet* 19 November 2013, Tocci 2005: 74, *Radikal* 30 September 2013a, b, *Haber7* 16 April 2013, *Time Türk* 7 November 2009, *Sözcü* 25 February 2013 respectively).

It was again during the JDP era that regulations on the celebration of national days were redrafted and the performance of nationalistic and militaristic ceremonies, rituals and procedures were abolished (*Radikal*, 5 May 2012). Among the national days, 19 May (the Commemoration of *Atatürk, Youth and Sports Day*) was celebrated as Atatürk's birthday and public participation carried a particular meaning; its abolition meant, in the eyes of Kemalists, that the government had put an end to Atatürk's legacy. By the same token, the "Atatürk International Peace Awards", established in 1984, was not awarded to anyone during the JDP era and was subsequently abolished on 17 August 2013 (*The Official Gazette* 17 August 2013, *Sözcü* 28 August 2013). Similarly, Atatürk's low-relief and the abbreviations of the Republic of Turkey (TC) were removed from the highest three state medals and badges; namely, the Order of Merit, Order of State and Order of the Republic (*Hürriyet* 5 November 2013). Last but not least, the review of school textbooks in terms of how much they complied with Kemalist principles were also abolished (CHP 13 September 2012).

Likewise, debates on a new constitution also clearly reveal attempts to further de-ethnicise nationhood practices. In its sample constitution draft between 2011 and 2013, the Kemalist Republican People's Party (RPP) suggested that citizenship may not be based on ethnic Turkishness but that Kemalist principles should remain as they are (*Taraf* 14 October 2011). The nationalist NMP (Nationalist Movement Party), while insisting on the use of "Türk milleti" (Turkish nation) also suggested that Kemalist principles (particularly laicism) are up for discussion and can be altered (*Samanyoluhaber* 5 April 2013). The pro-Kurdish Peace and Democracy Party (later Peoples' Democratic Party) also issued a draft which did not use the word "Türk" throughout nor did it give importance to any Kemalist principle (Ibid.). The JDP's 2012 draft constitution also made no reference to Turkishness or ethnic identification in its definition of citizenship (*Samanyoluhaber* 27 July 2012, *Ulusal Kanal* 27 July 2012). Their updated 2013 draft, however, while giving a non-ethnicity based definition of Turkishness (i.e., the old idea that everyone bound to the Republic of Turkey through the bond of citizenship is a Turk regardless of religion and ethnicity), articulated its intention to make citizenship as the only identification possible in the republic for citizens (*TRT Türk* 27 July 2012, *Sözcü* 25 February 2013).

These practices are all self-evident of the post-Kemalist and de-ethnicised "common" sense prevailing in the country. This has been the case despite the ascent of militaristic language surrounding the Kurdish issue after the resumption of conflict between the state and the PKK after June 2015, as anti-Kurdish rhetoric became more vocal among the nationalistic circles within the Nationalist Movement Party (NMP), Republican Peoples' Party (RPP) and partly the JDP too.

Nevertheless, the pro-Islamist elites, themselves of diverse ethnic backgrounds, have been the key entrepreneurs in the development of this new de-ethnicised nationhood norm and of the relevant cognitive frames. However, similar to Ottomania, this norm has been also supported by liberals such as the Second Republic supporters and other minority elites. In their support for the de-ethnicisation of nationhood, some elites from Islamic or liberal circles have made reference to Islam as a cement between Muslim communities, while others have championed Ottoman pluralism or the multi-ethnic and multi-religious structures of the country. The former was an idea used initially to call for the unity of Turks and Kurds under a sustainable conceptual umbrella, while the latter was more about providing a liberal and inclusive framework so as to practically bring both Muslims and non-Muslims under the banner of Turkish nationhood (Jacoby and Tabak 2015). In short, both contributed to the communicative and cognitive development of the norm of de-ethnicising Turkish nationhood.

To be sure, one can see in retrospect that Özal, as a pioneering figure in this regard, favoured both Otomanist and Islamic points of views stating that:

[j]ust as it was during the Ottoman Empire, it is possible today to transcend ethnic differences through Islamic identity. I believe that the most powerful single constituting element of identity in this society is Islam. It is religion that blends Muslims of Anatolia and the Balkans. Therefore, Islam is a powerful cement of co-existence and cooperation among diverse Muslim groups ... Being a Turk in the ex-Ottoman space means being a Muslim or vice versa.

(quoted in Yavuz 1998: 24)

To him, accordingly, "to be Turkish means to be Muslim" (White 2013: 101). Likewise, Naqshbandi religious orders and the Diyanet promoted this framework too, as a means for reimagining nationhood in Turkey (Yavuz 1998: 34). There were also secular but Ottomanist-oriented approaches. For instance, Prime Minister Tansu Çiller remarked that she viewed "the ethnic and regional richness of Turkey like the variation and coloration of a mosaic" (Grigoriadis 2009: 136). Çiller also rephrased "happy is the one who says I am Turk" to "happy is the one who says I am a citizen of Turkey" (Ibid.). This implies that de-ethnicised nationhood had the support of pro-Islamic and partially the secular-leaning wings of the political spectrum.

A similar stance was taken by Abdullah Gül, as discussed in the previous section, regarding the wrongdoings of the Kemalist governments, such as forcing people to declare themselves as "Turk" regardless of their ethnic background (see *Ensonhaber* 3 April 2013). He took a similar stance on the issue to Özal. Erdoğan also followed suit and in a noteworthy 2010 visit to Kosovo after which he gave a historical speech at the JDP party congress portraying his visit as a manifestation of an anti-nationalist foreign policy. He accordingly argued that "what constitutes a nation is not blood ties nor genetic codes, but history, culture, shared ideals, shared values" (*Kosova Haber* 9 November 2010). Therefore, focusing on Turkey's relations with Kosovo via the ethnic Turkish community and nationalism alone is fallacious. Erdoğan also remarked that:

> Separating those fell as martyrs while fighting for the same territory, flag, ideals and values based along ethnic origin, language or sect is the biggest mistake and the biggest form of disrespect to the martyrs, to this nation and the country. We are a nation gathered under the Republic of Turkey with a supra-identity, a nation interlocked around the same flag, the same national anthem, the same ideal and values.
>
> (Ibid.)

It was indeed this continuous and conclusive standing, in political sense, which led social anthropologist Jenny White to argue that Muslims in Turkey "have been able to provide a credible Muslim alternative vision of the nation and what it means to be Turkish" (White 2013: 182).

With regard to the secular support to de-ethnicised nationhood, former Chief of the General Staff, İlker Başbuğ, in a ground-breaking move, announced that in defining citizenship in Turkey, "the people of Turkey" (*Türkiyeli*) should be used instead of the "Turkish people" (*Türk halkı*) (*Radikal* 15 April 2009). It will be remembered that the military was traditionally the most staunchly Kemalist force in the country. Although the term was ultimately rejected by certain Kemalists such as the *Sözcü* daily, expression of this at the time was much welcomed by other Kemalists such as the Encümen-i Daniş, an NGO consisting of high-ranking retired military officers, administrators and politicians. They welcomed Başbuğ's *Türkiyeli* opening and asserted that "we agree on the use of 'people of Turkey', it is an inclusive phrase" (*Radikal* 17 April 2009a). *Türkiyeli* has long been embraced by the JDP and received official backing since 2004. For instance, the Working Group on Minority Rights and Cultural Rights, established under the Office of the Prime Minister, published a highly influential report in 2004 which stated that *Türkiyeli* would be the best way to mark national identity so as to overcome ethnic tensions brought by adherence to Kemalist ethnic nationalism (Grigoriadis 2007: 428, Grigoriadis 2009: 143, Oran 2004: 17, Oran 2011, *Haber7* 16 April 2013, *Radikal* 15 April 2009, *Radikal* 17 April 2009b).

Nonetheless, support of Kemalist segments of society for de-ethnicised nationhood was very fragile and did not last long. Soon, de-ethnicised practices were interpreted by conservative and Kemalist nationalists as a threat to "Turkishness" and the Kemalist Republic; indeed the fear of losing Turkishness has been very pronounced (*Gerçek Gündem* 7 April 2013, *Yeniçağ* 22 May 2013). The country was plunged into dispute over "what is sacred to the nation" (White 2013: 6). While liberal and Muslim elites highlighted the multi-ethnic character of society and stated their discomfort at attempts to assimilate the country into a single Turkish ethnicity, conservative and Kemalist nationalists considered any challenge to this as a challenge to the very "nature and essence" of the Turkish Republic. Indeed, nationalists and Kemalists have responded fiercely to the practices of de-ethnicisation and anti-nationalism.

For instance, Özcan Yeniçeri, a Nationalist Movement Party (NMP) MP, stated that "antagonism against nationhood is JDP's ideological fuel" (*Yeniçağ* 22 May 2013). He also labelled the JDP as "traitors" and to him the JDP era ha seen "everything national" lose its meaning – including national days celebrations. He also argued that the JDP has been shameless in daring to bring "Atatürk's Address to Youth" (see Appendix 3) into question by launching campaigns to remove this and the Kemalist youth oath "Our Pledge" from school curricula (Ibid.). NMP deputy-general Celal Adnan, similarly remarked that "[t]he recognition of linguistic pluralism in education and media will tear

Turkey part ... the JDP is antagonistic towards Turkishness under the camouflage of democracy ... Prime Minister [Erdoğan] is committing a hate crime. Our citizens' expression of their Turkishness is almost considered to be an offence" (*Yeni Şafak* 12 October 2013).

Yıldıray Çiçek, former general secretary of Ülkü Ocakları and a columnist for the nationalist daily *Ortadoğu* also remarked that the JDP's code of conduct is wrong, giving the following statements from JDP representatives as evidence: "With the JDP we all became free from [having to call ourselves] Turk" as stated by the party's Istanbul representative or the example from Erdoğan who argued, "that a newspaper uses the motto 'Turkey belongs to Turks' is immoral, shameful ... We have to come to accept the idea of 'people of Turkey' (Türkiyelilik)". For Yıldıray Çiçek, these examples clearly demonstrate the JDP's "antagonism to Turkishness" (Çiçek 2013).

This is part of a key reactionary frame, i.e. the idea that it has become "harder to declare him/herself to be a Turk in Turkey". It was in this context that people launched campaigns which ironically exclaimed "[I am] sorry for being a Turk" (*Yeniçağ* 23 April 2013). It was this feeling that led Bedrettin Dalan, an Ergenekon operation fugitive,[8] to state that "being a Turk has become something disgraceful" (*Hür Haber* 27 November 2007). Murat Bardakçı, a famous historian also complained that "expressing Turkishness is becoming [something] disgraceful" (*HaberTürk* 12 December 2013; Bardakçı 2009). A prominent composer and famous singer Feridun Düzağaç also argued that "I have become scared to say that I am a Turk" (*Mynet* 3 April 2013). It was due to similar concerns that by early 2013 hundreds of thousands of people in Turkey (but also including Turks in Kosovo, to which we will touch on in Chapter 8) had added the abbreviation T.C. to their Facebook names as a sign of protest.[9]

The novel act of favouring a sense of de-ethnicised nationhood by Islamist and liberal types, coupled with the opposing narrative created by nationalists and Kemalists against the increasing denunciation of nationalism and Kemalism, reveals the functioning of an anti-nationalist de-ethnicised nationhood norm. Likewise, the political and legal practices throughout also reveal the partly institutionalisation of de-ethnicised nationhood. Nonetheless, its institutionalisation was not solely sufficient for cross-border validity. De-ethnicised nationhood's translation into foreign policy was carried through at the governmental level, which adopted post-Kemalist Ottoman identity – it was aided by state institutional bodies and NGOs who also subscribed to the same identity in their cross-border activities. It was therefore the Ottoman state identity, which motivated such entrepreneurs to act according to the teachings of de-ethnicised nationhood.

In this sense, and having established that de-ethnicised nationhood's basic teachings are "anti-nationalism" together with an approval of the multi-ethnic and multi-religious structure of the country (inclusiveness), it was the Ottoman identity facilitated internationally mobilisation of de-ethnicised nationhood. Therefore, thanks to this relationship between the de-ethnicised nationhood norm and the Ottoman identity that the ethnicisation of the "Ottoman" as a Turkish civilisation has been given up; in other words, the Ottoman Empire was de-ethnicised. The contributions of, for instance, Bosnians or Albanians to Ottoman culture and civilisation have been boldly emphasised – both at home and abroad. In this sense, on the basis of agency, teachings[10] and identity inclination, de-ethnicised nationhood can therefore be said to share common ground with Ottomania.

In conclusion, de-ethnicised nationhood emerged through the entrepreneurial engagements of both pro-Islamists and liberals. Even seculars types occasionally contributed to this. Although this is rooted in Özal's ideas about (neo)Ottomanism, its true construction and institutionalisation was had during the JDP era. As a post-Kemalist norm, de-ethnicised nationhood's basic teachings are; anti-nationalism, anti-ethnic politics (ethnopolitics), multinationalism and a focus on the multi-ethnic structure of Turkey's society. In this sense, they share common ground with the norm of Ottomania. The reactions of nationalists and Kemalists to new de-ethnicised nationhood driven practices reveal that this norm has had constitutive influences. It is due to this that the emergence of this norm has been highly contested. Lastly, I may say that its translation into foreign policy was mainly through the Ottoman identity.

The Emergence of "Turkish Islam"

Turkey has long had concerns about radical Islam, both within secular and conservative governments. Accordingly, in the foreign policy realm, Diyanet, for instance, has long involved itself in "break[ing] the influence [of] the Salafist and Wahhabist associations" in the Balkans (Karadeniz 2011: 254) and recently the government has joined the global alliance against DAESH in Syria and Iraq. Moreover, people of all political persuasions see the need to take action against Wahhabism and DAESH (see Onur Öymen 2005: 247, İbrahim Özdoğan 2007: 135, *IHA* 25 September 2014, Dağ 2016). Several reasons can be listed for such a state of affairs, such as the desire to protect Ottoman cultural and religious heritage in the region, to preserve Ottoman/Turkish Islamic practices, and to fight against radicalism. Confirming them true, social anthropologist Jenny White has remarked that the underlying logic here is that "Turks of every political persuasion with almost one voice proclaim Turkish Islam different from and superior to other forms of Islam, particularly that practiced in the Arab world" (White 2013: 188).

I argue here that Islam can hardly be envisioned as a monolithic entity in terms of both the performance of the religion and the development of the institutionalised experiences. Thus, Islam has different representations and institutional outlets in different parts of the world based on political, cultural, societal and daily experiences and interpretations. On this basis and through a focus on the different representations of Islam, Hakan Yavuz identifies the Islamic experience zones as follows: Arab, Persian, Turkish, South Asia, Malay-Indonesian, African and Minority zones (Yavuz 2004: 215). To him, this diversity represents the tendency of "crafting and creating one's own way of being Muslim" (Ibid.: 218). This is what Şahin also suggested in arguing that "Islam is what Muslims make of it" (2010: 200).

The Islamic experience in Turkey, therefore, is considered to be distinct and indigenous practice of Islam due to specific political, cultural and societal experiences. However, its main distinction derives from the idea that Turkish Islam represents a genuine reconciliation between heterodox Islam and orthodox Islam and thus incorporates "the wisdom of Sufism with the historical experiences of modern Turkey" (Yavuz 2004: 218). The superiority of Turkish Islam, on the other hand, is argued to stem from the idea that it is moderate, pluralist, liberal, tolerant and modern while, for instance, so-called Wahhabi or Salafi Islam represents radicalism, fanaticism, extremism and intolerance (White 2013: 101, Özdalga 2006: 552, Aras and Caha 2000: 32, Tepe 2000: 59, Çitak 2010: 620). Moreover, Turkey is believed to hold a historical responsibility to "serve Islam", something it inherited from the experiences of previous Turkish Islamic states who had served Islam (Uğur 2004: 336). This idea is the major source for the cognitive construction of the exceptionalism and superiority.

The institutionalisation of the distinction and superiority of Turkish Islamic experience came to the fore in post-1980s Turkey – well within the scope of a general post-Kemalist turn. What prompted this was initially the rapprochement of Islam and the state. Along with this, retrieval of the Ottoman–Islamic sources of nationhood, and the envisioning of religion as a firm component of Turkish identity and a complementary bond between Turkey and kin communities have been influential in constructions of a transnational Turkish Islam. Moreover, the growth of a religious bourgeoisie and Islamic capital groups, coupled with new social, economic and political opportunity spaces, have also been constitutive in the "localization of universal faith and … the universalization of local Turkish understandings of religion" (Yavuz 2004: 218, Yavuz 1998: 22, Bulut 2004, Öktem 2010, 2012). Nonetheless, it was the Özal's and later the JDPs concerns for Turkish–Islamic cultural and religious heritage, which worked to operationalise the idea of Turkish Islam both nationally and internationally.

The 1980 military coup was a historical juncture in the evolution of the Turkish Islamic norm. This is because, as a post-Kemalist practice, the military authorised the post-junta governments to embark on favourable policies towards religion and to promote religious education and institutions as a bulwark against communism which had dragged the country into increasing internal conflict during the 1960s and 1970s (Çakır et al. 2004: 67–8, Akpinar 2007, Toprak 1990). Compulsory religious courses were introduced to schools, imam-hatip schools were promoted, the Diyanet was encouraged to promote Islam nationally and internationally, and religious movements were tolerated more than before (Atasoy 2005: 157). Although, these policies may be said to have led to the military coup in 1997,[11] Turkey's championing of "moderate" Turkish Islam did not change. Diyanet, for instance, was allowed to run cross-border operations and to support moderate Turkish Islam against radical Islamism among the Outside Turks in both the Balkans and Europe, even after the 1997 coup.

However, long before the country was dragged into a coup, as Turkic and Muslim states in Central Asia and the Balkans were gaining independence, both Diyanet and religious groups were promoted by the state to work towards rebuilding historical ties and to prevent the spread of "alien" forms of Islam among these communities (Korkut 2010: 126, Şen 2010: 63, Atasoy 2005: 156). Maintaining the practice of Turkish Islam was deemed a necessity when so-called radical Islamic practices were growing in influence throughout these regions. This idea was also dominant among secular factions in Turkey with former Prime Minister Tansu Çiller going so far as to state in Sarajevo in 1995 that "[i]n the Islamic World, there is the Turkey model and the radical Islam model. The Islamic world and the Balkans should adopt the Turkey model" (quoted in Solberg 2007: 429). Therefore, as a post-Kemalist practice, Turkey utilised religion, religious institutions and religious groups in foreign policy so as to make Turkish Islam internationally competitive. It was with this in mind that President Turgut Özal joined in the opening ceremony of Mehmed Akif Highschool (of the Gülen movement) in Albania in 1991 (*Abdullah Gül* 10 December 2009).[12]

In the 2000s, such concerns gained more prominence as the JDP came to power. TIKA and the Yunus Emre Institution were assigned the role of assisting Diyanet in running Turkish Islamic missions. The traditional assignments of restoring Turkish–Islamic and Ottoman architectural buildings/mosques, the dispatching of religious officials worldwide, publishing religious books in local languages, bringing children from mainly the Balkans to study in Turkey at imam-hatip schools and theology faculties, and taking initiatives to send humanitarian donations worldwide so as to strengthen religious solidarity between Turkey and the Muslim world have continued uninterrupted[13] (Korkut 2010: 131–4).

In the 1990s, despite this global vision, Diyanet's activities were mostly confined to the Balkans and Central Asia. Yet, by the time the JDP came to power, Turkish Islam was being promoted in a truly global way. For instance, concomitant to Turkey's broader opening up to Africa, the Diyanet intensified its concern for the continent and launched projects to make Turkey's experience of Islam known to African countries. Diyanet presented itself, and was approached by African Muslims, as "a test case for a synthesis of Islam and democracy ... [and] a model for the Islamic world" (Dere 2008: 299). Therefore, Diyanet (or "Turkish Islam") stood as an alternative Islamic interpretation for countries in search of a way out of radical Islam. This and similar other practices in Europe made Turkish Islam an internationally important and operant norm (Aydin 2008: 169).

Above, I described that "distinctiveness and superiority" have been the core cognitive frames utilised in the construction of Turkish Islam. Both Diyanet and religious groups, and even Kemalist groups, have been involved in the construction of Turkish Islam as a true model that should be embraced. All these parties, hence, have acted as both entrepreneurs and organisational platforms through which Turkish Islam has been institutionalised as a norm and an identity simultaneously.

In the scope of this institutionalisation and later of its translation into foreign policy practices, Diyanet, as a key entrepreneur, has long been utilised as "an instrument of foreign policy" and to endorse the idea that Turkey's Islamic experience matters to all Muslim countries in an age of modernity (Çitak 2010: 619–20, Öktem 2012: 41–4). As a part of post-Kemalist identity politics, Diyanet's Eurasian Meetings, the Eurasian Council, Diyanet offices abroad and religious officials with an international presence have been the main "conveyers" of the Turkish Islamic message (Öktem 2012: 42). They have been instrumental also in the transmission of distinct Turkish Islamic practices and structures of authority abroad (Landman 1997: 214). Exemplifying the transmission of such identities has been the national and international celebration of the Holy Birth Week[14] (14–20 April) as an authentic Turkish Islamic practice (White 2013: 9, *Diyanet Faaliyet Raporu* 2006: 52, *Diyanet Faaliyet Raporu* 2011: 44, *Diyanet Faaliyet Raporu* 2012: 37–46). During my fieldwork, I witnessed this celebration in Kosovo. It was done at the institutional level and I can confidently conclude that Diyanet was successful in creating, institutionalising and disseminating this Turkish Islamic norm.

Religious groups also contributed to the construction of Turkish Islam as a norm with international manifestations and as an internationally valid identity (Kuru 2005: 261). Among these groups, the Gülen movement has been the most influential and most effective one. The Gülen movement opened massive numbers of education institutions and very powerful business networks and media organisations (television channels, newspapers, magazines) in less than two decades after the 1980 coup (Ibid.). At the very core of its presence abroad, the Gülen movement claimed to be representing both Turkey and Turkish Islam (Balci 2003: 164–6). Their schools are known as "Turkish schools" and this was used by the movement in building relations (Ibid.: 167). In groups discourse, Turkish Islam is a pro-globalisation, peaceful and conforms to democratic values and principles. This provided them with a concrete basis for their opposition to violence, promotion of peaceful co-existence and their encouragement for inter-cultural and inter-faith dialogue as a typically Turkish Islamic practice.

Despite slight differences in their understandings of what Turkish Islam actually is, or in the practice of Turkish Islam, Diyanet and religious groups recognise each other. Although, their priorities are ostensibly different, however, they mutually subscribe to the practices they construct under the banner of Turkish Islam. This, in its very basis, confirms that Turkish Islam reconciles heterodox Islam and orthodox Islam (Yavuz 2004: 218).

Therefore, the institutionalisation of Turkish Islam and the construction of a relevant identity have been represented massively in both domestic and international politics. Their implications, particularly for foreign policy, are obvious. For instance, although the idea that "Islam is performed best in Turkey" has long been endorsed by Kemalist regime, by the time of the post-Kemalist turn in the country, for the first time in Republican history this idea became a foreign policy priority. Accordingly, state and societal level discomfort towards the so-called Wahhabi threat in the Balkans is also suggestive of such an international focus. Similarly, the nationwide and international celebration of the Holy Birth Week is an evident indicator of domestic and international institutionalisation even at the cultural and societal level.

In conclusion, Turkish Islam is an institutionalised post-Kemalist norm with imprints on Turkey's foreign policy. In its construction and institutionalisation, even the Kemalist military and seculars have played a role, yet the Diyanet and religious movements were the ones successfully acting as entrepreneurs and organisational platforms to promote national and international goals. Turkish Islam's internationalist appeal (Muslim solidarity) partly overlaps with the Islamic internationalism. However, they have contradictory teachings, as will be seen below. While Islamic internationalism considers the Islamic world as an entity, Turkish Islam is based on the idea of the distinctiveness and superiority of Turkey's Islamic experience and suggests a form of international competition with other Islamic teachings. It promotes the Turkish experience of Islam as a moderate, tolerant and pluralist path.

The Emergence of "Islamic Internationalism"

The history of how the "Turkish nation" was built is a story about the process of transformation from a religiously defined and organised society into a secular minded and nationally "behaving" community (Zürcher 1999). The Kemalist regime redefined the Islamic-Self and rebuilt it as a secular Turkish-Self which sought to force people to conceive of themselves as belonging to the Turkish nation rather than to the Islamic ummah or global community. Therefore, internationalist concern were focused on nationality rather than religion. This was the reason why ethnic identity was envisaged as the identification on which inter-state and inter-communal relations could be built (Yanık 2006: 5). Indeed, the excessive use of a rhetoric about "captive Turks" (those Turks living under communist regimes) while completely ignoring how Muslims suffered during the Cold War period prove the salience of this idea. This idea brought not only ethnic and national exclusion and isolation, but also religious indifference towards Islamic communities and countries. This was facilitated by the marginalisation and discrediting of Ottoman and Islamic history and the eventual decline in the idea of the unity of the ummah – a concept which lost its practicality and became empty rhetoric among small Islamic circles.

Historically speaking, in the political realm, although there were always some parties and politicians which called for more links to the Muslim world at the governmental and nongovernmental level, it was only with the rise to prominence of Necmettin Erbakan and his Milli Görüş (National View) movement that the necessity of developing economic and political relations with Muslim countries became a prominently spread idea (Dilligil 1994, Toprak 1984: 127). In its path to building fruitful relations with the ummah, Erbakan and the Milli Görüş movement established strong ties internationally with, for instance, the Muslim Brotherhood in Egypt and Syria and with the Islamic Salvation Front in Algeria (Robins 1997: 89). However, for Erbakan, the critical historical juncture came when the Welfare Party emerged as the biggest party in the 1994 local elections and then again in the 1995 general elections. Based on such confidence and with the motive for working for the cause of the ummah that Erbakan articulated his aim of building an "Islamic United Nations, Islamic NATO, an Islamic United Nations International Children's Emergency Fund, a common Islamic currency and an Islamic Common Market" (Ibid.). These institutions would be established, he argued, to meet the needs of the broader ummah. The ethnic cleansing of the Bosnian Muslims was the motivation which led him to think of the necessity of building a NATO-like joint military organisation among Muslim countries capable of intervening during such incidents. Erbakan's efforts to increase the Islamic Development Bank's (IDB) influence and involvement in the Islamic world were designed to encourage multilateral cooperation and solidary in the economic sphere (Robins 1997: 94, *Avrasya Bülteni* July 2006: 11–12). The establishment of the Developing-8 (D-8) group,[15] by Erbakan, was also designed with this purpose in mind, which eventually helped Turkey to rebuild and strengthen its broken ties with the ummah (Robins 1997: 88–9).

Although the 1997 military coup that toppled the Erbakan government on the grounds that his party was trying to change the regime of the country to an Islamic one and this made public opinion cautious towards building relations with Muslim countries and people, Erbakan's efforts to turn Turkey's attention towards the ummah eventually had constitutive influences on the JDP government. These initials forays to establish relations with Muslim countries in political and economic spheres were expanded to the societal and cultural realms by the JDP (Kösebalaban 2005: 31). The increase in ties with Muslims abroad in social and cultural spheres was made possible with the increasing activism in Turkish foreign policy, though abandoning Islamic references as a political programme (as with the WP) (Dağı 2005: 30). Eventually, this enabled the JDP to add "a layer of Muslim sensitivit[y] in foreign policy" without having to face accusations of *irtica* (religious reactionism) or Islamism[16] (Çağaptay 2012a). This was exemplified by Turkey's activist policies in Afghanistan, Myanmar, Africa, the Middle East and the Balkans. In these regions, Turkey, rather than relying merely on the intergovernmental level, opened the way for NGOs and humanitarian initiatives to encourage Islamic internationalist projects. It even broadened its focus on humanitarian engagement with both Muslims and non-Muslims. Therefore, different to the state-centrism of Erbakan in his pursuit of building ties with the ummah, the

JDP resorted more to NGO-backed humanitarian diplomacy and paid closer attention to the sufferings of Muslims worldwide and to the historical and cultural responsibility Turkey had towards them.

During the JDP era "solidarity with fellow Muslims" or "empathy with Muslims" have become key guiding principles in both institutional and societal levels (Çağaptay 2012a). This was materialised initially by the state institutions such as TIKA or YTB through delivering assistance and humanitarian aid to Muslim communities worldwide (see *Haber7* 15 September 2013, Orhan 2012: 78–9, Beylur 2012: 76–7, Atmaca 2012: 78–81, *Avrasya Bülteni* February 2005: 3, *Avrasya Bülteni* February 2008: 18–25. Ekmeleddin İhsanoğlu, a Turkish diplomat, also took over as the president of the Organisation of Islamic Cooperation (OIC) in 2004 (until 2014) – something which also facilitated the actualisation of Turkey's Islamic internationalism. Nonetheless, the JDP was not alone in this campaign. Economic and political circles with a religious agenda and other religious groups also backed such policies; with an eye to expending or giving a helping hand to the their overseas brothers. They had limited influence during the Özal and Erbakan eras, yet by the time the JDP came to power they too became part of the process of building and enhancing relations with the Muslim communities outside Turkey. Religious groups and humanitarian aid organisations became a stakeholder in reifying the societal level Islamic Internationalist consciousness which was increasing in Turkey. However, it should be noted that they owe this freedom of action to the general liberalisation of the country and to the EU accession process – both of which promoted the de-securitisation of religion and civil society.

Accordingly, it was within this scope that Kemalist and secular pressures on religious groups completely dissolved. These religious groups now run schools, do charitable works and act with more confidence than ever before. This freedom and confidence has enabled them not only to uphold charitable works in Turkey, but also abroad. Before the JDP government, only a few groups had schools or institutions abroad; however by the JDP era almost all religious groups have begun to operate internationally. Today, the different religious groups running cross-border missions include the Gülen Movement, Milli Görüş, Süleyman Efendi Group, Menzil, Naqshbandi, İsmailağa, Aziz Mahmut Hüdai, İskender Paşa, Haydar Baş, Sheikh Nazım Kıbrısi and the Yeni Asyacılar groups.

Along with these religious groups – and often together with them – many Islamic international humanitarian organisations have also acquired the organisational and financial capacities to run aid missions abroad. Today, among many others I can note, Humanitarian Relief Foundation (IHH), Kimse Yok mu Association, Deniz Feneri and Cansuyu Foundation along with Kızılay (Red Crescent) and Türk Diyanet Foundation all operate successful international programmes. Apart from the orientation of the current JDP government, these humanitarian aid campaigns also increase the sense of Islamic internationalist consciousness and activism in the country and stand as evidence of a self-evident post-Kemalist turn in Turkey. As a result, nowadays, it is very common in Turkey to send *qurbani* (sacrifice of a livestock animal during Eid al-Adha) or *zakat* (obligatory alms) abroad via these humanitarian institutions. In 2012, The IHH alone delivered more than £50 million worth of humanitarian relief worldwide (IHH 2012).[17] Moreover, as the official publication of YTB reports, the Turkish humanitarian organisations which delivered aid and assistance in Ethiopia in 2012 were Mahmut Hüdai Association, Kimse Yok mu Association and the IHH – all of which are pro-Islamic and religiously motivated organisations (*Arti90* January 2012: 79–81).

As can be seen, different to the Welfare Party, the JDP has resorted more to using civil society initiatives and humanitarian diplomacy, something which has also opened more space for the involvement of these civil society actors in the conduct of foreign policy. This paved the way for the construction of the Islamic internationalist norm with major civil society and public backing. Today, more people are involved in the process of building ties with the ummah. This indicates a change in cognitive and intersubjective understandings of the idea of the ummah.

In domestic politics, reflections of such a cognitive change were seen in, for instance, 1989 when Bulgaria forcefully moved hundreds of thousands of ethnic Turks out of the country, with many people in Turkey going out of their way to help. This was the same during the Gulf War when millions of Iraqi Kurds were given shelter in Turkey. The situation during the Bosnian and Kosovo wars was also the same (Bulut 2004). During the on-going Syrian Civil War, a similar collective mobilisation can also be seen. State institutions have created safe havens inside Turkey and supplied refugees with shelter, while Diyanet and religious groups have collected money in mosques to be used for the needs of the refugees. In the same vein, relief organisations such as the IHH, Deniz Feneri, Kimse Yok mu Association and many others have also launched appeals to raise money for needy people and children in these refugee camps. Similar concerns were activated during the ethnic cleansing of the Muslims in Myanmar, during Israel's use of excessive military force against the people of Palestine, or during the civil war in Somali and Sudan. Therefore, the constant suffering in many parts of the Muslim world and both civil and state initiatives to help these allowed for the reification of the norm of Islamic internationalism.

These policies and initiations have found audience in the Muslim world, and attempts to collaborate with Turkey in creating a sense of solidarity within the ummah have peaked during the JDP era. For instance, in Malaysia, the Malaysian Islamic Youth Movement (ABIM) organised a "Solidarity Rally" in Kuala Lumpur in mid-June 2013, in order to celebrate Turkey's constructive involvement in reviving the ummah and in putting the idea of "ummah consciousnesses" into practice (Özay 24 June 2013). The president of ABIM Mohammad Raimi stated in an interview regarding this rally that:

We sent Syria four [humanitarian aid] groups. This will continue ... Without getting support from Turkey, this is not possible. For example, in Mobarak era [Egypt] it was not possible to enter Gaza. Now, things have changed ... Malaysia's leadership to the Islamic countries can barely be claimed. However, it is obvious that this is done by Turkey. [Turkey's] influence within the Islamic Cooperation Organisation is remarkable. Interestingly [although Myanmar is our neighbour] we saw that the initiative in Rohinya [of Myanmar] was taken by Turkey. Minister of Foreign Affairs Ahmet Davutoğlu and Mr Erdoğan's spouse Lady Emine's visit to Myanmar was a significant episode. Surely, all these are the initiations Turkey embarked on in the scope of the concept of "ummah".

(Ibid.)

Given the above developments, it can be argued that at the societal level the norm of Islamic internationalism has been institutionalised to a large degree thanks to the efforts of religious groups and humanitarian organisations in various initiatives around the world. However, the political institutionalisation of the norm has yet to be completed and there is indeed no direct evidence that it can ever be so. This is because despite Turkey's promising Islamic Internationalist moves such as claimed ownership of the Palestinian cause, insistent legal and political actions against Israel's killing of civilians in Mavi Marmara, enhanced backing of the IHH to make its operations worldwide, and Syrian refugees policy, political discourses have not gone beyond Erdoğan or Davutoğlu's complaints about the artificial boundaries between Turkey and the Muslim communities or Abdullah Gül's suggestions that Muslim countries "find a solution to issues pertaining to the Islamic world, [before] others ... impose their own solutions" (Aslan 2013: 28, *Hürriyet* 17 September 2012, *Sabah* 21 November 2013). Nevertheless, the aforelisted Islamic internationalist actions suggest that the Islamic internationalism norm well and effectively functions without a need for firm political institutionalisation (see *Davutoğlu* 15 November 2012, *Davutoğlu* 4 February 2013).

The key presence of Islamic Internationalist consciousness and its smooth translation into foreign policy prove the presence of an Internationalist Muslim identity. This identity "emanated from a resurgence of Islamic values" and initially denoted a discomfort from dependence of Muslims on the West in Muslim affairs (Demirtaş-Coşkun 2008: 35). By the 2000s, however, this identity has been vocally and confidently taken on by the JDP in, for instance, the forging of relations with the Muslim countries or in intervening in Muslim affairs throughout the Middle East and later Africa (Warning and Kardaş 2011: 128). In addition to the abovementioned Islamic internationalism which was driving foreign policy acts, for instance, with a claim of "safe guarding the ummah's interests" the JDP also claimed "ownership of the Palestinian cause" or became involved in Muslim affairs in countries such as Somalia or Myanmar "as part of its [Islamic] civilisational duty" (Duran 2013: 94). As a proof of the external reception of this identity claim, it is now evident that Turkey is increasingly being viewed among Muslim communities abroad as a "spokesman" of the Islamic world which is part of the broader perception that Turkey has positioned itself at "the heart of the ummah after ... more than a century of walking history's margins" (Ibid.). These confirm that Turkey's Internationalist Muslim identity and the idea of Islamic internationalism have translated into a foreign policy agenda.

In conclusion, entrepreneurs and cognitive processes have functioned simultaneously and in an overlapping manner in terms of the emergence of the norm of Islamic internationalism. Accordingly, political developments such as humanitarian crises in Muslim countries and humanitarian-based discourses surrounding these have changed the cognitive frames in the minds of people regarding the ummah. Along with this, religious groups, state institutions and civil humanitarian initiatives have also worked as both norm entrepreneurs and organisational platforms for the creation of such cognitive frames and the institutionalisation of the Islamic Internationalist norm, where possible. The core teachings of Islamic internationalism are religious brotherhood, Muslim solidarity and unity of the ummah. This partly overlaps with Ottomania and Turkish Islam, yet this norm is also a distinct one in its own right. Moreover, together with de-ethnicised nationhood, Islamic internationalism is one of the most contested norms as secularist factions and Kemalists are all against considering Islam as the core of the country's international image in absolute terms. Nonetheless, as religious identity has been dominant throughout the JDP era, the Islamic Internationalist norm has also managed to inform foreign policy acts.

Conclusion

In this chapter, it was shown that there are four identifiably robust post-Kemalist norms concerning the country's understanding of Outside Turks and in developing relevant policies. These are: *Ottomania*, *de-ethnicised nationhood*, *Turkish Islam* and *Islamic internationalism*. The first stage of the elaborated norm lifecycle model, namely norm emergence, has been helpful and facilitative to understand why, when and how these norms emerged, institutionalised and influenced policy conduct. Accordingly, these four norms emerged under the unique environment created by the neo-liberal turn of the country and the EU harmonisation process whereby Kemalist taboos have been legally and politically broken. In the emergence of these norms, pro-Islamist elites and liberal circles have played a constitutive role. It is shown that the emergence of these norms were through political, historical, cultural, social, communicative and cognitive mechanisms and processes by which new identities, new intersubjective understandings and cognitive frames were constructed in post-Kemalist Turkey. These domestically constructed post-Kemalist norms are translated into policies and gained international mobility through institutionalisation and the functioning of relevant identities. The international mobility thus meant that post-Kemalist norms have gone beyond the tipping point, after which the domestic post-Kemalist norms became international ones and started to have cross-border influences.

This chapter provides the empirical grounds on which to explain the reasons why the way in which Outside Turks are comprehended has changed; it thus answers the first research question of this project, namely "how have post-Kemalist changes in domestic politics been reflected in Turkey's attitudes towards Outside Turks?". It has been shown in this chapter that the post-Kemalist norms of Ottomania and de-ethnicised nationhood generated a change in the way Turkey imagined co-national and kin communities abroad, whereby common history, culture and faith have become more concrete determinants in building ties based on elements other than ethnicity (see the Table 6.1. below). Therefore, Outside Turks have been re-constructed as communities with whom Turkey has strong historical and cultural ties and hence the ethnic ties have been underemphasised. In tandem with this, due to their championing of religious identity, Turkish Islam and Islamic Internationalism have facilitated Outside Turks' re-imagining as Muslim communities. The solidarity between Turkey and the Outside Turks thus have been re-coded along religious lines,

Table 6.1   Teachings of the post-Kemalist norms concerning Outside Turks

Post-Kemalist Norms	Teachings
Ottomania	Multiculturalism, supranational identity, multinationalism, pluralism
De-ethnicised Nationhood	Anti-nationalism, anti-ethnopolitics, multinationalism, supranational identity
Turkish Islam	Religious identity, distinctiveness and superiority of Turkish Islam, moderateness of Turkish Islam
Islamic Internationalism	Religious brotherhood and solidarity, unity of the ummah, supranational religious identity

rather than ethnicity or nationalism. In sum, due to the constitutive impact of these four post-Kemalist norms, Outside Turks' Muslimness or the cultural unity between Turkey and Outside Turks has gained importance, while ethnicity has lost weight in policy development.

In the chapter, the imprints of these post-Kemalist norms on foreign policy formulation and conduct have been shown; yet their constitutive and regulative roles in Turkey's policy towards the Outside Turks will be further elaborated on in the next chapter as Turkey's relations with the ethnic Turkish community in Kosovo are assessed.

CHAPTER 7

CASCADE OF POST-KEMALIST NORMS TO KOSOVO

Introduction

In the previous chapter, I showed the substantial role of identity politics in norm mobilisation. It is, moreover, identity politics which renders possible the norm cascade. Confirming this, the emergent post-Kemalist norms gained international mobility primarily through the post-Kemalist identity politics in Turkey's foreign policy and Kosovo, a country with undisputed historical and cultural ties with Turkey, and one of the prime destinations of diffusion since the late 1990s. At this juncture, this chapter provides a detailed response to the second research question raised in the Introduction, namely "how are Turkey's post-Kemalist domestic norms transferred to the Outside Turks locality in Kosovo?"

Kosovo, along with Bosnia, has attracted a great deal of attention in both official and societal levels in Turkey, particularly due to the bloodshed the country was exposed to throughout the 1990s, which ended up with Turkey, as part of NATO, intervening in 1999 and later sending troops to Kosovo as part of NATO's Kosovo Force (KFOR).[1] The focus on Kosovo intensified and gained novel characteristics during the JDP era thanks also to Kosovo's ethnic Turkish community's calls for help in their efforts to gain ethnic rights during Kosovo's UNMIK administration period (1999–2008). As the second largest Muslim-majority country in Europe (after Turkey) Kosovo's independence in 2008 witnessed a further development of good relations with Turkey.

Here, the Muslim character of both countries motivated Turkey to act confidently along identity politics lines.

Turkey's diplomatic, humanitarian and cultural presence in Kosovo has increased during the postwar period. Initially, a diplomatic coordination bureau was opened in 1999, which was eventually restructured as Turkey's embassy in Pristina following the country's independence in 2008 (Pristina.be.mfa.gov.tr). Along with Turkish military bases and a diplomatic coordination bureau, the third official body to open in Kosovo was a representation office of the Turkish Directorate of Religious Affairs (Diyanet) (*DHA* 16 April 2013). These were followed by the TIKA Kosovo Program Office in 2004 and the Yunus Emre Institute in Prizren, Pristina and later in Ipek in 2011 and 2013 respectively (*TIKA Faaliyet Raporu* 2006: 5, *Yunus Emre Bulletin* October 2011: 4). Intense high-level visits from Turkey officials facilitated the confident functioning of these institutional bodies and the development of Turkey's direct ties with Albanian, Bosnian and ethnic Turkish communities in Kosovo.

Moreover, Turkey also participated in post-conflict restructuring programmes in the security, economic, infrastructural and cultural spheres. In this scope, Turkey contributed to law enforcement and security capacity building and training efforts. Turkey also has a presence in the European Union Rule of Law Mission (EULEX) in Kosovo and provides assistance in training the Kosovo Security Forces (Balcer 2012: 228–9, *Balkan Insight* 20 September 2012). Similar help was extended during the restructuring of the religious authority (the Islamic Community of Kosovo – Riyaset) and in preserving Islamic cultural heritage in the country (Krasniqi 2011: 200). In this respect, Turkey's Diyanet, in collaboration with TIKA, has run several joint projects with the Riyaset and has contributed to reviving the Ottoman cultural heritage in the country by rebuilding and renovating hundreds of Islamic/Ottoman cultural artefacts. Furthermore, in this new era, Turkey's economic relations with and direct investments in Kosovo has also intensified (*Balkan Insight* 4 November 2010, Eralp 2010: 7, Yavan 2012: 255–61). Turkish firms have built the country's only civilian airport and main highroad linking it to Albania – the two centrepieces of Kosovo's international and national transport systems (Anastasakis 2012: 201–202, fn9). Turkish firms also have shares in banking, finance, energy and in the communication sector. Indeed, as the Deputy Prime

Minister of Kosovo, Mimoza Kusari Lila, has noted "7 out of the top 10 foreign investors to Kosovo are Turkish firms" (*Dünya* 14 April 2012).

It can be seen that Turkey has embraced a multi-layered approach in its policy and has not restricted its concern towards the ethnic Turks in the country. In reaching this end, the use of diverse diplomatic instruments has been employed effectively; yet, JDP's non-ethnic and non-nationalist tendency in its foreign policy was also determinative. Accordingly, the JDP emphasised the "birth of the second country in Europe with at least 90 per cent of its population being Muslim" with Kosovo having been conceptualised mainly as a Muslim country with whom Turkey shares a common history and culture (Demirtaş-Coşkun 2010: 73).

Accordingly, the central motive in the development of Turkey's Kosovo policy under the JDP rule was summarised by Foreign Minister Ali Babacan in a speech to Kosovo's Parliament on 13 January 2009:

> We shared a common history and fate for many years with the people of Kosovo ... The importance of Kosovo rests on the cultural and human ties stemming from this common history. As you all know, today a considerable number of Turks live in Kosovo. In Turkey, on the other hand, we have a large number of citizens with roots in Kosovo. This bond is the prime motive for us to show close concern to the Kosovo issue.
>
> (*Ali Babacan* 13 January 2009)

A similar policy orientation was uttered by Abdullah Gül during a visit to Turkey by Kosovo's president, Fatmir Sejdiu in 2010. Gül stated that:

> The great importance of Kosovo for Turkey stems from our historic cultural ties and the affinity, which exists between the two countries ... Turkey has deeply supported the friendly and brotherly country, Kosovo both before and after its independence. Our country became among the first countries to recognise Kosovo's independence ... In Kosovo there is an active Turkish community, in our country we have a large number of citizens with roots in Kosovo. This affinity, from the very beginning, is among the factors, which led us to show close concern to Kosovo.

The father of Mehmet Akif Ersoy, the Independence March poet, was of Kosovar descent, which demonstrates the historic and cultural ties between Turkey and Kosovo.

(*Abdullah Gül* 2 February 2010)

These speeches suggest that common culture and history have been the core motives in policy formulation, which is concomitant to the post-Kemalist transformation in policy making. The idea of a common history has been deployed as a legitimating factor in Turkey's involvement from the very beginning of tensions in Kosovo; by the time the JDP came to power, the cultural layer was added to this, referring to the religio-cultural unity between the two countries (Anastasakis 2012: 189, Altunya 2003: 119, Gangloff 2004).

In this sense, Turkey has been cautious to not make the ethnic Turkish community its primary concern in its Kosovo policy. Thus, "rather than prioritizing the ethnic Turks in Kosovo issue, [Turkey] mainly endeavoured to develop relations with the Albanians in the region" (Demirtaş-Coşkun 2010: 73, Gangloff 2004: 119). A member of the ethnic Turkish community confirmed this observation to me, arguing that "Turkey's foreign policy [towards Kosovo] is not nationalistic ... Turkey does not put [ethnic] Turks into the centre of its policy, it rather puts the Albanians" (Interview LE21[2]). My respondent from TIKA explained this by stating that "nothing would be different in Turkey's policy to Kosovo if the ethnic Turkish minority would not exist in Kosovo" because "Turkey does not look at Kosovo through an ethnic lens", just as it did wear an "ethnic lens" in its policy to Bosnia (Interview DM5[3]). This is confirmed also by a diplomat respondent from the Turkish embassy who argued that "we do not pursue an ethnic policy. At this point, even if there were no [ethnic] Turks in here, we would have had solid relations with Kosovo" (Interview DM7).

Despite Turkey's non-privileging of ethnic Turks in its Kosovo policy, kinship ties with Kosovar Turks are nonetheless never denied. The government has even felt the responsibility in terms of taking care of the ethnic Turkish community and has constantly lobbied for the community's inclusion in the plans for political restructuring and requested assurances from the government of Kosovo that their political representation is secure (*Radikal* 12 October 2005). For Turkey, the establishment of firm relations with Kosovo was an indirect yet sole way of enhancing the position of ethnic Turks in the country (Demirtaş-Coşkun 2010: 73). Turkey's vocal support for Kosovo's independence after 2005 and in terms of lobbying for increased international recognition has served this purpose well.

On the other hand, the Turkish community has always had good and direct access to Turkey's institutions, its diplomatic as well as NGO institutions – all of which have been in close contact with the Turkish community on the ground. The ethnic Turkish community has benefitted from this relationship in financial, cultural and political terms (Interview LE21). Moreover, members of the Turkish community follow political developments in Turkey very closely, visit Turkey frequently and contribute to the building of close relations between Turkey and Kosovo in both an international and transnational sense. They can even do political lobbying in Turkey through their transnational ties with political groups such as the secular Republican People's Party (RPP) and nationalist NMP (Nationalist Movement Party) so as to encourage the government in Turkey to support their nationalist cause (Interview DM4, Interview RG5;[4] also see *Bulut* 7 June 2013, Osman Durmuş 2009: 295). In the same vein, through their informal ties in Turkey, they can force TIKA or Yunus Emre Institutes in Kosovo to accept their projects, even after initially being rejected (Interview DM3).

As the above-reviewed policy framework suggests, Turkey's approach to Kosovo was had within the scope of identity politics and Turkey's influence was made possible by the presence of a high number of Turkish institutions and religious groups operating at the grassroots level in Kosovo. In this sense, the international mobilisation of Ottomania, de-ethnicised nationhood, Turkish Islam and Islamic Internationalism have been provided by state institutions such as the Turkish embassy in Pristina, TIKA, Yunus Emre Institute, Diyanet and the presidency for Turks Abroad and Related Communities (YTB) along with religious groups such as the Gülen movement, the Süleyman Efendi Group, the Menzil Group and the Erenköy Group. Ministerial and prime ministerial level visits, but also the local post-Kemalist elites, have also been facilitative in this sense.

Turkey's institutions have acted as the prime actors of norm diffusion and socialisation, yet each institutional body is responsible from the conveyance of different norms depending on their identity inclinations. For instance, while Diyanet's practices mobilise mainly the

"Turkish Islam", Yunus Emre Institute has mostly acted according to the Ottomania norm. TIKA has conducted post-Kemalist practices of all kind. Alternatively, Türk Taburu has introduced and institutionalised Kemalist practices.[5] These differences derive mainly from the identity differences among the institutions, which are noticeable also to the members of diplomatic mission. The diplomat respondent in Kosovo reviewed this as follows:

> There is an identity difference among Turkey's institutions in Kosovo ... [and] this is reflected in their activities ... The military [Tabur], Yunus Emre or YTB represent different identities. This derives from the political landscape in Turkey ... In YTB, the people in charge are close to the government and share its ideology. This is well reflected in its institutional identity ... The Tabur carries the identity of the Turkish Armed Forces [which is Kemalist[6]], yet in its activities it finds a middle way ... These institutions work separately from the embassy as much as they can ... They differ from each other, they reflect different identity behaviours ... The government subscribes to the Ottoman idea [and] ... in traditional [foreign policy] institutions this is not seen any more as odd. People no longer find the use of Ottoman language words strange ... [By the foreign policy missions] Islam is now told as part of Turkish history, which was not done previously ... The naming of Yunus Emre is a deliberate choice. It blends Turkish history, culture and arts with Islamic history, culture and arts. [Thus] Yunus Emre Institute represents the Turkish Islam [Türk İslamı], not merely Islam ... Similar to what happens in Turkey, in here, these institutions tell us 'Let's unite upon Islam' ... [Therefore, in short,] the changes in Turkey are reflected here, too.
>
> (Interview DM7)

This goes a long way in portraying the identity differences and its implications for various "norm diffuser actors". In addition to state institutions, local elites also employed social learning practices to transfer norms from Turkey and to make the community adhere to these norms. For instance, the Turkey Alumni Association in Prizren (Türkiye Mezunları Derneği-TÜMED) has been a key local institution that has long worked for the idea of Ottoman ethnic accord, the ummah and Turkish Islam in Kosovo. Due to this devotion, it managed to build strong and conclusive ties with Turkey's official institutions in Kosovo. In this respect, it is not surprising to see that "when TÜMED was officially established, all of its office equipment were supplied by TIKA" (Interview LE8). The local norm learners also invited Turkey's religious groups to Kosovo and gave them use of facilities, organised events of a post-Kemalist nature such as commemorations of Mehmet Akif and the idea that he represents Albanian–Turkish brotherhood, or, for example, in assisting Diyanet or Yunus Emre Institute in serving the cause of Turkish Islam.

In short, the cascade of the post-Kemalist norms concerning Outside Turks to Kosovo has taken place in the scope of Turkey's identity politics and has been facilitated by Turkey's institutions in Kosovo and local norm learners. Turkey's religious groups also played constitutive roles. Below, I have given detailed accounts of the cascade of each post-Kemalist norm and of the conduct of post-Kemalist foreign policy.

Ottomania's Cascade

TIKA's office in Kosovo has been the most effective entrepreneur of Ottomania. This was mainly due to its financial capacity and special concern for culture and history. I showed previously that TIKA was established with nationalist sentiments in mind in the early 1990s. However, by the time the JDP government came to power, its mission was redefined and commenced embodying pro-Ottoman, pro-Islamic and non-nationalist orientation. In this vein, TIKA has channelled its financial capacity and concern for culture and history to mobilise the post-Kemalist norms in Kosovo. The trails of all four post-Kemalist norms have been evident in its activities, yet Ottomania has a special place here. In this sense, although many of its activities in promoting the Ottoman/Turkish culture and language were taken over by the Yunus Emre Institute after its establishment in 2011, TIKA continues to conduct and support activities in the cultural field by which Ottomania is mobilised internationally. As an indicator of this diffusion, the basic motive and area of involvement of TIKA is introduced by a respondent from TIKA in the interview I recorded follows:

The cultural heritage is the main area of investment of TIKA ...
This is because this heritage is not merely an historical artefact or
architectural artefact. These are the explicit expression of your
[Turkey's/Ottoman Empire's] historical contribution to here
[Kosovo] ... These artefacts are giving the identity to this
land and differentiate here from other places of the world.

(Interview DM5)

TIKA, therefore, recalls Ottoman values and identities through
re-erecting historical and cultural artefacts. Yet, more importantly,
re-erecting the Ottoman architectural heritage evokes the desire
of re-enactment of the Ottoman as a "culture of living" in Kosovo.
In this sense, TIKA frames the Ottomans as a model for dealing with
cultural and ethnic diversity, a model of peaceful co-existence, a
pluralistic collective memory, an inclusive "social contract" based on
multiculturalism and multi-ethnic experience, a cure against the
nationalist destruction of societal relations and a cure to the crises of
nationalism and nation-building in Kosovo (Interview DM5). Thus, as a
diffusive act, the Ottoman era ability to enable co-existence in Kosovo is
used as an example, which should be implemented even today.

Likewise, Yunus Emre Institute, again a norm entrepreneur, has been
involved in introducing and promoting Ottoman culture, values and
identities in Kosovo with a primary emphasis on brotherhood and
solidarity between Turkey and Kosovo. In this sense, for instance, a
Yunus Emre official stated that:

[W]e are primarily trying to find out the things that represent our
common culture, particularly with the Albanians. However, we do
not discriminate [between ethnic groups] hence do events for [and
fund the projects of] Turks, Albanians, Bosnians, Roma people,
Torbeshis or Goralis. There was 600 years of Ottoman rule and
there indisputably exist a great common culture ... We are trying
to highlight this culture in our activities ... We are uttering
brotherhood and solidarity.

(Interview DM3)

The promotion of common culture, therefore, takes the form of a call to
show endorsement to the idea of the Ottoman Empire as a living culture.

Moreover, along with TIKA and the Yunus Emre Institute, high-level visits to Kosovo from Turkey have also been an important way to convey Ottomania. For instance, in his address to thousands who lined Shadirvan Square in Prizren,[7] many of whom were ethnic Turks, Recep Tayyip Erdoğan also championed the idea of Ottoman inter-ethnic accord:

> Prizren[8] serves as a model of tolerance and of culture of co-existence to the world. In the world those who want to see how differences co-exist need to come to Kosovo, to Prizren. We have carried out successful projects to preserve this cultural heritage in Kosovo, with the support of the Kosovo state. TIKA continues its efforts to hand down this cultural heritage to the next generations.
>
> (*Kosova Port* 3 November 2010a, *Kosova Haber* 3 November 2010)

As a diffusive act, moreover, local norm entrepreneurs also argue for the need to adopt the Ottoman model as a more inclusive framework in terms of promoting inter-ethnic relations. A leading member of the Turkey Alumni Association (TÜMED) expressed that "TÜMED does not want to work excessively on Turkishness. This is because TÜMED is a multi-ethnic association; it has Albanian and Bosnian members along with Turks" (Interview LE8). This multi-ethnic focus is also reflected in the association's preferred areas of interest: reifying the idea of "ummah" in Kosovo. The ummah, here, represents the method deployed by the Ottoman Empire to deal with the multi-ethnic Muslim communities, which also enabled communities to co-exist all the while protecting their own identities. As my respondent argued throughout:

> Since the Ottoman Empire ruled the world for 600 years via recourse to the idea of the ummah – and nobody lost their identity – we similarly need to act according to the understanding of ummah [in Kosovo] ... [Thus] we can only cultivate bonds with Albanians through subscribing to the idea of ummah; with nationalism we lose such bonds.
>
> (Interview LE8)

All these suggest that Ottomania has been diffused to Kosovo. The socialisation of the community hence commenced with the successful diffusion of Ottomania to Kosovo and has been upheld through the same norm-diffusing actors and through similar practices. My informant from the TIKA office argues that Turkey's large institutional presence in Kosovo – with non-nationalist, pro-Islamic and pro-Ottoman attitudes – have become a factor in mending inter-ethnic relations between Muslim communities, which reveal the functioning of Ottomania:

> During the Yugoslav era ... Albanians were suppressed and Serbs tried to use the Turks against Albanians ... More precisely, the [solidarity] ties between Muslim communities, particularly between the Turks and Albanians, were attacked ... Initially, due to this policy a negative view was developed between Albanian and Turkish communities. [However] for the last 15 to 20 years this has begun to change and relations have gradually relieved thanks to the independence [of Kosovo] ... With Turkey's influence these relations have become normalised.
>
> (Interview DM5)[9]

Therefore, it appears that Turkey did not content itself with merely conveying Ottomania to Kosovo; it also worked to make the Turkish community embrace this. I will discuss whether my respondent from TIKA is right or not on this score in the internalisation chapter (that is, the final chapter) addressing whether relations were normalised or not. Yet, this quotation above evidently shows us that Turkey's Ottomania-driven acts have been constitutive for the ethnic Turkish community and for inter-communal relations in the country.

The socialisation of the community into Ottomania has been run through a couple of interrelated and multiculturalism-informed practices relating to restoring inter-ethnic relations. Accordingly, the socialisation of the ethnic Turkish community into Ottomania has been done via promoting key figures such as Mehmed Akif – someone who represents the shared history and culture between Albanian and Turkish communities. Moreover, this is done via the promotion of an agenda aimed at uniting Muslim ethnic groups, and promoting multi-ethnic associations, which take the Ottoman experience as a reference point to produce solutions to contemporary problems of the country. The processes of exemplifying the Ottomans as a "culture of living" and adjusting inter-ethnic relations have been shaped by the acts of deconstructing the dominant nationalist cognitive frames and opening more room in politico-cultural circles to "Ottoman ethnic accord" discourses.

First and foremost, the promotion of historical figures such as Mehmed Akif that represent the shared history and culture between Albanian and Turkish communities has been a catalyst for restoring the inter-ethnic relations. Accordingly, for instance, TIKA organised "Mehmet Akif Ersoy Day" which featured poetry competitions and symposiums to commemorate his life. Moreover, 2011 was announced as "the year of Mehmet Akif" by the Kosovo government (*Kosova Haber* 12 March 2011a). In these events, Mehmet Akif was presented as "one of the most significant symbols of Turkish–Albanian brotherhood" (Ibid.). It was with reference to this bond that Adem Demaci, a Kosovar political activist and author, stated in the opening ceremony of the event that "the national anthem of Kosovo has no lyrics. We are waiting for a Turk to write its lyrics" (Ibid.). This is a reference to the fact that Mehmet Akif, an ethnic Albanian, wrote the lyrics of the national anthem of Turkey and that an ethnic Turk would write the lyrics of the national anthem of Kosovo. The organisation included a symposium titled *Mehmet Akif: the Poet of Our Civilisation* which was organised by TÜMED. In this symposium, TIKA's country coordinator Adem Urfa stated that "Mehmet Akif is a joint symbol of Turks and Albanians. Mehmet Akif's personality stands out as a proof of how close the two nations are to each other" (*Kosova Haber* 12 March 2011b). Turkey's ambassador to Pristina, Söngul Ozan, also remarked that "Mehmet Akif, as the poet of a joint civilisation, has been one of the finest symbols of the centuries old friendship and brotherhood" (Ibid.). In the scope of the commemoration events, his much-loved work, *Safahat*, was recited during a "poetry night" and was also enacted as a play in Kosovo's national theatre in Pristina (*Kosova Haber* 9 March 2011). This event was the fifth of its kind to be organised since 2007.

To give another example, TIKA has worked to build additional classrooms and provided technical and equipment assistance to Mehmet Akif Primary School, in Mehmet Akif's hometown of Prekaz (*TIKA: Kosovo – Projects and Activities Booklet* 2009: 19, *TIKA Kosova Proje ve Faaliyetleri* 2006–7: 12). The school was brought into service in a ceremony featuring Ahmet Davutoğlu, the Minister of Foreign Affairs at the time, in attendance. After opening the school, Davutoğlu and his envoy visited Mehmet Akif's ancestral village, Sushitsa. In the village, Davutoğlu met with Ersoy's relatives and kissed the hand of Ersoy's eldest relative. He ended this ceremony by saying that "anything that is related to Ersoy is of paramount importance to us. His family is the family of the Turkish nation, his house is the house of the Turkish nation, and his hometown is the hometown of the Turkish nation" (*Kosova Port* 28 August 2011).

Similarly, having taken Mehmet Akif as an example of ethnic accord in the county, in the opening ceremony of Yunus Emre Institute in Pristina in 2011, Ahmet Davutoğlu remarked that:

> Our Kosovar brothers are like the members of our family, Kosovo is like a hometown to us. We have such a deep-rooted shared culture, which provides a firm basis for walking to the future together with confident steps. Mehmet Akif, an iconic figure for Turks, is from Kosovo and this alone means a lot. Our history is together, our future will be together, no one can separate us from each other.
>
> (*Yunus Emre Bülteni* October 2011: 5)

Alongside this, Davutoğlu also reminded to an Albanian interviewer that there were 28 prime ministers of the Ottoman Empire of Albanian descent and that Mehmet Akif and Sami Frasheri[10] (Şemsettin Sami) were both crucial historical figures who had served both Ottoman and Turkish culture[11] (*Kosova Port* 5 September 2012). It was in this vein that Yunus Emre Institute has organised events to commemorate Sami Frasheri along with Mehmet Akif to underscore the role of Albanian-descent historical figures in imagining this idea of Ottoman ethnic accord (Interview DM3).

Secondly, there is an attempt to actualise the Ottoman model coming from local multi-ethnic associations, by which the agenda of uniting Muslim ethnic groups is tried to be achieved. TÜMED has been the prime example of such efforts and has long declared its intention of not being restrained in its area of activity solely to the ethnic Turkish community. This is despite the fact that its entire governing body is formed of ethnic Turks. Another association which serves the Ottoman cause is AKEA (Association for Culture, Education and School).[12] This is a multi-ethnic association founded by Albanians.

TÜMED has close relations with AKEA. My respondent from TÜMED described AKEA as follows:

> It is not a Turkish association. It is founded by Albanians. [However] when you enter their office, you see the coat of arms of the Ottoman Empire. It is led by an Albanian, yet, he likes speaking Turkish, [and] he is very fond of Turkish people in Kosovo.
>
> (Interview LE8)

AKEA, like TÜMED (and sometimes in collaboration), organises events which underscore common culture, values and identities among Kosovo's Muslim communities. For instance, the annual Prizren Book Fair (established in 2009) features books in three languages: Albanian, Turkish and Bosnian (*Dünya Bizim* 16 August 2012). This is also embraced as a motto of the event. TÜMED and similar-minded members of the ethnic Turkish community contribute to and join this event to foster the idea of ethnic cohesion among Muslim communities in the country (Interview LE21). AKEA also collaborates with TIKA. As Ilir Gashi, the Prizren coordinator of AKEA, reports:

> We have very close relations with Turkey. We are trying to learn from the experiences of our brothers in Turkey. After all, Istanbul was our capital city for five centuries. We mainly collaborate with organisations such as TIKA and the IHH. With TIKA, we mainly work together in cultural activities such as publications, symposium organisations. We, for instance, published Alija Izetbegović's book and organised a symposium to honour him with contributions from TIKA. With the IHH, we organised and continue to organise humanitarian aid activities.
>
> (*Dünya Bizim* 16 August 2012)

TIKA assists AKEA in many ways, including with technical issues and facilities, such as refurbishments made to AKEA property, such as its auditorium, and the central heating and elevator systems (see *TIKA Faaliyet Raporu* 2009: 75, *TIKA: Kosovo – Projects and Activities Booklet* 2009: 45, *TIKA Kosova Proje ve Faaliyetleri* 2006–7: 45, *Avrasya Bülteni* November 2009: 13).

Two other organisations working for an increased sense of Ottoman/ Islamic values and identities and who collaborate with the other pro-Ottoman and pro-Islamic elites in the Turkish community and with TIKA are the IDEA Association and the PENDA Association. The former is a cultural organisation, close to the Justice Party of Kosovo and "promotes the idea of multi-ethnicism and Islam" in Kosovo (Interview LE21). The Justice Party, meanwhile, imitates the discourses and policy approaches of the Turkey's JDP. It even copied the constitution of the JDP for its own party (Interview LE21, Interview LE11). When the IDEA Association was founded, it was TIKA who provided necessary assistance to purchase office equipment (*Rubasam* 15 December 2012). PENDA, on the other hand, is an organisation in Kosovo which brings together the alumni of divinity schools in Turkey and three out of thirty founding members are ethnic Turks (Interview LE21). This organisation also has a particular concern for the idea of Ottoman ethnic accord and the Islamic experience of peaceful co-existence, yet their real importance comes to fore in their collaborations with Diyanet in terms of combating the "*Wahhabi* menace". I will deal with this in the Turkish Islam section of this chapter. Nonetheless, all three Albanian-majority associations have ethnic Turkish members, work closely with the ethnic Turkish community, and, more importantly, are supported via institutions from Turkey such as TIKA and Diyanet. Together they take the Ottoman experience as a reference point in finding solutions to contemporary problems. Along with these, TIKA also supported joint associations such as Fidan Turkish-Albanian Women Association and MESK Multinational Kosovo Association in terms of technical expertise and in the events such as the Turkish Cinema Week (see *TIKA Faaiyet Raporu* 2008: 75, *TIKA: Kosovo – Projects and Activities Booklet* 2009: 29–31, *TIKA Kosova Proje ve Faaliyetleri* 2006–7: 45).

Thirdly, a similar pattern of utilising the Albanian community to restore the idea of harmonious inter-ethnic relations along Ottoman lines has been seen in Balkan TV's (Balkan RTV) approach to the issue. As my respondent from Balkan TV argues:

In Kosovo, the ethnic Turks are not interested in forming good relation with the Albanians; they turn their face merely to Turkey ... In a normal situation, the ethnic Turks should feel close to the Albanians; however, the Yugoslav experience and nationalism separated them. In order to bring them back together, Turkey deploys Ottoman jargon and underlines experiences of multiculturalism and multi-ethnic Islamic civilisation. It, therefore, underlines the Albanians' and Bosnians' contributions to it, along with that of the Turks. By the same token, Balkan RTV promotes such ideas of brotherhood. It does so through supporting religion, shared culture and shared civilisation in its broadcasting. In Kosovo, the values of Ottoman/Islamic civilisation and religious knowledge are needed and this is what we try to provide with Balkan RTV.

(Interview RG5)

Nonetheless, my respondent was quite pessimistic about the ethnic Turkish community's ability and willingness to show endorsement to the Ottoman-themed idea of inter-ethnic relations. Therefore, similar to TIKA and TÜMED's cooperation with Albanian associations, Balkan TV has shifted its focus more towards the Albanian community in re-casting inter-ethnic relations along Ottoman lines. The respondent puts this down to the fact that:

It is more likely to see the development of a Turkish-friendly movement among the Albanian community ... The Turkish community cannot be an instrument to transform the Albanian community, yet in the Albanian community there are certain signs of this ability [to transform the Turkish community's attitude]. The reluctance among the ethnic Turkish community to collaborate with the Albanians in line with Muslimness makes things difficult for future relations.[13] This is also how Turkey comprehends the issue.

(Interview RG5)

Balkan TV[14] thus endeavours to socialise the ethnic Turkish community to Ottoman values and identities by increasing the Albanian community's attachment to the Ottoman past, through embracing a multi-ethnic and multilingual broadcasting policy (in Turkish, Albanian, Bosnian languages), and finally through broadcasting religious programmes which underlines the sense of shared religious identity (balkanrtv.com).

At this juncture, it is worth mentioning that Balkan TV was founded with financial support from TIKA. More precisely, Balkan TV was allowed to acquire the equipment and hardware from the now-defunct Yeni Dönem TV, founded in 2005 but which closed down in 2008. It was TIKA who had also funded this earlier TV station. When TIKA opened its country office in Kosovo in 2004, one of the first things it did was to provide support for *Yeni Dönem* newspaper[15] to establish a TV channel under the same name. As reported in TIKA's Avrasya Bulletin "the entire studio equipment and hardware of Yeni Dönem TV, which began test airing in December 2005, were supplied by TIKA" (*Avrasya Bülteni* May 2006: 6). This TV project was actualised to promote multiculturalism in Kosovo and to enable the Turkish community to co-exist and to integrate with other communities (*TIKA Faaliyet Raporu* 2005: 130–1). In the opening ceremony of the TV channel, Beşir Atalay,[16] stated that:

I believe that Yeni Dönem TV, which will also be broadcasting in the languages other than Turkish [namely Albanian, Bosnian and Roma], will contribute to the future of a democratic and inclusive Kosovo.

(*Avrasya Bülteni* May 2006: 6)

Nevertheless, Yeni Dönem TV did not last long. In 2008, due to the nationalistic orientation of the governing body of the television and newspaper, TIKA withdrew its support and forced the channel to hand over administration – including all its facilities - to someone else entirely (Interview LE4). This is when Yeni Dönem TV was renamed "Balkan RTV" with an entirely new governing body and operational philosophy.

In the scope of "recalling" Ottoman history and identity in Kosovo, fourthly, Turkey launched a campaign to have phrases and narratives denouncing the Ottoman Empire and Turks removed from school textbooks. Official Kosovar historiography, following similar patterns in Albania, has come to view the Ottomans and Turks as the enemies of the Albanians for having "occupied" and subjugated them for hundreds of years. Some even blame the Ottomans for conducting a "genocide" of the Albanians (*Kosova Haber* 26 August 2011). Such arguments create a negative image of the Ottoman and thus Islamic history. Moreover, such narratives were seen as an obstacle in the way of building sustainable relations between Turkey and Kosovo and between Muslim communities in the country. The emphasis on Mehmet Akif and Sami Frasheri should be seen in this context and designed, to a certain degree, to soften such nationalistic claims and to foster closer relations between communities. Changes to the official history curricula textbooks was first demanded by Turkey's former Minister of Education Ömer Dinçer, in an official visit to Kosovo in 2011 though this move caused a fierce reactions among some in the Albanian community at the time (*Kosova Haber* 22 August 2011). Ahmet Davutoğlu, in response to such outcries, stated that:

> History cannot be changed, but its interpretation changes ... A nation cannot demand another nation to change its history ... However, the way a nation perceives its own history can change. We challenge our history textbooks not only in Kosovo, but also in Turkey. We want to eliminate all prejudices from textbooks ... [In similar manners] we founded joint commissions, for instance, with Greece to discuss the ways to remove these prejudices ... We [therefore] suggested the formation of [a similar] joint Turkish–Kosovar intellectual commission.
>
> (*Kosova Haber* 27 August 2011)

The examples show how the Ottoman history and identity of Kosovo and of the communities living in the country are recalled. There is, clearly, an attempt to cast the Ottoman image in a positive light.

The final socialising act was an attempt to increase the level of integration of Turks in Kosovo in political, social and cultural terms. Turkey is uncomfortable with the isolation of ethnic Turks from the majority Albanian community. To this end, the learning of Albanian by Turks has been heavily supported. Indeed, my respondent from the embassy stated that:

> We want the ethnic Turks to not face integration problems and are working on this. We support the community's efforts to learn Albanian. For example, people in Mamusha[17] live in isolation and don't know Albanian ... [Therefore] with the support of Yunus Emre Institute we are helping this community to learn Albanian.
>
> (Interview DM7)

My informant from TIKA similarly remarked that "[y]ou can neither contribute to, nor live in this country without having knowledge of Albanian and by having enmity towards the Albanian language" (Interview DM5). In this sense, in Mamusha TIKA, Yunus Emre Institute, Diyanet and local associations (Alperenler Association) have together opened language courses to support the learning of Albanian and consequently to increase societal rapprochement (Interview DM1; Interview LE24). The use of multiple languages at the events organised by Turkey's diplomatic missions or of local post-Kemalist associations also serve this same cause. For instance, in a commemoration of Ottoman Sultan Murat in 2010, the prayers and memorial services were delivered in both Turkish and Albanian (*Avrasya Bülteni* September 2010: 7). Similarly, in events commemorating Mehmet Akif, his poems have been recited in both Turkish and Albanian (*TIKA Faaliyet Raporu* 2011: 57).

In short, as can been seen, Turkey "endeavours to protect the Ottoman identity of the people in [Kosovo] and tries to remind them the Ottoman values", as argued by my respondent from TIKA (Interview DM5).

De-ethnicised Nationhood's Cascade

Whether Turkey shows concern here [in Kosovo] in an ethnic sense is of great importance in the political agenda of the ethnic Turkish community.

(Interview RG5)

Despite the Turkish community's desire for a bold form of ethno-politics (as can be seen in the quote above) Turkey, nevertheless, refrains from focusing entirely on ethnicity and ethnic identity in its policy towards Kosovo. As was dealt with in the introductory section above, the lack of ethnic concern and appeals to nationalism in Turkey's approach is pretty clear.

Indeed, TIKA stands against placing ethnicity at the core of politics in Kosovo and expresses its discomfort at the building of a Kosovo – a country with 95 per cent of its population declaring themselves "Muslim" and 92 per cent "Albanian" – as a state built on an ethnic basis alone. For TIKA, an ethnicity-based politicisation of communities is an obstacle to peaceful co-existence in the country. It causes ethnic fragmentation among the Muslim communities and between Muslim and non-Muslim communities. Therefore, for TIKA, Kosovar Muslims' focus on ethnopolitics threatens the capacity for peaceful co-existence among the Muslim communities in Kosovo. My respondent from TIKA explains this as follows:

> In one way or another and in spite of the turmoil, there exists a societal peace in here [Kosovo] ... These people, without the need of external imposition, have developed their own co-existence experience. The externally imposed and constitutionally recognised [ethnic] minority rights have converted Kosovo into an open-air prison for ethnicities. This means that ethnic rights break the naturally developed ties between people ... If you go and talk to a Turk s/he will soon start complaining about Albanians and others. If you go and talk to Albanians they complain about Turks and other ethnic groups ... Therefore, [the externally imposed ethno-political organisation of state-society and inter-ethnic relations] only create ghettos: A Turkish ghetto, a Bosnian ghetto, an Albanian ghetto, a Roma ghetto, a Serbian ghetto. This is to say that "live in your own ghetto and do not care about mingling with others".
>
> (Interview DM5)

Therefore, TIKA encourages non-ethnic politics and complains about the ethnic fragmentation in the country, which it argues did not exist during Ottoman times. In this fashion, TIKA also complains about ethnic Turkish community's sole reliance on ethnopolitics. As my respondent from TIKA argues, the ethnic Turkish community shows no concern for country-level problems or the problems of other ethnic communities in Kosovo; all they care about is the Turkish community and their ethnic rights. The respondent also remarked that:

> [o]ur co-nationals in Kosovo should develop territorial belonging and belonging to this state as much as to their ethnic belonging. They should not prefer one to another. Turkey does not have such a view. Turkey does not support the Turkish community's exclusivist acts of ethnocentrism. Turkey follows a rational and

integrative policy [a policy which seeks to unite ethnicities into a broader umbrella] in Kosovo.

(Interview DM5)

There is no doubt that the unifying factor for TIKA is Ottoman history and Islamic culture. We can also mention YTB's activities in Kosovo in terms of its student exchange programme – something which is also revealing about Turkey's non-emphasis on nationalism. To recount briefly, Turkey's "Great Student Exchange Programme" has been altered in that "the old system", as the diplomat respondent remarked "ethnic Turks and other nations [in Kosovo] were given separate places, whereas, now they are all applying to the Balkans Undergraduate Scholarship Program [of the Great Student Exchange]. In this system there is no ethnic favouritism" (Interview DM7). Therefore, there is neither an upper limit nor a guarantee for how many ethnic Turks would be granted a scholarship. The positive discrimination towards ethnic Turks which was dominant before, thus, has been removed. They became equal to other communities in Kosovo in terms of the possibility of being awarded scholarships. Along with YTB, universities in Turkey also allocate places for students coming from the Balkans and even here, these universities refrain from awarding these to only ethnic Turks. As the diplomat respondent remarked accordingly, "Trakya University [of Edirne in Turkey] allocates places to the student coming from the Balkans, in which there is no ethnic discrimination made. When its rector came to Kosovo, ethnic Turks demanded positive discrimination, but the rector refused this as a matter of principle" (Interview DM7). Furthermore, in the old system, Turkish-speaking ethnic Turks who received primary and secondary education in the Turkish language in Kosovo were exempt from sitting a Turkish-language exam so as to enter a university in Turkey; however, with this new programme they are now obliged to take it[18] (Interview DM7).

Concomitant with this diplomatic institutional approach, in his address to a crowd of thousands in the Shadirvan Square in Prizren in November 2010, Recep Tayyip Erdoğan made no reference at all to blood or race ties when addressing ethnic Turks. He treated ethnic Turks rather as "brothers in religion" (Interview LE37). Erdoğan also suggested that everything be done to preserve the Islamic and Ottoman heritage of the country and the history of peaceful inter-ethnic coexistence with their "Muslim brothers" (*Kosova Haber*, 9 November 2010). The "brotherhood" he referred to, therefore, is imagined as being a fact of life in Kosovo among the various Muslim communities. This tendency has been noted by the local community too, as one of my respondents reported that "when Turkey's politicians visit the ethnic Turkish community, the most necessary feature they highlight is the shared history, rather than ethnicity" (Interview LE21). Confirming this, in a speech, Erdoğan portrayed his visit to Kosovo as a manifestation of an anti-nationalist foreign policy and underlined the common history and culture. He also remarked that:

> What constitutes a nation is not blood tie nor genetic codes, but history, culture, shared ideals, shared values ... what we have done for our citizens, co-nationals, related communities, oppressed [and] victim communities indispensably reveal the way we understand nation and nationalism. The poet of our national anthem, Mehmet Akif, is an Albanian. He is from Ipek in Kosovo. You would never see racism in Mehmet Akif ... He never highlighted his Albanianhood ... So our ties with Kosovo stem from history, from culture [and] values ... There is no need to talk the same language ... What we have seen in Kosovo is the harmony of Albanian and Turkish speakers.
>
> (*Kosova Haber* 9 November 2010)

Therefore, considering Turkey's relations with Kosovar Turks as being built on ethnic nationalism is a fallacious argument; rather, we see clear evidence that the ethnic Turkish community is called on by Turkey to not resort to nationalism. Neither does Erdoğan utilise the idea of 'co-national" in his speech when referring to Kosovo's Turks. He suggests rather that culture, values and history are the cement, which can build and hold relations between people. A similar attitude can be seen in the approach of religious groups from Turkey operating in Kosovo. When religious groups refer to 'Turk' or 'Turkish', there is no ethnic emphasis, nor should this be seen as a reference to nationalism. This is the case in defining both the ethnic Turkish community in Kosovo and the Turkish people in Turkey. To these religious groups, regardless of their current residence, Turks are the successors of the Ottomans and the preceding Turkish-speaking Islamic states (Seljukid Empires and others) which had given a great service to Islam. The way my respondent from the Süleyman Efendi group tried to articulate this is instructive. He sees Fatih Sultan Mehmet as a Turk and so was his great-grand son Süleyman Efendi, the founder of the Süleyman Efendi group (Interview RG1). The respondent from the Erenköy group also admits that they define themselves as "Turk", yet with a deeper motive of representing the Ottoman and Islamic forms of national/societal belonging (Interview RG4). One of the officials from the Gülen movement also remarked that "it is historically not possible to detach Ottoman and Turk from each other [yet] having taken into account the other nations' contribution to it, Ottoman is not a solely Turkish civilisation" (Interview RG2). In this sense, these members of religious groups are proud to be part of a nation that served the Islamic cause, yet they are against imagining the Turkish nation in mono-ethnic lines. To them, the Turkish nation represents a heterogeneous and diverse group of Turkish-speaking Muslim people.

Such practices which exhibit a non-concern for ethnicity and non-nationalism demonstrate the conveyance of the norm of de-ethnicised nationhood to Kosovo. The socialisation of the community into these norms has been done through simultaneous de-ethnicised nationhood-induced discursive and behavioural interactions. For instance, as a respondent from Balkan TV in Prizren argues, "Turkey is careful about not describing Ottomans as ethnically Turkish, it draws attention rather to the indisputable contribution of the Albanians and Bosnians" (Interview RG5). It is, similarly, due to this that the Yunus Emre Institute is "careful to not to serve only a certain ethnic group in [its] activities" (Interview DM4). It, in this sense, "treat[s] all ethnic groups equally, [does] not discriminate based on language, religion, [or] race . . . [and does] not [tolerate/support] micro-nationalism [in Kosovo]" (Interview DM3).

Turkey's institutions, in the scope of socialisation, thus promote religiously defined relations among Muslim communities, denounce the re-building of Kosovo along ethnic lines, and encourage a non-nationalist social and political atmosphere in the country.[19] For this reason Islamic history in the country is viewed from the perspective of the Ottomans, which the Albanians and Bosnians – along with the Turks – took part in building. This history is often recalled via cultural activities. TIKA, moreover, uses its economic resources to eliminate nationalistic sentiments among the ethnic Turkish community. With this in mind, one of officials from the now-defunct Yeni Dönem TV/ newspaper argued that "the reason why Yeni Dönem was closed is because of its nationalist worldview – something which, from the perspective of Turkey, harms both the ethnic Turkish community in Kosovo and Turkey as a country"[20] (Interview LE4). Similar arguments were made by other locals in explaining why Turkey's institutions do not support the activities of nationalist associations such as the Filizler Kemalist Turkish Culture and Arts Association or "Turkevi" (the Turkish House[21]) (Interview LE9). These are many examples of the way Turkey's backing to groups is used as a means to socialise a community away from nationalism.

Nevertheless, the most direct call for adherence to a de-ethnicised concept of nationhood has come from Erdoğan during his visits to Kosovo. During one of these, he is reported to have argued that "do not insist on having your IDs written in the Turkish language ... take them even though they are in the Albanian language ... *Stop emphasising all the time that 'we are Turks'*. Unite upon Islam with your Albanian brothers" (Interview LE4, Interview LE9, Interview LE6, Interview LE2, *emphasis added*). This statement is reported also in the following form:

> Turkey does not show any concern to Turkishness over here. I heard this from the Prime Minister, Erdoğan, with my own ears ... Erdoğan responded to ... Orhan Lopar's[22] saying "we act upon the sake of Turkishness ..." with the words "forget about Turkishness, what have you done for the cause of Islam [*Türklüğü boş ver, sen İslamiyet için ne yaptın?*]".
>
> (Interview LE8)

To emphasise this suggestion, Erdoğan also gave a post-visit assessment speech, remarking that "Mehmet Akif is an Albanian, but never brought his Albanianhood to the fore. This should be comprehended well; it should be understood well" (*Kosova Haber* 9 November 2010). The argument here is that the Turkish community should not bring their Turkishness to the fore. Erdoğan's message seems to have been well received by the community, as one of my respondents (during my scoping visit) stated that:

When Erdoğan says "do not insist in Turkishness", many may find it positive in that he is helping to sustain Muslim identity but this leaves the ethnic Turkish community defenceless as Turks. While Turkey is a cure-all for the woes of the communities in Kosovo, it cannot provide a cure to the problems of Turkishness.

(Pers. Comm. SVN3)[23]

However, some members of the local community share Erdoğan's sentiments. They imagine the Turkish nation with reference to the multi-ethnic Ottoman Empire and argue for the necessity of moving beyond ethnicity. These individual norm learners, some of whom are ardent supporters of an anti-nationalist worldview and promote the idea of an ummah, are those who "managed to learn how not to be Kemalist, albeit being raised as Kemalist through the education system of the Turkish community" as described by a prominent norm-learner and a Turkey graduate (Interview LE21).[24] To the informant, a student's worldview and ideology change during their time studying in Turkey; some of them becomes members of religious groups, others lose their nationalist inclinations. This is the reason why s/he confidently argues that "ethnic Turks who studied in Turkey move beyond ethnic worldviews" (Interview LE21).[25] Confirming this, a respondent from TÜMED argued that resorting to ethnic nationalism ruins Kosovar Turks' chances of relating properly to other Muslim communities in Kosovo. The respondent suggested that Turks should subscribe to the idea of ummah and subordinate their ethnic identities to this. The respondent therefore remarked that:

Nationalism will get us nowhere ... I said this also in a meeting in Turkey. All our politicians were in the meeting. [Upon my articulation of this] Amet Davutoğlu's adviser talked to me privately [and showed close concern for my argument]. What I am saying is that we will not achieve anything with nationalism.

(Interview LE8)

Indeed, in addition to activities with a multi-ethnic focus, these local norm learners have been trying to break the idea of privileging ethnic identity over religious identity. They, therefore, are locked in a fight with the following nationalistic saying: "I am first of all a Turk, then a

Muslim". They are the proponents of an inverted form of this saying (Interview LE8, Interview LE24).

Finally, the role of religious groups is also part of this struggle against nationalism. A local elite, at this juncture, defines the role of Turkey's religious groups as follows:

> Turkey's religious groups know well how to tackle non-religiosity [*dinsizlik*] and Kemalism [*Atatürkçülük*]. They now have to teach this to us. Their necessity stems from this and we need to facilitate their visits here. They convey to us their experiences gained in Turkey, which enables us to deal with the Kemalist elites here ... Today, the Turkish community itself invites Turkey's religious groups to Kosovo to be able to cope with the Kemalist elites.
>
> (Interview LE18)

Confirming the quotation above, in my own meetings with officials from religious groups, I learned that they strongly opposed attempts by Kemalist nationalists to disrupt the unity among Muslim communities in Kosovo. My respondent from the Gülen movement in Prizren even went as far as to argue that this disruption went too far for him/her and that "s/he no longer invites people who [insistently] declare themselves as Turks to their events" (Interview RG3). Another way to deal with this is proposed by the Erenköy group who has been "us[ing] both Albanian and Bosnian along with Turkish [in their events] in order to show that [they] treat equally to all [Muslim] communities" (Interview RG4). My respondent from the Süleyman Efendi group also argued that "in Kosovo in the name of education, the Turkish community had merely been taught about Atatürk until 2000s [*2000'lere kadar eğitim yat-kalk Atatürk'müş*]", which is something they intend to change (Interview RG1). As a socialisation method, therefore, through religious education, these groups have been "compensating" for previously nationalist education policies enacted by Kosovar Turks.

Turkish Islam's Cascade

As seen above, the rebuilding or renovation of Ottoman cultural artefacts has long functioned as a way to convey Ottomania. Rebuilding is also a result of the functioning of another post-Kemalist norm, which is Turkish Islam. In this sense, Turkish Islam's diffusion into Kosovo can reveal itself in, for instance, TIKA's decision to re-erect the Murat Bey mosque in Janjevo (Yanova). In the words of my respondent from TIKA:

> As regards the issue of Salafism, an Arab comes and says to the local people [when they see an old Ottoman mosque] that "your mosque is in decay, lets demolish this and rebuild a nicer one". We [often] encounter such situations [and] try to prevent this from happening. For example, there is one reconstruction project we will begin in the coming days – that of the sixteenth century Murat Bey Mosque in Janjevo. It was decided that this was to be demolished. [The reason was that] it was in decay and had lost its historical character . . . The local community was provided funds to build an apartment-style non-historic mosque.
>
> (Interview DM5)

Re-building the mosque here meant not only preventing the fading away of Ottoman cultural history, but also of preventing so-called "Salafis" (used interchangeably with "Wahhabi") from gaining ground and replacing Ottoman/Turkish Islam with "Salafi Islam" in Kosovo. This practice may also be seen as another example among many that works to convey the post-Kemalist norm of Turkish Islam to Kosovo.

Nonetheless, it has been Diyanet which has played the most important role in the diffusion of Turkish Islam to Kosovo. According to the respondent from the Diyanet office in Prizren, the organisation's presence in Kosovo is necessary because:

> [t]here exist several madhhab-based [sectarian] disputes in the world and this region [the Balkans and Kosovo] has to be particularly protected from such disputes. Turkey's Diyanet and Kosovo's Riyaset [therefore] need to build a close relationship in order to prevent people from turning their back on their cultures [but also to promote] the performance of worship according to our madhhab. Thus, Turkey guides people based on the historically present madhhab and forms of worship.
>
> (Interview DM1)

An official from Diyanet's office in Mamusha similarly remarked that:

> [f]or Diyanet, the presence of religious missions in Kosovo is
> significant because during the Tito era, Tito told the Muslim
> community that "if you would like to acquire religious education,
> go to the Arab countries, because Turkey has abandoned the
> religion". Therefore, since the Tito era, particularly our Albanian
> brothers, have been acquiring religious education in Arab
> countries. None of them went to Turkey due to what Tito said.
> The returnees, however, came back as devotees of Salafism, which
> is not something which is part of the four true madhhabs.
> Unfortunately, they have offices in many Albanian mosques in
> Kosovo. Diyanet, therefore, feels obliged to have a mission in
> Kosovo. Diyanet does not want the Hanafi School to disappear
> from these lands.
>
> (Interview DM2)

These declarations affirm Diyanet's promotion of Turkish Islam and the
functioning of such a norm. As a means for norm diffusion, moreover,
Diyanet sends religious books which it has published, assigns permanent
religious officials, and delivers regular services in mosques in Prizren,
Mamusha and Janjevo. Diyanet also brings Turkish Islamic religious
rituals to Kosovo such as the Holy Birth Week. It has long been
celebrated in Kosovo by Diyanet in vast religious gatherings.

The international mobilisation of "Turkish Islam" owes, however, as
much to the work of Diyanet as to independent religious groups. This
norm represents a common ground for the varying religious groups of
Turkey operating at the grassroots level in Kosovo. This is the case
despite these groups differing in other doctrinal issues. It does so
because these religious groups are Turkey-centric and share a belief that
"Turks brought Islam to Kosovo and they will sustain it." This
constitutes the rationale behind their activities in Kosovo.
My respondent from the Süleyman Efendi group articulated this as
follows: "Muslimness came to these lands from Turkey, now it is again
coming from Turkey, inshaAllah {with the help of God} this time it
will be far stronger than before" (Interview RG1). The respondent from
the Erenköy Group, with reference to the Ottoman "material {cultural}
and spiritual {religious} legacy in Kosovo", stated similarly that

"Ottomans laid a foundation here that will last forever" (Interview RG4). They therefore give themselves the responsibility of sustaining this legacy and "deliver[ing] services in Kosovo on behalf of Turkey" as "Turkish Hodjas"[26] (Interview RG4).

In this sense, Turkey's religious groups attribute a special meaning to their presence in Kosovo and a special role: sustaining Ottoman/Turkish way of Islam. To play this role, they not only try to make people more observant in religious rituals and well-informed about religious ideas, but also fight against what they see as "alien" Islamic factions. In this respect, while nationalism, secularism and Christian missionaries are all considered as posing a challenge to the religious identity of Kosovar ethnic communities, it is so-called Wahhabism that is considered the biggest threat by Turkey's religious groups in Kosovo, a view shared by Diyanet.

The Süleyman Efendi group is the most vocal religious group in declaring this as a threat. This is because "Wahabbis are antagonistic towards Turkish Islam and towards Turks" and because they "disregard the service of Turks to Islam" not only in history but today, too (Interview RG1). Therefore, they reject what they see as "Wahhabi practices" and seem themselves as locked in competition with them in terms of which practice of Islam will dominate in Kosovo.

The Erenköy group shares such a perception and sees Ottoman cultural and religious legacy in Kosovo as being attacked by so-called Wahhabis. As a respondent from the Erenköy group argued:

They see the crescent [put on the dome of the mosques or on the top of the minarettes] as the symbol of Turks. The crescent is [widely] used in mosques, for instance, in Algeria, Morocco or England. You might have noticed, here the crescents are removed from the domes of mosques and replaced with the letters of Allah in Arabic ... Why does this happen in some mosques? They want to break the Turkish influence ... It is understandable to see the markers of Arab architecture in mosques built by Arabs. It is reasonable ... However they change the authenticity of our [Ottoman] mosques, destroy graveyards which are the historical testimonial of our [Ottoman] presence in here ... [Thus] there is an Arab influence here ... 90 per cent of the hodjas over 40 or even those between 30–35 years old are educated in Arab countries ... they brought this culture legally or illegally, publicly or secretly to here. Therefore, we can talk about a religious fragmentation in Kosovo.

(Interview RG4)

The Gülen movement also sees Wahhabism as a threat. A respondent from the movement remarked that "Hocaefendi [Fethullah Gülen] says that one of the two things we are going to battle against is Salafism ... Wahhabis are the cause of Islamophobia and the phobia against the religious orders [*tariqahs*]. Indeed, the phobia seen against religious orders in Kosovo over the last two decades is because of them" (Interview RG2).

Indeed, the above gives us an acute insight into the functioning of the idea of Turkish Islam in the discourses of Turkey's diplomatic missions and religious groups. Turkish Islam has gained international mobility through the entrepreneurial involvement of Turkey's official missions and religious groups operating in Kosovo. Yet, along with these, local entrepreneurs have also taken a role in norm transfer. However, their role becomes apparent mostly during the socialisation of the community into such norm(s).

In socialising the local community into Turkish Islam, the most constitutive acts have been conducted by Diyanet. The respondent from Prizren's Diyanet office informed me of the reasons behind its strong involvement as follows: "Diyanet is in Kosovo to orient the performance of religion [Islam] and to ensure its true practice" (Interview DM1). The intention of interfering and socialising the community into certain practices is self-evident here. The first socialising act is related to the "threat of Wahhabis" and can be seen, for instance, in Diyanet's collaboration with local associations in preventing its spread. Accordingly, for instance, "when TÜMED asked for assistance in keeping the ethnic Turkish community away from the madhhab-based disputes", Diyanet gladly accepted this and funded their projects (Interview DM1). Similarly, TÜMED's request for a partnership in organising an event on Sufism, whereby "Wahhabi" claims made against it could be challenged, was positively responded to by Diyanet and a panel was organised accordingly (Interview DM1). It is clear that Diyanet's close cooperation with the Riyaset is also made within the scope of battling so-called Wahhabism.

The second socialising act which needs to be mentioned here is Diyanet's support for the Holy Birth Week. This can also be seen as part of an attempt to institutionalise such norms in Kosovo. Diyanet has been celebrating Holy Birth events in Kosovo for many years and celebrations are attended by the ethnic Turkish community, the Turkish diplomatic mission including the embassy and Turkish Tabur, religious groups from Turkey and local Riyaset offices (Interview DM7, also see *Yeni Dönem* 20 May 2004, *Yeni Dönem* 21 April 2005, *Kosova Haber* 26 April 2012). Nonetheless, the local community is not a passive recipient of these Turkish Islamic practices. They willingly cooperate with Diyanet and take part in the organisation of this event. For instance, in Mamusha, the municipality, local schools and associations all joined the Diyanet in preparing the 2012 celebrations of this event. The respondent from the Diyanet office in Mamusha recalls this as follows:

> This year we [Diyanet and MABED][27] prepared a Holy Birth programme which was attended by the primary and secondary school children. There were religious talks, religious song performances by students from Qur'anic schools . . . We [even] organised a Holy Birth Football Trophy for secondary school children.
>
> (Interview DM2)

Besides the events organised in Mamusha, Diyanet has in cooperation with TIKA also organised events, conferences and commemorations of various sorts in other parts of Kosovo too. These include Prizren, Janjova and Pristina (*Kosova Haber* 26 April 2012). Indeed, what makes these practices constitutive is that each year the Holy Birth events are built around a theme as defined by Turkey's Diyanet. This theme then becomes the basis on which all other activities are built. The official from Diyanet and my respondent in Mamusha explains this as follows:

> The Holy Birth used to be celebrated only in Turkey. Praise be to God, today it is celebrated all over the world. Each year, the Religious Authority in Turkey chooses a theme and the celebrations are prepared based on that theme.
>
> (Interview DM2)

The theme of the 2012 celebrations was the importance of religious brotherhood in Islam.

As a third example of a socialising act, Diyanet also encourages locals to send their children to imam-hatip schools (madrasas) or theology faculties in Turkey rather than to Arab countries. In a similar vein, for those graduates of Turkey's theology faculties Diyanet suggests that they apply to the Kosovo Riyaset so as to become official imams or teachers in Kosovo's mosques and madrasas. Diyanet, by the same token, "requests from [the] Kosovo Riyaset that they facilitate the hiring of Turkey graduates to relevant positions by arguing that 'they will build the necessary bridges to transfer the education structure, culture and ideas they learned in Turkey to Kosovo'" (Interview DM1). In line with this, Diyanet has also built close relations with Riyaset. The latter supports Diyanet's imitative for more Turkish preachers in its official structures (Interview DM1). This is because the Riyaset follows the Hanafi school of Islamic law, and sees its authority as under threat from the so-called Wahhabis. Thus it shares a similar approach to Diyanet and encourages cooperation in a bid to strengthen its hand in running anti-Wahhabi projects. Indeed, the Prizren Riyaset Office supports Diyanet, TÜMED and PENDA's activities of this kind and encourages cooperation of this kind (Interview LE21; also see Kosova Haber 26 April 2012).

Finally, Diyanet also exports books from its publishers to Kosovo, including copies of the Qur'an, textbooks for Qur'anic education, Islamic encyclopaedias and classroom equipment for Qur'anic schools – all of which are disseminated for free (Interview DM2). Nonetheless, many of these books are in Turkish and their use is thus restricted to mosques with Turkish congregations. Last but not least, the sending of imams, both on temporary and permanent missions to Kosovo has also been part of this socialisation project.[28]

Along with Diyanet, the Yunus Emre Institute has also taken a keen interest in the promotion of Sufism and has utilised figures such as Yunus Emre and Rumi (known as "Mevlana") to promote Turkish Islam. For instance, the Yunus Emre Institute organises a "Rumi Week" (Mevlana Haftası) full of events which include panel discussions on Rumi's philosophy and influence in the Balkans, but also events such as Sufi music concerts (Kosova Haber 19 December 2011; Kosova Haber 25 December 2011). Indeed, it is such interests which push the Yunus

Emre Institute to cooperate with Doğruyol, a local cultural association, and facilitates their aim of organising Sufi music concerts and the showcasing of Sufi dances during the month of Ramadan (Interview DM3). Another local association in cooperation with institutions from Turkey to promote Sufism has been TÜMED. With the financial support from Diyanet and the Yunus Emre Institute, TÜMED organised a panel on *Islam and Sufism* in 2012 where "Wahhabi" arguments against Sufism were challenged by local members of Sufi orders. The main aim of the event, therefore, was "to tell people that Sufism is something good" (Interview LE8). Such endeavours are had with the aim of trying to promote the idea that Turkish Islam is a genuine reconciliation between heterodox Islam and orthodox Islam and the idea that "Wahhabi Islam" is not. TÜMED's cooperation with Diyanet and the religious authority of Kosovo in organising such events denouncing the harm done by "Wahhabism" thus unites Albanians and ethnic Turks in belief (Interview LE8).

Efforts by other religious groups to socialise the community into Turkish Islam are similar to Diyanet's agenda and those of other local associations, mainly in terms of their approach to "Wahhabism". However, their socialising efforts have been carried out mainly in terms of everyday practice of religion. For instance, these groups have all published books and journals in Albanian and Bosnian along with Turkish in order to amplify their message – something which has sought to keep Turkish Islam at the fore. Moreover, they have sent students to Turkey for religious education and opened private schools, student dormitories, Qur'an schools and cultural associations which have increased the prominence of Turkish Islam. Their organisation of weekly religious talks, Qur'an recitation gatherings and kermises[29] provide the necessary platforms for them to convey their message, such as calling female Muslims to wear the hijab (Interview LE8). Their participation in "Holy Birth celebrations" which Diyanet organises, Rumi commemorations run by Yunus Emre, or events of the local associations such as TÜMED, Alperenler or Doğruyol also serve the same cause. On the other hand, the rest of their activities, are focused on their own organisational agendas of bringing some religious practices performed in Turkey to Kosovo. For instance, *mukabele*[30] and *tespih namazı*[31] were first brought to Prizren by the Süleyman Efendi group and today it is quite common in some mosques in particularly Prizren during Ramadan (Interview

RG1). Nonetheless, religious groups are not alone in promoting their activities; some local community members have fiercely supported their cause too. They provide all the necessary facilities and networks to bring these groups from Turkey to Kosovo. For instance, when Menzil group opened an office in Prizren, it was done so through the invitation and assistance of an ethnic Turk in Kosovo (Interview LE8). Last but not least, another factor has facilitated the emergence of religious groups from Turkey in Kosovo: returning graduates who studied in Turkey. As the same local elite argued:

> We have friends who joined religious groups during their studies in Turkey. [Upon their return] they formed a branch of these groups [in Kosovo] ... [Therefore] there are people influenced from these groups' ideologies who then brought them here.
>
> (Interview LE8)

Islamic Internationalism's Cascade

In terms of foreign policy conduct, the functioning of "Islamic Internationalism" manifests itself in the form of acts which champion religious identity and which are done by norm entrepreneurs. These promote the idea that it is necessary to hold Islam as a conclusive identity. In this fashion, the legacy of Islamic culture and civilisation in Kosovo has been constantly recalled and the religious identity has been actively performed. Belonging to the Islamic ummah has been promoted. In relation to this, as the second manifestation, Islam has been utilised as way to reconcile between different ethnic groups. These are therefore the patterns of acts through which the idea of Islamic Internationalism is spread in Kosovo and how the socialisation takes place.

This Islamic Internationalist stance, from the very beginning, has led diplomatic mission members and the high-level officials to promote the Islamic history of Kosovo which existed under the banner of the Ottomans. It is always emphasised that in building this Islamic civilisation both Albanians and Bosnians, along with the Turks, have taken part. Emphasising this is seen as a necessity because in order to be able talk about the present Islamic ummah, they believe that the shared Islamic history and culture of the past must first be recalled. With this in mind, there has been a concerted effort to "de-ethnicise" the Ottoman Empire and to recall, in particular, the role of Albanians during its existence. The functioning of such references has been seen also in the diffusion of the norm of Ottomania. Nonetheless, these attempts to remind people of the past have functioned different in the diffusion of the norm of Islamic Internationalism. This was done to underscore the necessity of holding the feelings of Muslim sensitivity, Islamic consciousness and Islamic brotherhood. The legacy of Islamic culture in Kosovo and brotherhood between different ethnic groups was also highlighted. As Bekir Bozdağ, a former minister in charge of Outside Turks, stated in the opening ceremony of the Alaaddin Madrasa in Gilan (which was refurbished by TIKA):

> There are plenty of things binding us together. We are the heirs of the same history, of the same culture. We are representatives of the same civilisation. We are subscribers of the same faith. We are tarred with the same brush.
>
> (*Kosova Port* 11 August 2012)

This is just one among many other statements articulated by officials from Turkey who promote the idea that religion should continue to be the strong link, and the bases upon which policies are developed, between Turkey and Kosovo. Accordingly, Ömer Dinçer, the former Minister of National Education, also argued in a 2011 visit to Kosovo that:

> We see all the problems Kosovo faces as if they are ours and we are striving to solve them. Turks, Albanians or any other ethnic group: you are all our brothers. We will try to meet the responsibilities of brotherhood and will stick to it as much as we can ... It is necessary to create a [well-functioning] multi-ethnic and multi-religious environment and to live in peace, as brothers.
>
> (*Kosova Port* 19 August 2011)

The emphasis on religious brotherhood is clear in both statements. Yet, what makes these visits important is that both visits were conducted during Ramadan which gave the visits extra special meanings. I have already shown in the introduction chapter that for the last couple of years

Turkish state officials in charge of Outside Turks visit these communities during Eid celebrations (Bajram). This is done on a directive from Erdoğan and is part of a process whereby the "Muslimness" of Turks has been experienced, performed and promoted. In this scope, for instance, Ahmet Davutoğlu, visiting Kosovo in Ramadan 2011, stated the rationale behind his visit thus:

> In our tradition, nights such as Laylatul-Qadr [Qadr Night] and Eid-ul-Fitr [Ramadan Bajram] are spent at home. By coming to Pristina during Laylatul-Qadr and by being in Kosovo right before the Ramadan Bajram we wanted to say this: Our Kosovar brothers are part of our family [and] Kosovo is our home ... Our history is common, our future is shared and no one can separate us from each other.
>
> (*Kosova Port* 27 August 2011b)

Davutoğlu's visit to Kosovo during Ramadan where he partook in fasting and prayers with the local people expressed a strong sense of religious identity and brotherhood – discursively, representatively and behaviourally. Bülent Arınç,[32] also visited Kosovo in 2011 where, before breaking his fast with guests who had gathered at the Shadirvan Meydan, argued that:

> Our great power derives from our faith. We will continue rebuilding the dilapidated [Islamic] artefacts in Kosovo. The adhan [prayer call] will be recited everywhere. We will spend many Ramadans together.
>
> (*Kosova Port* 12 August 2011)

In this way, religious identity and a sense of brotherhood was "performed". Moreover, feelings about Muslim sensitivities, solidarity, empathy with one another and Islamic consciousness were also promoted discursively and representatively. Nonetheless, while Turkey prioritises Islamic brotherhood in the country, the facts on the ground are characterised by an over-zealous concern with ethnicity and the dominance of ethnopolitics. These are considered a serious threat to the Islamic unity in the country, which Turkey has tried to counter by presenting the Ottoman/Islamic experience of peaceful co-existence[33] as a model which Kosovo should embrace. With this in mind, my respondent from TIKA argued that[34]:

Islam provides the grounds for ethnic communities in Kosovo to ease relations, to tolerate each other and to unite. If you rule this out and develop a more secular and more ethnicity-based order, all of this will disappear. Namely, the historically built ability to co-exist in tolerance will disappear. Here, we do not impose a religious life to people. We consider the religion as a culturally unifying factor.

(Interview DM5)

A similar consideration was articulated by my informant from Balkan TV in explaining why Turkey needs to utilise religious identity. The respondent accordingly stated that:

Ethnic Turks are Kemalist, nationalist and non-religious, while Albanians are under Catholic control and racist, the only grounds upon which to bring these two communities together is via religious identity, which is Muslimness.

(Interview RG5)

Therefore, Islamic Internationalism initially manifested itself as a call to remind people of the idea of religious brotherhood as part of efforts aimed at transforming ethnically divided inter-communal relations in Kosovo in favour of a religiously defined relation. The targets for this policy are mainly ethnic Turks who are, according to Turkey, overly concerned about ethnicity and is something which has been highly criticised by Turkey. I will touch on this issue below. In this respect, Islam is suggested as a cure for ethnic Turks and their relationship with Albanians and other Muslim communities in the country. Admittedly, my respondent from the embassy argued that "this government [JDP] views [Kosovar] Turks in terms of its wider aim of giving priority to Ottoman and religious identities" and "institutions tell that 'Let's unite upon Islam'" (Interview DM7). Therefore, the functioning of Islamic Internationalism here is about the transformation of the ethically minded Turkish community into a religiously motivated community.

An anecdote from the early 2000s exemplifies this well. Abdullah Gül, former Minister of Foreign Affairs, visited Kosovo in 2003 and responded to complaints from local ethnic Turks (my local respondent tells me) mainly regarding the alleged "assimilation the ethnic Turkish community is being exposed to" in Kosovo (Interview RG5). Gül responded as follows: "You constitute 90 per cent of Kosovo, how can you become assimilated?" (Interview RG5[35]). The "you" refers here to the Muslim communities in Kosovo, suggesting that any assimilation they could encounter could only be of a religious kind and, therefore, to challenge such assimilation the Turkish community should work with their Albanian "brothers". Turkey thus chooses to give priority to the Muslimness of ethnic Turks and approaches them accordingly.

Turkey's overwhelming emphasis on religion and religious identity has been observed by the local Turkish community too. Many of my respondents confirmed that the religious motive is priority in Turkey's (JDP's) approach to Kosovo, yet it is more about politics of identity rather than an attempt to make people religiously observant (Interview LE4, Interview LE12, Interview LE6, Interview LE2, Interview LE8, Interview LE21). "No matter how one keeps it under wraps" a local respondent argued, "religion is in everything [that Turkey does]" (Interview LE25). "They try to Muslimise us, Muslimise Turkishness" another respondent remarked in describing the way Turkey approaches the Turkish community in Kosovo, something which reveals Turkey's involvement in trying to socialise this community into an Islamic Internationalist worldview (Interview LE6).

The local community however is not a passive recipient but often also the drivers of such a religious approach. The local norm learners, similar to Turkey's institutions and high-level officials, have long resorted to the idea of ummah as a way to transcend the ethnic nationalism among the ethnic Turkish community in Kosovo. This refers to those who "went beyond ethnic lens" in the Turkish community as defined by one local norm learner (Interview LE21).

A leading member of TÜMED and a prominent norm learner articulated their motive in initiating and propagating a religious worldview as follows:

> Since the Ottoman Empire ruled the world for 600 years using the idea of ummah with nobody losing their identity in the process, we similarly need to act according to the understanding of ummah [in Kosovo] ... We, [the ethnic Turks in Kosovo] have talked forever

about the Turkish language and Turkishness. As a matter of fact, nationalism can take us nowhere. We cannot generate an impact with it but only negative reactions. Yet our leaders and elites do not understand this. I personally believe that if we resort to the idea of ummah, rather than to nationalism, we could achieve more ... [Among the ethnic Turkish community in Kosovo] the [religiously] conservative minded people have respect toward Albanians and Bosnians, while a nationalist demonises Albanians ... [Thus] we can only cultivate bonds with Albanians through subscribing to the idea of ummah; with nationalism we lose these bonds.

(Interview LE8)

Nonetheless, in order for this to be realised, the respondent argued that "Turkey ... has to serve the cause of Islam in Kosovo [and] support those who serve this cause here" (Interview LE8). Apparently, TÜMED reflects similar concerns with Turkey's institutions on the necessity of religious identity and ummah in promoting inter-ethnic relations. They emphasise the Islamic history and culture of the country and act as a multi-ethnic/multicultural association. Accordingly, for instance, they do not want the Ottoman Empire to be ethnicised and are "careful about not describing Ottomans as ethnically Turk and [instead] touch upon the indisputable contributions of the Albanians and Bosnians to the Empire" (Interview RG5). As the respondent from TÜMED went on to argue, "TÜMED does not want to work excessively on Turkishness. This is because TÜMED is a multi-ethnic association [hence] it has Albanian and Bosnian members along with Turks" (Interview LE8[36]). This multi-ethnic focus is also reflected in the association's preferred area of interest: reifying the "ummah" (or the sense of Albanian, Bosnian, Turkish brotherhood) in Kosovo (Interview LE8).

Last, but not least, Turkey's religious organisations also contribute to the reification of the ummah in Kosovo. In Ramadan 2013, the Kimse Yok Mu humanitarian organisation (organically linked to the Gülen movement) came to Kosovo to distribute food aid. The statement of one of the members reflects well the cause it serves:

The consciousness of being an ummah becomes reified through these kinds of events. After having seen our brothers in Kosovo, we feel so glad for having come here! I cannot help but become emotional when I see people speaking Turkish and living as a Muslim hundred miles away from Turkey.

(*Kosova Port* 23 July 2013)

These discursive, behavioural and representative norm-guided acts suggest that the diffusion and socialisation of Islamic internationalism has occurred through a similar pattern of acts. Therefore, since the early 2000s, due to the diffusion of Islamic internationalism, there is an observable effort being made to mobilise the ethnic Turkish community towards an Islamic worldview and the idea of ummah is gradually gaining ground. In this sense, Islamic internationalism has diffused in due course and attempts to socialise the community have been made accordingly. Below I present other instances through which Islamic internationalism is diffused to Kosovo and adherence to it is promoted by norm entrepreneurs.

A notable example is Turkey's eagerness to build the biggest mosque in Kosovo, Pristina, in order to "protect" the religious identity in the country. My respondent from the embassy explained this as follows:

The Prime Minister recently told us that Turkey will build a gigantic mosque in Pristina. There is a huge Cathedral in the city centre. Kosovar people demand the building of such a mosque from Turkey and argue that "we are Muslim. It is inappropriate that the biggest building in city is a cathedral. This misrepresents the identity here, we need to show that Kosovo is Muslim land". Upon hearing this demand, Turkey announced its decision to build a mosque in Kosovo. Turkey looks after Islam here and {brings} the Muslim identity of Kosovo {to the fore}.

(Interview DM7)

The preparations for the building of the mosque continue to this day. In late June 2014, the president of the Diyanet, Professor Mehmet Görmez and Grand Mufti of Kosovo, Naim Ternava came together in Pristina to discuss issues affecting the Islamic community in Kosovo, including the building the Pristina mosque (*Kosovo Port* 21 June 2014).

Moreover, JDP organises pro-ummah events in Turkey which are attended by organisations from Kosovo such as TÜMED. In explaining his/her experience in one of these events, my informant from TÜMED stated that:

> Turkey definitely attaches importance to the ummah . . . It does so by giving support to associations. In the coming days the Balkan Youth Workshop will take place where we will discuss how youth like us [pro-ummah] can become more influential in Kosovo . . . discussions will go on for three days . . . It is organised by the AK Party [JDP of Turkey].
>
> (Interview LE8)

The workshop mentioned here was held on 16–18 May 2013 and was hosted by the Bayram Paşa Municipality in Istanbul. The opening remarks of the workshop were given by Ahmet Davutoğlu, Suat Kılıç[37] and Mehmet Görmez, and the closing remark by Bekir Bozdağ. Participation from such high-ranking politicians and state officials suggests that the government placed much importance on the event. Confirming what was argued in the above quote, one of the key themes of the event was "religious life and opportunities for cooperation".[38]

Conclusion

In this chapter, by way of a response to the second key question this book aims to answer and through employing the mechanisms suggested in the second stage of the framework for my analysis of overseas implications of domestic norms (Figure 4.2), I have shown the ways in which the post-Kemalist norms concerning Outside Turks have been translated into foreign policy acts, how they gained international mobility and thus worked to cascade to the Outside Turks locality in Kosovo.

In so doing, I have given a detailed account of Turkey's post-Kemalist foreign policy conduct towards Kosovar Turks.

Ottomania has been diffused to Kosovo in many ways. It was promoted and shown endorsement via official promotion campaigns whereby Kosovo's Ottoman cultural identity was mentioned, and the framing of the Ottoman as a model for peaceful coexistence of different ethnicities was promoted as a cure to the virulent nationalism, which led to war in the Balkans in the 1990s. It was also presented as the solution to the challenge of nation-building in postwar Kosovo. The agents of diffusion here were TIKA, the Yunus Emre Institute, high-level Turkey officials and local norm entrepreneurs. The socialisation of the community into such norms has been done by the same agents.

De-ethnicised nationhood, on the other hand, was diffused to Kosovo through the constitutive involvement of TIKA, YTB, Yunus Emre Institute, high-level officials from Turkey, religious groups and local norm learners. These institutions and/or individuals did not show any concern to the ethnic Turkish community's expectations for a bold ethno-politics. They rather, as diffusive acts, tried to act upon anti-nationalism. The socialisation of the community into these norms has been done via a parallel process of championing going beyond ethnicity. The motto of these efforts has been Erdoğan's direct call for adherence to de-ethnicised nationhood and his call to *"stop constantly emphasising that 'we are Turks'"*.

The diffusion of Turkish Islam has mainly been done under the banner of preventing the spread of so-called Wahhabism, which is thought to be gaining ground in Kosovo. In this respect, TIKA, has, for example, prevented "Wahhabis" taking over Ottoman mosques in a bid to "defend" Ottoman culture, while religious groups have also "protected" Ottoman religious legacy in the country with the claim "Turks brought Islam to Kosovo and they will sustain it." The socialisation of the community to Turkish Islam, however, was done through more constitutive acts, such as re-institutionalising Turkish Islamic practices or forming alliances against the so-called Wahhabi threat. Diyanet has been the principal norm entrepreneur in this regard yet it has also been accompanied by the Yunus Emre Institute, TIKA and local norm learners, along with religious groups from Turkey.

The diffusion of Islamic Internationalism is about the introduction of frames such as religious brotherhood, religious identity and ummah to the ethnic Turkish community. These frames were attempting to redefine the inter-ethnic relationship among the Muslim communities in Kosovo. High-level officials from Turkey, TIKA, Diyanet, the Yunus Emre Institute and local norm learners have been the principal entrepreneurs relevant to this norm mobilisation process. The socialisation of the ethnic Turkish community into such a norm is part of an effort to transform the ethically acting Turkish community into a religious thinking and acting one. In this scope the notions of

Muslim sensitivity, religious solidarity, the idea of empathy with fellow Muslims, and Islamic consciousness have been promoted discursively and representatively. Moreover, the actors above prefer to treat ethnic Turks as a religious community rather than an ethnic one. Through visits during religious festivals, the Muslim Turkish identity is performed and promoted by them and this has been one of the most constitutive socialising acts conducted by Turkey.

As these empirical findings suggest, and confirming Checkel (1999), the cascade of the post-Kemalist norms to Kosovo had a constitutive influence on the ethnic Turkish community through the involvement of norm entrepreneurs both in Turkey and among the ethnic Turkish community in Kosovo (both norm setter, norm taker and norm learner entrepreneurs are involved). The diffusion of the norms and the socialisation of the community, therefore, was made possible by the active and identity-inclined involvements of Turkey's diplomatic missions, religious groups from Turkey and local norm entrepreneurs. They are therefore both the agents of diffusion and of socialisation, confirming Finnemore and Sikkink (1998: 902). In another confirmation of Finnemore and Sikkink, the cascade of post-Kemalist norms can be seen as part of a deliberate process rather than a "contagion" practice; their mobility and functioning is provided for by agents with a certain identity and cognition (Ibid.). Nonetheless, the match between the social and cultural characteristics and identities of the norm-setting and norm-taking communities have also been facilitative in the norm cascade, thus paving the way for successful diffusion of the norms (confirming Checkel 1999: 86, Cortell and Davis 2000).

Moreover, during the cascade stage, norm diffusion and the local community's socialisation took place in an inter-related manner. The norm-diffusing acts have functioned also as socialising acts. This confirms two things. Firstly, between diffusion and socialisation mechanisms there is no sequential relationship. Secondly, the functions that are suggested for norm-induced acts in the literature hold true. Accordingly, a norm-induced act conveys the norm that drives such act and the conveyed norm calls for adherence. The former is a diffusive and the latter is a socialising act. By way of confirmation, as seen above, the conduct of the post-Kemalist acts functioned as a means for both diffusion and socialisation.

In sum, the second stage of the framework embodies the capacity to explain domestic norms' international mobilisation and functioning abroad. However, without the internalisation section, full comprehension of the socialisation efforts remains incomplete. This is because the functioning of the post-Kemalist norms will also be revealed by reactions to it by the target community. The diffusive acts and socialisation efforts will be unfolded by the community itself. Therefore, the next chapter will reveal contestation of post-Kemalist norms and the degree to which they have become internalised in Kosovo. This way, the implications and tentative influences of these will be disclosed.

CHAPTER 8

LOCAL RESPONSES TO POST-KEMALIST SOCIALISATION

Introduction

In the previous two chapters, I traced the emergence of the post-Kemalist norms concerning Outside Turks and their diffusion to Kosovo through post-Kemalist foreign policy practices. In this chapter I elaborate the extent of the internalisation of these norms by the Kosovar Turkish community by looking at the local responses to the socialisation efforts of norm entrepreneurs. In so doing, I aim to disclose how these norms are understood by the Kosovar Turks, what are their implications for them, and the scope and degree of influence these norms have had on the community. The chapter starts with the perceptions of the Turkish elites about Turkey's broader approach and influence on Kosovar Turks, which affirm the presence and functioning of post-Kemalist norms in Kosovo. It then moves on to the individual post-Kemalist norms and the extent of their internalisation by exploring argumentation and contestation surrounding these norms.

In Chapter 7, I mentioned briefly that the Kosovar Turkish community perceives Turkey's approach towards them as Islamic-oriented and non-nationalist. This is a common opinion in the community at all levels. For instance, as some local elites stated:

Unfortunately, today, Turkey's policy is a bit different than before. It is based more on religion (Interview LE17).

Turkey approaches Kosovar Turks in an Islamic sense, rather than with nationalism (Interview LE12).

I do not see nationalism in JDP's policy towards the Turkish community in Kosovo ... It is more prone to holding a religious viewpoint (Interview LE1).

Turkey's JDP government does not care at all about Turkishness ... Turkey's non-concern for Turkishness and over-concern for Islam is reflected in Turkey's relations with Turks in Kosovo (Interview LE34).

We did not see such a religious approach until the early 2000s (Interview LE2).

These perceptions and considerations not only suggest that Turkey's approach during the JDP era is different than that of previous governments, but it also confirms that which was admitted by Turkey's diplomatic mission members and discussed in the previous chapter. Therefore, the community is aware of the message given by Turkey's JDP and of the change in approach towards them. Nonetheless, the observations of local elites do not stop there, they have more to say about this change, because to them this change in Turkey has profound impact on the community; whether the influence is positive or negative depends on the political leanings of the individual.

Those who see Turkey's pro-Islamic and anti-nationalist approach as positive also argue that sustainable relations with the majority Albanians requires the silencing of (ultra)nationalist voices among the Turkish community. In this sense, this group sees the rhetoric of ethnic politics from Turkish nationalists in relation to other Kosovar communities as merely feeding the antagonism among the majority Albanian community. Turkey's approach of recalling the Ottoman and Islamic civilisation and tolerance, in this sense, helps to politically and institutionally bring Turks and Albanians together, which was not possible during the warring period of the 1990s and during the Turkish community's struggle for ethnic rights in the early 2000s (Interview LE25, Interview LE21, Interview LE8).

On the other side of the debate, those who view Turkey's influence as negative for the Kosovar Turkish community mainly argue that state and NGO "officials' emphasis on religion has damaged Turkishness" (Interview LE15). This is because, as articulated by a local academic "[the] Islamic oriented policy of Turkey ... has partly caused ... a decline in Turkish language, Turkish culture, Turkish literature, Turkish education, Turkish nationalism, [and in] everything related to Turkishness" (Interview LE5). This occurred, according to the same respondent, because Turkey "harmed Turkish nationalism which kept the Turkish community alive through publications, media, culture and education" (Interview LE5). Therefore, nationalism is considered as a source of both national production and survival. It is, moreover, considered as a way of protecting against counter-nationalisms coming from the Albanian and Bosnian communities. In a local academic's words, "the Turkish community needs nationalism to balance other nationalisms [and] if only other nationalisms decline, we could [then] talk about a policy other than [alternative to] nationalism ... [Despite Turkey's approach] Albanians have not changed their nationalist attitudes towards Turkishness, and nor have the Bosnians" (Interview LE5). To such people, therefore, Turkey's pro-Ottoman and pro-Islamic policies "are not so productive" meaning that to be able to survive the adverse effects of Turkey's policies the "Kosovar Turks [have to wait] for Turkey to conduct a foreign policy that would support them in national[ist] projects ... because only through this can [Turkish] nationalism survive" (Interview LE5).

Making a value judgement about whether the change in Turkey's approach has had a positive or negative impact on the community is not the purpose of this study. I can say, however, that this remains a contested issue. Indeed, as argued by local elites and observed directly by me also, the constitutive impacts of this change in Turkey's approach has manifested itself in a division within the community. More precisely, as a local teacher and a journalist put it, there has been a "polarization ... along secular nationalist and conservative lines" within the community (Interview LE13, Interview LE1). The "conservatives" (as they are referred to by secular nationalist and a title they also use for themselves) are those who find the JDP's approach agreeable. The secular nationalists, on the other hand, see the new approach as anti-Turkist and ultimately destructive. The first group has occasionally acted as a group of post-Kemalist norm entrepreneurs, something which was elaborated on in the previous chapter. The second group, on the other hand, acted forcefully as the "resistance" to this and has struggled to impede the internalisation of post-Kemalist norms. The relationship between these groups, however, cannot be described merely as a zero-sum one, because this division within the community does not always represent a clear-cut demarcation of interests or self-identification. Indeed, a local academic argued that:

> Even though the Kosovar Turks do not like such fragmentation within the community, they are unable to overcome it ... This is because, in essence, they embody all those values. They do not find the Islamic view odd because it is part of them; they do not find the nationalist view odd because they are as nationalist as those in Turkey. No matter how much they try to find leftist ideas odd, they cannot because they are modern as well.[1]
>
> (Interview LE5)

As can be seen here, the cultural context is very influential to the way the community responds to socialisation efforts. This also shows that two poles have emerged out of a blending of nationalist, religious and secular values. In this sense, illustrating the norm structure before the division (before the ethnic Turkish community was exposed to post-Kemalist norms) is useful to better understand their responses to the issues we have already raised, but also to inform us more about how the community functions.

The historical records suggest that the ethnic Turkish community has had a commitment to Atatürk and his reform agenda from the early days of Yugoslav rule in Kosovo. During this period, Atatürk was a historical and national figure who was revered in schools and in literature and used as a tool to inculcate in Turks a sense of nationality, and in building and sustaining their ethnic identity. Indeed, it was within this context that Kosovar Turks were transformed from a religious community to a nationally thinking and acting community (as with other cases of Outside Turks explored in Chapter 2). Accordingly, after the community was given the right to education in their mother tongue in 1951, teachers used all available means to "cherish the Turkish identity and consciousness", with Atatürk serving as the necessary figure to impose a national sentiment to children (Interview LE2). A respondent confirmed this by telling me about that the education they received during 1950s:

Atatürk was imposed on us since the early days of education in Turkish language schools. For example, in the beginning we did not have Turkish history courses at schools, but our teachers skilfully filled this gap. Atatürk was the lead figure they relied on to teach us about Turkish history.

(Interview LE35)

With the opening of the *Tan* newspaper in 1968, the community began producing literary, academic and cultural forms of national expression, again, inspired by the legacy of Atatürk as the central figure. For staff at the newspaper, as reported by İskender Muzbeg, the former editor-in-chief of *Tan* "Atatürk revolutions and Atatürk's thoughts became the main source of enlightenment and inspiration" in their quest to use *Tan* to maintain Turkish national identity, language and culture –an endeavour which lasted for many years (*Atam İzindeyiz Booklet* 2009: 64). Similar responsibility was borne also by the cultural associations of the community. Through music, theatre, arts and literary productions, these associations, the oldest two of which were founded in 1951, managed to reify Turkish identity and Atatürk in the minds of the people. They did this by organising commemorations, concerts, theatre plays or poetry nights centred on Atatürk and on Turkish national days (*Doğruyol 30. Yıl Monografisi* 1981: 54).

By way of confirmation, a local secular nationalist figure, Ferhat Derviş, narrates how the community gained a national consciousness as follows:

[The socialist government] allowed us to bring books on Atatürk from Turkey ... [and] the right to be taught Turkey's national history ... [this] made us embrace the things we read ... After reading about Atatürk's life and revolutions from books, we learned about his qualities as a soldier, a politician, a statesman ... Revolutionism, Secularism, Nationalism, Republicanism, Populism, Statism all became our principles ... The articles and poems written in Kosovo about Atatürk in the newspapers and bulletins also encouraged our development as Kemalists. It was due to our traversing of Atatürk's path that we managed to protect our education, culture and nationality in these lands. In Kosovo every single Turkish intellectual succeeded in becoming Kemalist [becoming Atatürk]. The secret of our success was following Atatürk's principles and thoughts.

(*Atam İzindeyiz Booklet* 2009: 71–2)

Atatürk was therefore utilised in educating the community about the national Self with nationalism – an unquestioned and "natural" way to act in the cause of sustaining national identity. The same was the case also during the 1990s. Indeed, even towards the time of the collapse of Yugoslavia, sustaining national identity continued to be the prime purpose of many in the community and in so doing a nationalist political struggle was organised based on Atatürk and his principles, which were thought to be the best way to preserve national identity and culture (*Tan* 30 May 1992[2]). In the 1990s Turkish identity gained political representatives and Atatürk was employed by these to further promote and institutionalise their national identity against Serbian and Albanian pressures and a general state of war. The community lived through the war by embracing Turkish identity and through taking a low political profile while devoting much of their time to sustaining Turkish language education and Turkish language publications. Last but not least, the 1990s was also a time when the community re-invented their religious values. This will be dealt with in detail below but I can say here that this was done by reinventing a religious character in Atatürk's personality. The religious values therefore were not imagined as a replacement political ideology; they were remembered as an authentic part of Turkish culture and were kept strictly in the cultural realm.

The coming of the Turkish military troops (Turkish Tabur) to Kosovo did not change this structure much. When the Turkish Tabur came to Kosovo after the NATO intervention in 1999, the Turkish community was already nationalist, and knew and wrote about Atatürk as a means to assert their national identity. This tendency facilitated the Tabur's approach to the Turkish community in confidence as the institutional representative of the Kemalist state, in a similar vein, the community, from the very beginning, welcomed the Tabur's presence in Kosovo and thought of this as an end to almost a century-long absence (Recepoğlu 2004: 75). It was within such a context that the Tabur was seen as the savour of the community; savour from possible Serbian massacres during the war and problems after the war which affected the community's ethnic rights. Some community members commented on this that:

> The Tabur has done an excellent job here. If you have found me here as a Turk, this is by the help of Tabur. Otherwise, you would have found me here either murdered or displaced.
>
> (Interview LE6)

Tabur's image in the eyes of the local community enabled it to institutionalise certain Kemalist practices in Kosovo, many of which were happily accepted as they had long been embraced and celebrated by this community. In this vein, for instance, Tabur initiated the celebrations of 23 April Children Festival, 19 May Youth and Sports Day, 30 August Victory Day, 29 October Republican Day, 10 November Atatürk Commemoration Day – all of which were commemorated via mass celebrations which featured the participation of students and the general public (for details of these celebrations see the following sources *Yeni Dönem* 1 November 2001, *Yeni Dönem* 15 November 2001, *Yeni Dönem* 25 April 2002, *Yeni Dönem* 5 September 2002, *Türkçem* May 2013: 36, *Mehmetçik Kosova'da Booklet 1* 2002: 247–59, *Mehmetçik Kosova'da Booklet* 2009: 97–9, Recepoğlu 2006: 142).

In organising these events, Tabur always collaborated with local associations. Tabur appreciated their efforts and spoke highly of their services in increasing "the love of Atatürk" among the Kosovar Turkish community and also their "embrace of Atatürk with devotion" (*Mehmetçik Kosova'da Booklet 1* 2002: 267). In a similar vein, with the "support and encouragement of the officers in the Turkish Tabur" local Kemalist civil society organisations were founded. These included the Kemalist Thought Association (Atatürkçü Düşünce Derneği-ADD) in Gilan in 2000 and Zübeyde Hanım Turkish Women's Association[3] in Prizren in 2001 (Recepoğlu 2007: 86, 80). The community did not deem Tabur's campaigns odd at the time; in fact, they were happy that they could proudly express their identity and long commitment to Atatürk in spaces created by Tabur. By the same token, the Turkish Tabur did not aim to change things within the community, except by allowing for Turkish identity to be represented institutionally.

As can been seen, for the community, Atatürk and nationalism functioned initially as a way to learn about their national-Self and later became sources from which they could cherish national identity. Tabur gave them more courage and institutional support to declare this more vocally. Therefore, I can say that before the community was exposed to post-Kemalist approaches, it had a strong sense of national identity with a strong commitment to Atatürk and his principles. Accordingly, nationalism has historically been a dominant norm in the community. With the coming of Tabur to Kosovo, this did not change, but actually provided the community with comfort in that the community came to believe that Turkey was happy about their nationalism and commitment to Atatürk. However, by the time the JDP came to power in Turkey and due to the functioning of post-Kemalist norms afterwards, some community members, including many graduates from Turkey began, in due course, to change their views in ways which went against the dominant norm and perspective highlighted above. As will be seen in detail below, they questioned the validity of nationalism, began to view it as destructive for the community and tried to deconstruct and replace it with ideas of non-nationalism, multiculturalism or a devotion to the ummah instead. This change in approach to nationalism within the community scared nationalists and forced them to adopt a reactionary state of mind whereby they embraced nationalism and Kemalism even more than before, seeing these as the only way to maintain their national identity. There is indeed a mutually constitutive state of affairs taking place here.

In short, a secular nationalist versus conservative division came out of this norm structure. Although the depiction of the division is quite rough, it is a consistent illustration of how the target community elites are grouped as a result of the functioning of post-Kemalist norms. The first constitutive implication of Turkey's new policies for Kosovar Turks therefore is division within community. This impact is key to tracking the arguments taking place between community elites regarding post-Kemalist norms and also enables us to uncover the impact of other norms too. This also provides us with a good starting point to move to an analysis of individual post-Kemalist norms and the arguments taking place around them.

Responses to Ottomania's Functioning

The functioning of Ottomania in Kosovo has had implications in three main domains, namely (1) the restoration of inter-ethnic relations,

(2) recalling of multicultural forms of belonging, and (3) multi-ethnic local agendas in daily life and politics. The different responses with regards to embracing or rejecting the Ottomanist perspective is highly dependent on the position of the person being addressed in the conservative vs. secular nationalist divide. There is, however, a considerable amount of intermingling; for instance, some secular nationalists admit the necessity of such an approach in formulating sustainable and peaceful inter-ethnic relations in Kosovo, as can be seen in the above quotations. Nonetheless, this does not change the fact that there is a substantial number of elites who fiercely oppose the use of Ottoman analogies in thinking about the present Turkish community in Kosovo. This group has produced a reactionary discourse against the functioning and increased influence of Ottomania.

The relationship between Albanian and Turkish communities has been on the rocks since the Yugoslav era, yet it went from bad to worse in the 1990s and early 2000s due to the constant calls by Albanians for ethnic Turks to join the war against Serbia. More importantly, the situation deteriorated when some Albanian political elites initially wanted to deny basic rights to ethnic Turks after the 1999 war (Interview LE5). This relationship was arguably relieved thanks to Turkey's official engagement with the Albanian political elite and their promotion of the idea of ethnic accord which had existed during Ottoman times as a basis for Kosovo's post-war settlement. This is precisely what was argued by the respondent from TIKA, as noted in the preceding chapter (Interview DM5). The respondent would appear to be right in their assertion to the extent that through my own interviews and observations, I saw that Ottomania has provided elites (both Turkish and Albanian) with the necessary cognitive frames to rethink inter-ethnic affairs in the country. An interview with a local elite in Mamusha is also instructive here:

> After the [coming to power of the] Erdoğan government, Turkey does not see Albanians different from Turks, it approached both of them equally ... This strengthens the Turks' position in Kosovo and has led to a positive change in the way Albanians and Bosnians think about Turks.
>
> (Interview LE22)

Albanians and Turks now cooperate in social and political activities such as establishing education and youth associations or joining forces to form a Conservative Party in Kosovo, a party with a pro-Islamic and pro-Ottoman agenda. This was also due to a change in how Albanians saw their own history – something which was generated by the functioning of Ottomania and its promotion by Turkey and local norm entrepreneurs. Many nationalists in the Albanian community have long perceived the Ottoman period in Kosovo as destructive (something which also forms part of the "official" history taught at schools). With the increase in nationalism in the 1990s and early 2000s, this further exacerbated this sentiment. Turkey's decision to join the 1999 war was not enough to reverse this. However, by the time the JDP came to power things begun to change drastically. Turkey began to pay more attention to a number of issues: it actively glorified the role played by Albanians and Bosnians in the Ottoman Empire and Islamic civilisation, gratefully acknowledged their contributions to the Dardanelles Wars, constantly underlined Mehmet Akif's Albanianhood and promoted Sami Frasheri's contribution to the Turkish language[4] despite his notoriety among nationalist circles in Turkey. This helped in altering opinions about not just Frasheri but also facilitated the Albanian community's embrace of their Ottoman past. This change is narrated by a local journalist as follows:

> In the JDP era huge changes have been experienced [in Kosovo].
> For example, the Albanian community's views on Turkey have
> been altered. In the Albanian language education, in history
> courses, antagonism against the Ottoman [Empire] was previously
> widespread. [Although] [t]here are still chapters or articles in
> those books depicting the Ottoman Empire as invaders, brutal and
> destroyers ... due to Turkey's policy, in the community level this
> [hostile] attitude has softened. As journalists, we observed that
> until a few years ago any journal article against Turkey was readily
> supported with those who did not back the article less than 10 per
> cent. Today, this ratio is around 50 per cent. There shows an
> incredible influence in this sense.
>
> (Interview LE1)

Today, therefore, there is a growing number of Albanians who believe that the Ottomans were not as evil as was previously thought and that they owe the presence of the Albanian nation today to the Ottomans, because the Ottomans protected their culture and language. There is even "a new trend that the religiously motivated Albanians of Kosovo consider themselves as the remnants of the Ottomans" (Interview LE21). Therefore, "the Ottoman consciousness has awakened among the Albanian and Bosnian communities in Kosovo. They now want to protect the cultural heritage and realise projects with the Ministry of Culture of Kosovo for this cause" (Interview DM5). It is, again, in this vein that "Kosovo and Turkey [are working] together to make changes to history textbooks" (Interview LE1) and the Ministry of Education of Kosovo have launched projects to remove "insulting expressions towards Turks in the textbooks ... and the maps showing South East Turkey as Kurdistan ... [and] Eastern Turkey as Armenia" (*Kosova Haber* 1 March 2011).

This rapprochement positively contributed to the relieving of the inter-ethnic tensions. The Albanian majority, in this sense, for instance, partly gave up suppressing the Turks. This is necessary because in the early 2000s Albanian political groups were "threatening the ethnic Turks with refusing them to education in the Turkish language at schools – an issue of life and death for the Turkish community" (Interview LE14). This change has also allowed for post-Kemalist norm entrepreneurs and Turkey to make use of the Albanian community to transform Kosovar Turks. This confirms what my respondent from Balkan TV said (see the preceding chapter): attaching the Albanian community to the Ottoman Empire can also be an instrument to transform the ethnic Turkish community.

The embrace of Ottoman history and Islamic civilisation by Albanians – something which the Turkish community did not expect due to nationalism and antagonism towards the Turks often expressed by some Albanians – has also had the effect of making Kosovar Turks more confident in identifying with their Ottoman past. Historically, the Ottomans was a legacy only for ethnic Turks; now it is becoming part of the history of the Kosovo state and the Albanian people. The restoration of Ottoman buildings and cultural artefacts and the intense interest in these from tourists and local people have contributed to this idea. For instance, the Sultan Murad tomb, restored by TIKA in 2009, became Kosovo's most visited place in 2011 (*TIKA Haber* 23 January 2012). Turkey was, in a sense, restoring not only the history of ethnic Turks in Kosovo, but also the history of Kosovo as a whole. Kosovar Turk history thus became the history of the land they had settled on. This has made it easier for ethnic Turks to embrace Kosovo as a homeland.

During the socialist era, the homeland for the Turkish community was Yugoslavia, as declared to me proudly by the elderly among the Turks. They had "martyrs" who fought and died during the "liberation war" between 1941 and 1944 while fighting on the socialists' side (Yusuf 1976: 18). Members of the community, during the socialist era, wrote a poem on these "martyrs". Moreover, the Yugoslav revolution and Tito who made Yugoslavia a homeland for the Turks were also central themes of the literary production produced by the members of the community throughout this period (Ibid.: 98–9). By the time Yugoslavia was on the verse of collapsing, however, the true homeland of the Turks was imagined to be Turkey (Interview LE5). This is initially because of the insecurity Turks felt amid mass killings in the 1990s. Yet, moreover, the killing of Muslims in Bosnia for being "Turks" and the destruction of the historical Ottoman sites/artefacts made them feel detached from the idea of imagining Yugoslavia or Serbia as a homeland. Nonetheless, by the 2000s, with the restoration of security in Kosovo which the Turkish Tabur provided to the community, Turkey's large institutional presence in Kosovo and the activities aimed at restoring historical heritage sites seems to have contributed to the development of the feeling of political and cultural belonging to Kosovo. For the ethnic Turkish community, between Turkey and Kosovo there is now a clear distinction with regard to homeland/fatherland in discussions. Accordingly, while Turkey is commonly described as the fatherland (or motherland), Kosovo is the homeland, a fact admitted to me by many senior members in both conservative and secular nationalist circles.

The functioning of the third domain, "Ottomania", also began to be reflected in the daily life and politics of the local Turkish community – that is, a new multi-ethnic local agenda was introduced. The Turkish community already had the experience of coexisting peacefully with other groups during the socialist era. However, the 1990s and the war led these communities to mostly live in isolation from one another, with Turks focusing only on maintaining their Turkish-language education and culture. The NATO intervention led to a period of mobilisation by the Turkish community in the struggle for ethnic rights in a legal sense after these were scrapped following the war (these rights were enshrined in the 1974 Yugoslav Constitution). This led the Turkish community and its political party, the KDTP, to focus exclusively on the problems and concern of Turks in Kosovo. The political agenda of the Turkish community and the programme of the KDTP were limited to ethnic issues concerning the community. However, today, there has been a shift towards following a more inclusive agenda vis-à-vis Albanians and Bosnians. Indeed one party official from the KDTP argued that in election campaigns his party does not emphasise Turkishness and focuses instead on the common problems of Turks, Albanians and Bosnians (Interview LE19). With this, they are seemingly trying to attract not only the votes of ethnic Turks, but also those from other Muslim communities.

Nonetheless, with regard to the multi-ethnic local agenda introduced by the functioning of Ottomania, the most ground-breaking development occurred in the establishment of multi-ethnic associations and the advent of multi-ethnic political parties. Although, in the general discourse of the community "the Turks are expected to vote only for the Turkish political parties [and this] is a prerequisite for being Turk", there are now some groups within the community which were founder members of the Conservative Party and which were candidates for local elections meaning that they were, in effect, competing with the ethnic Turkish party, KDTP, for the Turkish community vote (Interview 21, Interview LE12). Yugoslav-era joint programmes were mostly done for the sake of socialist unity whereas today the concern is more culturally defined and has a focus on ideas of Ottoman era inter-ethnic and religio-cultural relations. Therefore, nationalist cognitive frames are being seen, by some, as destructive and must be replaced with a new multicultural framework – and this is thanks to the functioning of Ottomania. This however, does not mean that nationalist frames have been replaced altogether. They continue to function and shaping the societal and political agenda of the community.

In another example, the multi-ethnic local agenda manifests itself in the representation of Mehmet Akif as the symbol of brotherhood, and shared history and culture. Mehmet Akif's Albanianhood has been proudly articulated by both Turkey's institutions and the local conservative elites and is seen by these groups as a way to deepen the societal and political level relations. To do this, they mention him often so as to inform both Kosovar Turks and Albanians about his legacy. In one instance, the Yunus Emre Institute even organised a Turkish national anthem recital contest. In discussions about this with a local elite in Mamusha, it was argued that the contest "caught the attention of the Albanian students at the school and they learned about Mehmet Akif" meaning that, to him at least, it was "Yunus Emre that made Albanians aware of Mehmet Akif" (Interview LE22).

This is part of a process whereby the adherents of Ottomania try to restore inter-ethnic relations in Kosovo by underlining multicultural forms of belonging which were present in the past and by adopting a multi-ethnic local agenda in daily life and politics. However, these have mostly appealed to the conservative elites of the community while the adherence of secular nationalists continues to be limited. Moreover, in some instances, the functioning of Ottomania has actually made the secular nationalists more reactionary and extreme in their arguments.

Among them, for instance, some of the leading secular nationalist elites stated in discomfort that "Turkey over-propagates Ottoman culture" (Interview LE4). This approach, to them, "ties the Turks' hand which will end with Turks losing all their privileges" (Pers. Comm. SVN4). Here, the privilege comes to mean their being "Turks". They therefore "do not want to be compared to others" and make strong statements about their history in Kosovo as (former) conquerors (Interview LE34). The "Ottoman approach" to cultural unity and brotherhood thus does not appeal to them and they fiercely deny the idea of the Ottoman as representing shared ground between them and Albanians. At this juncture, they more often make use of the idea of the Ottomans to support their nationalistic stances and stand strongly against the post-Kemalist initiations of de-ethnicising the Ottoman Empire. To them "the Ottomans were Turks" and they themselves stand as proof to this Turkish presence in Kosovo (Interview LE38). They also argue that:

The Ottomans in Kosovo [for the Turkish community] are considered Turkish; however, Turkey's [referring here to the current JDP-era] Ottomans are not Turkish. To us, Ottoman means Turk. However, the government in Turkey comprehends the Ottomans by putting forth other nations' contributions to it. They in a way are trying to show the Ottomans as a multinational civilisation.

(Interview LE34)

Secular nationalist elites, in this sense, support the preservation of Ottoman artefacts "because they are the proof of [the Turks'[5]] presence in Kosovo" (Interview LE12). To them, the demolition of the "old Ottoman mosques" or the destruction of "Ottoman graveyards" are attempts to "root out Turkishness from Kosovo" because "those Ottoman symbols were also the symbols of Turkishness" (Interview LE15).

Although the secular nationalist elite argue that the Ottomans were Turks, the claim that the presence of Kosovar Turks in Kosovo began with the Ottomans is an uncomfortable truth for them. They are not at ease with such arguments made in history textbooks written by Albanians. Indeed, one of my historian respondents argued that those Albanians who wrote the history textbooks for the Turkish community during the socialist era were "illiterate about Turkish history ... [because they] began [discussions of] Turkish history [by referencing] the Ottoman Empire" (Interview LE2). For my respondent, however "long before the Ottomans, [the ancient Turkic clans such as] Avars, Pechneneks ... Kumans, Albuzs ... came to the Balkans" (Interview LE2).

Another important event mentioned in this vein is the Dardanelles Wars of 1915. Secular nationalist elites equivocally disagree with framing this as a multi-ethnic (Ottoman) struggle against a common foe and in highlighting the participation of Albanians and Bosnians to the war effort. They narrate the war and subsequent victory as a purely Turkish endeavour. The *Yeni Dönem* newspaper's narration of the event exemplifies this:

> The foundations of Turkish independence were laid in Dardanelles [war] ... Mustafa Kemal's iron will created the victory of Dardanelles, in return Dardanelles created Mustafa Kemal [Atatürk]. Tens of thousands of young and elderly Turkish soldiers, who had the consciousness of Turkish blood and who were willing to die maintaining Turkishness, joined this war; 250,000 martyrs were made in Dardanelles. Nonetheless, the enemy was defeated with the leadership of Mustafa Kemal Atatürk.
>
> (*Yeni Dönem* 21 March 2002)

Another issue that secular nationalist elites show discomfort towards is the idea that Mehmet Akif represents a "multi-ethnic figure" and that he was "Albanian". They both deny Mehmet Akif's Albanianhood and are annoyed with Turkey's constant emphasis of this. They argue that "Turkey unnecessarily emphasises that Mehmet Akif is an Albanian. There is no need to always stress this" and that "[w]e consider Mehmed Akif a Turk, an Ottoman" (Interview LE2, Interview LE4). In their writings about Mehmet Akif, they either claim that he is a Turk or make no reference at all to his ethnicity. For instance in an article about Mehmet Akif, Altay Suroy Recepoğlu – now a member of the Constitutional Court of Kosovo – makes no references at all to the Albanian roots of Mehmet Akif in a book written by him about the ethnic struggles of the Turkish community (Recepoğlu 2004: 59). In the relevant part, Recepoğlu instead quotes a sentence from a poem by Mehmet Akif where Akif denounced the building of an Albanian state and argued that this was not Islamically justifiable (Ibid.). Though Recepoğlu does not say that Mehmet Akif was a Turk, he nonetheless argues that "his homeland was Turkey and he was in love with the Turkish nation" (Ibid.). During a Mehmet Akif commemoration event organised by the Kemalist Filizler Association in 2013, an erstwhile MP, Fikrim Damka, similarly stated that:

We are proud to commemorate Mehmet Akif, the defender of Turkish ideology, and would like to argue against those who try to introduce him differently.[6] We have to put a lid on this, because, in essence Mehmet Akif is a Turk ... It is necessary to unfold the [Turkist] ideology hidden in his writings. He was an ardent supporter of such an idea [Turkish ideology] both during the foundation of the Republic of Turkey and during the Ottoman era.

(*Kosova Haber* 28 December 2013)

Taking this into account, it is necessary to highlight here that contrary to how the ethnic Turkish community imagines Mehmet Akif to have been, there is no doubt about his ideological leanings according to most academics. Mehmet Akif contributed to the Islamist thought in Turkey and was known for his ardent anti-nationalist stance (Mardin 2005: 152). Yet, the secular nationalists need him to be represented as a "Turk" and a Turkish nationalist in order to achieve their own nationalist agendas.

In conclusion, Ottomania has been less successful in deconstructing the dominant nationalist frames introduced by conservative elites and mentioned in the introduction – rather, it has fed the growth of nationalism in some ways. This norm has not been internalised en masse by elites in the Kosovar Turkish community, as many of them continue to ethnicise the Ottomans or Mehmet Akif as "Turkish". Yet, there is a growing number of associations and intellectuals both among the Turkish and Albanian community that have begun to consider the Ottomans as a "joint" civilisation and to admit the contribution of Albanians and others to the building of such a civilisation. In this sense, adjusting the inter-ethnic relations along Ottoman lines is referred to more often than in the past, and has been promoted discursively as a cure to the disintegration of the Muslim communities along national lines.

Responses to De-ethnicised Nationhood's Functioning

In the introduction above, I argued that the Kosovar Turkish community sees Turkishness as the prime lens to be worn in policy making and in regulating relations with other communities. Ethnopolitics and nationalism, in this sense, have been the primary tools used to sustain "Turkishness". This has historically been the dominant norm, generated by arguments such as "Turks living outside of Turkey must be nationalist, otherwise, they will vanish" or "I have to be Turk to exist. I exist only if I am a Turk. If I am not a Turk, I do not exist" (Interview LE3, Interview LE6). Via nationalist expressions, therefore, elites have practised and hoped to sustain Turkish ethnicity and culture. This has been reflected in several domains which I noted in the introductory section above.

In the realm of politics, for instance (as nationalist elites hold) in order to be considered an ethnic Turk in Kosovo one must vote for an ethnic Turkish party. This is because of the belief that ethnic Turkish party/parties must survive in order to protect Turkishness in Kosovo. Accordingly, along with cultural associations, it has been particularly the KDTP – the biggest political party of the ethnic Turkish community – which, according to a senior member, has "successfully protected the education, culture, customs and tradition" of the Turkish community (Interview LE19).

In the realm of education, this nationalism manifests itself in a similar claim that one must go to Turkish schools in order to be able to remain an ethnic Turk and in order to avoid assimilation. Education is a very important issue because it has traditionally been the prime means by which the ethnic Turkish community has historically learnt to become and to "act like a Turk". In the absence of education, they argue "the sense of Turkishness would not have been developed adequately and the community would have been assimilated" (Interview LE35). Therefore, they see that the day the community was granted the right to education using their mother tongue (1951) as the time when Turkishness in Kosovo (and Yugoslavia) was born from the ashes. Since then, most members of the community who studied at university have become teachers. Those who went to Turkey for university education by 1993 onwards, especially the first generations, similarly in the main studied pedagogy and became teachers. In tandem with the role of education in building and sustaining national identity, a retired education inspector and the author of many history textbooks used by the Turkish community, and also one of the experts who took on the role of preparing the history course curriculum in Kosovo, Bedrettin Koro, argues that the history course curricula and textbooks used by the Turkish community aim to:

1. Make the Turkish students disposed to sustaining secular (*laic*), democratic, national and modern values through making sure that the students understand the place of Atatürk's principles and revolution in the fatherland's (that is, Turkey's) social, cultural and economic development.
2. Make the students take responsibility in protecting and further developing the (*Turkish*) cultural heritage (in Kosovo) through making them comprehend the core elements and processes forming Turkish history and Turkish culture.
3. Make them comprehend the formation of national identity, the elements constituting such identity and the necessity of protecting national identity.
4. Make the students embrace and defend Atatürk's world view and thoughts.

(Koro 2011: 13)

Koro's arguments have a reactionary character; yet many of the points, particularly the ones related to Atatürk, have long been aimed for in the agenda of the community elites. In this sense, through a nationalistic stance towards education, elites managed to develop a national consciousness among community members, and schools have been the means by which the community was taught about how to act as a Turk.

In tandem with education, another realm of nationalist practices through which Turkishness has been practised and the community has been ethnically mobilised is the media. The relationship between these two fields is articulated by a former teacher and journalist as follows: "[o]nly through our involvement in education and journalism did we manage to secure the national [ethnic] consciousness of Kosovar Turks" (Interview LE35). Today, the Turkish media is constituted by a number of online news portals and one or two small-scale and irregular weekly newspapers. However, this does not dissuade them for casting a role for themselves in contributing to the ethnic struggle of the community. Accordingly, the founder of one of the news portals stated in our meeting that:

> I established [the news portal] with an ethnic consciousness, I established it to contribute to Turkish media, to Turkishness [in Kosovo]; because there is a constant struggle to sustain Turkishness in here ... If our education, culture and media get muted, we will die down.
>
> (Interview LE31)

This represents a continuity of the traditional role of media and journalists within the community. Historically speaking, the *Tan* newspaper facilitated the community's development of their ability to use Turkish language and to learn about Turkishness. A former manager of the *Tan* newspaper articulated the importance of *Tan* for the community as follows:

> The *Tan* newspaper was an academy, a publishing office and also a society where the Turkish people's national struggle was organised. The issues of how to act in the political realm [or] who to propose for certain positions etc., were discussed within the newspaper ... This continued until 1999, when it was closed down.
>
> (Interview LE35)

Accordingly, media contributed to the community's practice of nationalism and Turkishness thanks also through efforts to make the community learn literary uses of the Turkish language. To a local academic, national themes "such as Turkishness, Turkish identity, Turkish consciousness, fatherland, Turkey and Atatürk" found a place in the literature produced by Kosovar Turks only after the *Tan* newspaper was established (Interview LE5). Before the *Tan* newspaper, literature in Turkish "discussed mainly issues to do with children, mothers, the homeland, brotherhood, union, freedom [and Tito] which were more of interest to wider society" (Interview LE5). As a turning point, the 1990s brought about a new nationalist agenda to the media and literary practices, in the scope of which some community members began to refer to the world-wide Turkish nation in their literary productions and established extensive contact with wider audiences in Turkey and in the Turkish-speaking (Turkic) world (*Türk Yazarlar Derneği* 1996: 53, *Tan* 17 November 1990, *Tan* 29 August 1992, *Tan* 21 November 1992[7]). This is concomitant to the community's reference to Turkey as their "homeland" (mentioned in the Ottomania's internalisation section above). This was due to the community's search for a way out of the war engulfing the Balkans and due to the uncertainty they felt about their future in Kosovo. The media continued to play a similar role after the 1999 war and was mainly interested in arguing for the protection of ethnic rights. Tabur's presence in Kosovo and its assistance to the community, such as the institutionalisation of national day celebrations, were warmly welcomed by most.

Therefore, confirming the arguments made in the introduction, nationalism has historically been a dominant framework for the community as a way to practise Turkishness. The post-Kemalist norms in general and de-ethnicised nationhood in particular were conveyed to and commenced functioning within such a context. This generated two, largely opposed, consequences. On the one hand, due to the successful socialisation efforts some community members became ardent adherents of de-ethnicised nationhood and there occurred a shift in their approach to nationalist (and Kemalist) dominant frames. On the other hand, others embraced nationalist frames more strongly and begun to praise Atatürk more vocally.[8] These two opposite approaches were embraced by secular nationalists and conservatives which have together mutually contributed to a gradual reification of Kemalist and post-Kemalist attitudes.

In this sense, anti-nationalist conservative elites complain about that "Turkishness has become a full-time occupation in Kosovo [*Türklük Kosova'da meslek haline geldi*]" meaning that they see Turkishness as becoming the only purpose worth living for and the sole point of view which has to be embraced in managing relations with the Kosovo state and other Muslim communities in the country (Interview LE37). There are numerous examples of nationalist acts which have generated discomfort among anti-nationalists or moderate elites. For instance, a moderate artist argued that:

> It is necessary for the Turks of Kosovo to know about the national days of Turkey; however, they should not forget that here is Kosovo territory ... Teachers' Day is already set by Kosovo, but you are, in addition to Kosovo's Teachers' Day, also celebrating Turkey's Teachers' Day. Why?
>
> (Interview LE10)

Confirming such a view, another respondent argued that "these national days are [the] special days of Turkey and make sense in that specific context", but they are "irrelevant for the local Turkish community [here in Kosovo]" (Interview LE25). These celebrations and commemorations, to those opposing them, are merely working to blur the boundaries between Kosovar Turks and Turkey in the minds of the former, thus posing a serious threat to the community as it prevents the community from developing a sense of belonging to the state of Kosovo. Other conservative elite also argued that:

> The Yunus Emre Institute organised a painting contest among school children under the theme 'homeland'. Many of the contestants sent paintings about Turkey and Atatürk. This is not a healthy situation. Turks, while not knowing anything about Kosovo, knows everything about Turkey. This is an unhealthy situation. Kosovo carries all the necessary qualities to be considered a homeland. Turkey should be the fatherland, not the homeland.
>
> (Pers. Comm. SVN5)

Another concern arises here regarding the over-emphasis on Turkishness and ethnic-nationalism among conservative elites. These are thought to be jeopardising the Turks' current state of affairs with other communities and considered an obstacle to peaceful co-existence in Kosovo. A concern in this vein is articulated by a moderate journalist as follows:

> There are teachers making students recite "Our Pledge"[9] in schools . . . This started after the Tabur came. Why would you need Our Pledge to be recited? You are going to protect your identity, but we did so for 80 years without reciting Our Pledge . . . At the events organised by the Turks, the Turkish national anthem is always played [and in many of them this is the only one played – not the Kosovo one].
>
> (Interview LE13)

As a result of this ethnic-nationalism, for the adherents of de-ethnicised nationhood, the new generation has been raised with no desire to learn the Albanian language, nor to be part of the Albanian-led state and culture (Interview LE16). With the influence of the Great Student Exchange project, students think only of Turkey and Turkishness and there develops a deficit in developing a sense of belonging to the Kosovo state. This, to them, signals the potential for future integration problems at both the societal and state levels. Such issues have led some community members to cooperate with Turkey's diplomatic missions and with religious groups from Turkey who work at the grassroots in Kosovo so as to work towards socialising the Turkish community towards post-Kemalist norms. I have given an account of these socialisation efforts in Chapter 7. The efforts of local norm entrepreneurs and groups coming from Turkey have borne fruits to a certain degree and several important changes have been made. There is now a growing anti-nationalist sentiment in the Kosovar Turkish community.

Indeed, many parents have become concerned about the future of their children in Kosovo. The conservatives' constant refrain that "students who were educated in the Turkish language are having problems learning Albanian" – which means that they are facing problem in perceiving themselves as members of Kosovar society – have convinced some community members to make changes and "Turks have started registering their children to Albanian-language schools" (Interview LE21). This is a contentious issue for nationalists, whereas for conservatives it is a step in the right direction towards creating harmonious relations with Albanians and other Muslim communities. Indeed, community members have begun to send their children or have personally joined courses – organised by official state institutions from Turkey or local entrepreneurs – to learn Albanian.

Another change, more precisely a diversification, has occurred in the field of literary production. Until the early 2000s, the community's literary voice could best be described as purely "nationalist". However, today there are authors who write about Islam and the Islamic experience of the community. In this sense, as one of my academic respondents argued, after 2002 there occurred two core changes in Turkish literary production in Kosovo. On the one hand, "young writers shifted to far-right nationalism in their writings . . . as a result of an effort to keep Kosovar Turkishness alive" while on the other "a number of new literary voices emerged in Kosovar Turkish literature with writings featuring religion as a [key] theme. They use Ottoman language words in their writings . . . that follows the ideas of literature in Turkey . . . used mainly by rightist and Islamic literary circles" (Interview LE5). These new writers have distanced themselves from the socialist-era literary nationalist writings and have instead "focused on the rich sources of Turkish literature" which blends Ottoman Turkish and Islam (Recepoğlu 2006: 56–7). It is with such developments that a local conservative proudly argued that Kosovar Turks are moving beyond ethnicity in terms of worldview.

De-ethnicised nationhood has evidently generated some changes in the way the community acts politically and culturally, particularly for conservative circles. These changes have however led to a secular nationalist reaction against these changes. Yet, it should be borne in mind that both post-Kemalist socialisation and Kemalist/nationalist resistance to the former have taken place simultaneously and thus we can say that those changes are mutually constitutive. While the embrace of post-Kemalist norms by some elites has motivated a Kemalist counter-reaction, the latter nationalist and extreme nationalist acts have also motivated conservatives to expend more effort in socialising the community into post-Kemalist norms.

We listed the initiatives run by post-Kemalist norm adherents above and we now list the nationalist responses to them.

In the political realm, the reactionary discourse took the form of blaming those who voted for or became candidates for an Albanian-majority party as having "converted to Albianhood", something which was argued by a prominent political figure in the Turkish community during an interview (Interview LE15). The necessity of voting for Turkish parties thus became a prerequisite for remaining a Turk. A conservative respondent shared his/her experience about this issue as follows:

> People criticised me for becoming a candidate for city council elections as part of an Albanian (majority) party. If you pursue education in Albanian language and vote for an Albanian party, you cannot be a Turk. If you are a Turk you must be educated in the Turkish language, you must vote for the Turkish party. This is a [dominant] consideration.
>
> (Interview LE21)

Indeed, in the realm of education, too, nationalist elites are critical of every alternative to Turkish-language education. This can be seen in their criticism of those who chose Albanian-language education. A high-ranking elite interviewed during my scoping visit had this to say about the issue: "if a Turkish child goes to school which instructs in the Albanian language, s/he starts acting like an Albanian" (Pers. Comm. SVN6). A stronger argument came from a local education expert "[i]f an ethnic Turks goes to education in Albanian language, s/he loses his/her Turkishness . . . The education in Turkish language is the main path for maintaining their ethnicity in Kosovo" (Pers. Comm. SVN3). In another example, when Recep Tayyip Erdoğan suggested to the Turkish community that they go to Albanian-language schools, parts of the community reacted fiercely. Here is one of the reactions of a local teacher:

> Prime Minister Erdoğan was ripped to pieces by the Turkish community when he said that they should not insist on Turkish education and suggested they pursue education in the Albanian language instead . . . We are very sensitive to Turkish education; if we managed to protect our Turkishness under Yugoslav rule, we can [better] sustain it today. We do not want Turkey to act in this way . . . We want Turkey take care of us not as Kosovar people, but as Turks.
>
> (Interview LE12)

A similar response was given to one of the former Turkish military commanders in Kosovo when he suggested to the community that they might form mixed classes. Below is a response to such advice by a local politician:

> The Tabur commander suggests forming mixed classes where both Albanian and Turkish students could come together. This is wrong. It is the reflection of a lack of knowledge about [how things work] here. What keeps the Turks alive in Kosovo is Turkish-language education, its sustenance is vital. If the classes conjoin, half of the teachers among the Turkish community will fall out of work. Then, the Turks will vanish.
>
> (Pers. Comm. SVN7)

They therefore do not tolerate discussions about alternatives to Turkish-language education and they cannot stand non-nationalist policy alternatives.

The functioning of post-Kemalist norms makes secular nationalists feel that "it has become harder for one to declare him/herself a Turk" in Kosovo.[10] Therefore, to them, the JDP government jeopardises the survival of Turkishness and makes it harder for them to survive as Turks in Kosovo. A local nationalist elite presented the hardships they face thus: "Turkey is in Kosovo but we have not relieved yet. We should have felt relieved. Rather, we are expending much effort today to protect our Turkishness" (Pers. Comm. SVN4). The closing down of *Yeni Dönem* newspaper in 2008 for its heavily nationalist stance or the lack of funding given to Türkevi (Turkish house) from official sources in Turkey due to the same reason has contributed to the surfacing of such feelings according to nationalist elites (Interview LE4, Interview LE14). Such a discomfort stemming from the alleged harm done by Turkey's policies towards Turkishness in Kosovo was articulated in several different contexts. A local academic, accordingly, stated that:

> With the JDP's coming to power in Turkey, Turks in Kosovo have lost ... Turkishness has lost ... the Turkish community in Kosovo has become so worried, because [they knew that] JDP was not going to give importance to Turkishness.
>
> (Interview LE6)

Expressing a similar discomfort, a local artist argued that:

> We have withstood wars, yet we still feel that we are in danger,
> even though Turkey is in Kosovo with all its means ... The
> motherland, Turkey, comes and annihilates the Turks here ...
> You can be a brother in religion [and history] with Bosnians or
> Albanians ... but I am a true brother to Turkey, I am a Turk ...
> Am I a biological child or just a kin to you?.. I fought for
> Turkishness here in the absence of you for a century; you
> cannot treat me as you treat Albanians or Bosnians.
>
> (Interview LE10)

Another nationalist argued that:

> We have always been "co-nationals" ... but now they do not dare
> to call us Turk ... The Prime Minister Erdoğan came to here and
> gave a speech in Shadirvan. He did not call us "Turks", not even a
> single time ... They do this intentionally; their aim is to establish
> a Muslim nation not a Turkish nation ...
>
> (Interview LE9)

In a similar tone, a nationalist teacher claimed that:

> Erdoğan keeps calling for "unity in Islam with your Albanian
> brothers" ... If they had the chance, they [the JDP] would ask us
> to close down the KDTP and form a new Muslim party with other
> ethnic groups.
>
> (Interview LE14)

In another development that has sparked condemnation from nationalist
circles, some community members, as a post-Kemalist practice, began to
questioning the legacy of Atatürk. This was a very shocking development
for secular nationalists who equate being Turkish to loving Kemal
Atatürk. This act is depicted by a local journalist as follows:

> Atatürk's legacy was never discussed this much before.
> [However] today his name is mentioned very often and the
> way Atatürk is perceived by the community is changing. Due to

the conservatives within the community, people now say about Atatürk that he was an alcoholic ... This is said by both old and young people ... There are even teachers among the new generation spreading the seeds of hostility towards Atatürk.

(Interview LE13)

A nationalist elite also noted that:

It is so sad that the children we send to Turkey through the Great Student Exchange programme are coming back hostile to Atatürk; they were Kemalists before going to Turkey [and we thought that] they would come back as more dedicated Kemalists ... Our children are brainwashed by some anti-Kemalist circles in Turkey regarding Atatürk's deeds.

(Interview LE9)

Having seen that most of the post-Kemalist norm entrepreneurs are graduates from Turkey, this quotation reveals the extent of the impact of de-ethnicised nationhood on the community. Secular nationalists have dealt with such denunciations of Atatürk with much discomfort. It was a disturbing development for them. In this sense, the ten days' long commemorations of Atatürk (the 10 November commemorations), while it is only a one day commemoration in Turkey, is, in addition to its other functions, also a response to such anti-nationalist and anti-Kemalist shifts within the community.

This reactionary stance has also been supported by the Tabur. Although its capabilities were limited, it fuelled the contestation of post-Kemalist norms, and contributed to the Kemalist resistance and prevention of post-Kemalist norms being fully internalised. By sticking to the traditional Kemalist approach to Turkishness, Tabur promoted ethnic Turkishness discursively and representatively in support of local nationalists mentioned above. It was at this juncture that, for instance, the aforementioned ten days' long commemorations of Atatürk or "Teachers' Day" were organised in a joint venture by local nationalist circles and the Turkish Tabur.

The celebration of the yearly "Teachers' Day" in the Turkish military base in November is also a case in point, with invitations sent out to all teachers. As an example, in 2005 the Turkish Tabur organised a poetry and painting contest for this celebration. The theme of the Teachers' Day contest was based on the idea of "Atatürk as the head teacher".[11] In another example, the motto of the 2008 Atatürk Commemoration week which was jointly organised by Filizler Kemalist Turkish Culture and Arts Association and the Turkish Tabur was "Atatürk, we are on your track" (*Atam İzindeyiz Booklet* 2009: 2). Ferhat Derviş, the head of Filizler Association argued for the importance of Atatürk to Kosovar Turks during the opening speech to the above that: "we learned how to be Turk from Atatürk ... A Turkish community who does not follow Atatürk will eventually fade away [lose its Turkishness], regardless of the place it is settled" (Ibid.: 28). He suggested that the local community must hold onto the legacy of Atatürk more tightly. To him, this was needed, not because of the threat that the Albanians or other communities pose to ethnic Turks; it was needed to protect national identity, not surprisingly, from Turkey's post-Kemalist influences. Atatürk, at this very juncture, is attributed with the meaning of resistance to post-Kemalist Turkey. One of my self-declaredly Kemalist academic respondents accordingly stated that:

> No matter how far they push to take Atatürk out of Kosovar Turks' daily lives and cultural events, it is impossible to achieve this ... When you say Kosovar Turkishness, Atatürk is at the epicentre of such nationalism. Some groups try to bring forth denunciations of Atatürk and spread these among the Turkish community; they cannot achieve it ... This is because Kosovar Turks firstly value Atatürk as their townsman [*hemşeri*][12] and they, secondly, believe that they owe their Turkish consciousness and nationalism to Atatürk.
>
> (Interview LE5)

In this fashion, those special festivals were part of the practices of Kemalism that gave the Tabur the required opportunities to deliver Kemalist messages more directly and to recall the Kemalist imagination of Turkish identity, as part of resistance against post-Kemalist norms. Tabur therefore has been making use of the institutionalisation of these Kemalist practices as a way of opening alternative discursive fields against the dominant post-Kemalist institutionally backed discourses. It is this stance which made one of my secular nationalist respondents to argue that "our Tabur acts responsibly and behaves sympathetically in saving Turkish identity" (Interview LE5).

In short, Turkey's non-concern for ethnicity has had anti-nationalist constitutive influences in Kosovo and created an elite with a commitment to going beyond ethnicity in their relation with the Kosovo state and other communities. On the other hand, the functioning of de-ethnicised nationhood has also caused a sharpening of nationalist discourses within the community whereby nationalism has gained a reactionary character and generated resistance against post-Kemalism. Moreover, the ethnic Turkish community and the Turkish Tabur have made use of Atatürk to prevent the internalisation of post-Kemalist norms in general and de-ethnicised nationhood in particular. Atatürk has been cast as a historically significant to learning about and cherishing their national identity. However, after the coming of post-Kemalist norms to Kosovo, Atatürk has become a tool to fuel reactionary positions against post-Kemalist norms and a tool to 'protect national identity'.

Responses to Turkish Islam's Functioning

Islam has been present in Kosovo as a daily practice and a representation of identity for centuries. It was historically represented in the form of two intermingled institutional bodies: on the one hand the Caliph and the supreme religious authority in Istanbul, the capital of the Ottoman Empire and, on the other, the diverse *tekke*s throughout the Balkans. The former was based on the Hanafi School of Law, while the other was mostly based on Bektashi Orders. When the Ottoman Empire withdrew from Kosovo in 1912, the religious legacy left was mainly in the form of mosques, later run by the Yugoslav religious authorities, and tekkes, many of which were closed down during the following decades. Today, in Kosovo, Islam is institutionally represented by the central religious authority (Riyaset) on the one hand and a handful of tekkes on the other. We may also note a third actor to come the fore in the 1990s, that is, a broadly defined group of "Salafi" Muslims. People in Kosovo, including the Turkish community, mostly follow the Riyaset and the Hanafi School, while acknowledging the authenticity of the local tekkes. However, more recent manifestations of religious thought are contested as "foreign". The

Turkish community supports the Diyanet's close relations with the Riyaset in Kosovo and their joint efforts to preserve what they see as an Ottoman version of official Islam. This also strengthens the Turkish community's positive view of the Riyaset. Similar fondness has not been shown to Salafi religious groups. The functioning of Turkish Islam and the ethnic Turkish community's socialisation into it, therefore, have taken place within this given cultural context and have been culturally validated within this scope.

This cultural context, in the case of Turkish Islam, has been advantageous as it has provided norm entrepreneurs of all backgrounds, from Turkey's diplomatic missions, religious groups and local norm entrepreneurs, with the necessary ground to operate. In many instances, these operations are very much welcomed by the community. The first of these is related to joint efforts to protect Ottoman artefacts from Salafi – or, as the community calls them, "Wahhabi groups" – and their alleged aims to destroy these. In this sense, for instance, when TIKA "rescued" the Murat Bey mosque in Janjevo from being destroyed and rebuilt in an "Arab" architectural style, the local community came to greatly appreciate this. As mentioned earlier, Ottoman artefacts are vital in the eyes of Kosovar Turks for their cultural and political survival as an ethnic group. In a second example, similar to the first, the protection of the dominant religious culture in their community is also of profound importance to the Turkish community. It is with this in mind that the actions of norm entrepreneurs have been validated, while any move against this is denounced. A local nationalist, in this sense, stated in the interview that:

In the Balkans, particularly in Prizren, there is a moderate Islam, there is a tolerant Islam. It is tolerant to other religions ... This state of mind was created by a centuries, long Turkish Islamic tradition, it is our tradition, it is our world view. While there is this tradition here, some groups try to break this ... [These] Wahhabi groups are very dangerous for the Turkish community ... There are Turkish religious groups operating in Kosovo, for instance, Süleymancıs. They call themselves Turks and they mind their own business. They do not stand in the way of our local associations. They do not become rivals to us; they do not compete with us. When we need assistance, they support us, however [the Wahhabi groups] try to impose their own culture as a true Islamic belief. [The Wahhabi groups say to us that] "Your culture is wrong". [We in response say to these groups that] My culture [Turkish religious culture] is different than yours [referring to the so-called Wahhabis here].

(Interview LE9)

In the above quotation, it is evident that "Turkish Islam" is considered to be an authentic belief and the so-called Wahhabi one to be alien and posing a threat. In this sense, the community became more welcoming towards the post-Kemalist norm entrepreneurs' socialisation efforts in the scope of Turkish Islam. Nonetheless, it would be misleading to argue that their closeness to Turkish Islam is because of the so-called Wahhabi menace. In fact, the idea of a Wahhabi threat is not central to Turkish elites: elites reason Turkish/Ottoman Islamic practices as tolerant, moderate, and more apt to the cultural context in Kosovo. They therefore consider such practices superior to the so-called Wahhabi-Islam. As a consequence of such arguments centred on claims to superiority, they oppose so-called Wahhabi-Islam. It is at this juncture that, despite the discourses on the threat that Wahhabism poses, elites confidently and proudly argue that "Turks have nothing to do with the Wahhabis" (Interview LE17). Below are two concomitant observations about the issue, one by a local elite and the other by a Diyanet official:

Wahhabism does not have any appeal among the Turkish community because the Turkish community learn religion from their families and does not want an outsider to teach their religion to them (Interview LE34).

Wahhabism has almost no influence among the Turkish community. This is because Turks in Kosovo are culturally committed to [Turkish Islam] . . . There is religious consciousness among the Turks. Even though they are not practising Muslims, they have managed to protect themselves through saying that we follow Turkey in religion (Interview DM1).

If the community is seen as immune to Wahhabi Islam, why do we see so much discussion about it? The perceived danger, in this respect, is the idea that there are "alien" groups targeting the Turkish identity. Accordingly, the so-called Wahhabis are considered hostile to Turkish/ Ottoman culture and its religious legacy, two of the core components of Turkishness in Kosovo. It is in this context that local elites support Turkey's efforts to preserve Ottoman heritage in Kosovo.

Moreover, another reason why local elites give support to the Turkish Islamic causes is that the community has long known of and supported the promotion of figures such as Yunus Emre and Rumi. These two are part of the local culture with Yunus Emre, for example, known as "Baba Yunus, an important figure for the local Sufi orders and the common people" (*Atam İzindeyiz Booklet* 2009: 71). Moreover, Yunus Emre's contribution to the development of the Turkish language has always been acknowledged, with the community organising a celebration of his 650th birthday in 1971 (*Tan* 8 January 1971). Likewise, the community has also organised "Rumi Week" events and commemorations ever since the 1990s which were followed with the establishment of Kosovo Mevlana (Rumi) Culture Association in December 2005 (Recepoğlu 2007: 97, 226). In this sense, having remembered the "Wahhabis" as having been against Sufism, the community elites have welcomed these historical figures' use against the so-called Wahhabi threat and they alike have readily utilised them as local authentic representatives of the practice of Turkish Islam (*Doğruyol Derneği 60. Yıl Kataloğu* 2012: 53, *TIKA Faaliyet Raporu* 2008, *Yeni Dönem* 20 October 2005).

However, not every protectionist move has been welcomed by the community. For example, religious groups which attempt to make the wearing of the hijab, a traditional practice among women in the community, has led to contestation from some members of the community, particularly from the secular nationalist circles. This is because some of the teachings of Turkish Islam, particularly as regards the performance of the hijab or the growing of the beard, are contested issues in the community with debates about these on-going. It is at this juncture that the community starts seeing the functioning of Turkish Islam as a threat, despite the fact that it is through this practice which cultural and religious heritage is being taken care of and indeed welcomed by this community. Their criticism of religious groups begins at this juncture. The argumentation taking place about hijab is instructive:

Recently, unfortunately, there has been an increase in the wearing of the hijab ... it is mainly the Süleymancıs who make [Turkish] girls wear the hijab ... Among the teachers [of the Turkish community], up until 5 or 6 years ago none wore it ... Due to the influence of religious groups there are now teachers wearing the hijab (Interview LE9).

Teachers historically never used the hijab in Kosovo [he refers to the post-1951 era]. Hijab is something new here. People still do not show much interest, yet there are some among the youth ... They wear hijab ... This is because of the religious groups from Turkey operating in Kosovo ... I personally prohibited my family to go to the meetings of those religious groups (Interview LE4).

By the 1950s no one wore hijab in schools ... [however] wearing the hijab has been revived recently ... [and] in the future there will be [more] hijab-wearing teachers in schools (Interview LE1).

Turkey's Islamic groups, such as the Nurcus and Süleymancıs try to transfer the Islamic organisation and structure from Turkey to here ... they are mostly influential in making women wear the hijab.

(Interview LE5)

Discomfort at the influence of religious groups is uttered mostly by the secular nationalist elites. Nonetheless, there are elites, particularly among conservative ones, who do not see the hijab's gaining public appearance as an adverse development. They confirm however that the influence of religious groups from Turkey has led to an increase in the number of hijab wearers in this community. A conservative norm entrepreneur admittedly argued that:

The religious groups in Kosovo have played an important role in the increase of the hijab wearers in Kosovo, but particularly among the ethnic Turkish community.

(Interview LE8)

Contrary to secular nationalists, conservatives are not annoyed at the site of the Turkish women wearing the hijab, nor do they find it odd (Interview LE5). In fact, they are rather supportive. A Diyanet official argued that:

There is now a number of covered [wearing the hijab] teachers working in Turkish schools. In Mamusha it is even promoted. Moreover, at the municipal level the major himself encourages them to not hesitate in wearing the hijab during work.

(Interview DM2)

The division between conservatives and secular nationalists becomes clearer here. While the conservatives are happy that hijab is becoming popular, "[t]he hijab ban in the public sphere is viewed as something good" by secular nationalists (Interview LE31). They therefore "do not see the hijab as a prerequisite" for being or remaining Muslim (Interview LE8). A secular nationalist justifies their approach to hijab as follows:

We are already Muslims. We have not diverted much from religious values. We still do the mawlids and *kandil*s, and fast in Ramadan. We never ignored these religious values.

(Interview LE31)

The discomfort felt by secular nationalists at the influence on local practices of Islam therefore turns to a discomfort of religious groups in general. Religious groups from Turkey therefore have become securitised, denounced and demonised in a way similar to the so-called Wahhabi groups. It is in this scope that a local secular nationalist confidently argued that "[w]e call the religious groups deviants" (Interview LE4). Still, they continue to trust and follow the Diyanet. This is because, to one official from the Süleymancı group:

Turks don't want their religion to be thought to them by religious groups. To them, the only legitimate religious authority to come to Kosovo is Atatürk's Diyanet.

(Interview RG1)

As an institution founded upon the decree of Atatürk, this makes the Diyanet more acceptable in the eyes of the Kosovar Turks. A local nationalist, accordingly, argued that "Diyanet is fine but the religious groups are dangerous" (Interview LE2). Indeed, a local administrator from the Turkish party boldly declared that "KDTP has no relationship with religious groups, [but] it does [have a relationship] with Diyanet"

(Interview LE19). Such a secular nationalist approach is also found in the organisation which holds firmest to the Kemalist identity – the Turkish Tabur with one informant from the Turkish community similarly arguing that the Tabur is "distant from religious groups" (Interview LE16). This is because, to my respondent, "they do not share the same political identity as the Tabur" (Interview LE16). Here, the identity in question is undoubtedly Kemalism. Therefore, the Diyanet is thought of as a good Kemalist institution, while religious groups are in some respects a threat to this. This is because there are indeed certain things that Diyanet does for the community which serve to promote Turkishness. A local nationalist, for instance, argues that "Diyanet's presence in Kosovo contributes to the Turkish community ... through [if nothing but] delivering khutbah and sermon in Turkish language in the Sinan Pasha mosque" (Interview LE17). Diyanet's role was influential also in persuading families to send their female children to school, when a new high school was opened in Mamusha in 2008. Accordingly, Diyanet officials accompanied officials from the Tabur and the Zübeyde Hanım Association (a local Kemalist women association) when they visited homes in Mamusha to talk to families regarding registration of their daughters to high school (Interview LE26, Interview LE22, Interview DM2). This affirms the secular nationalist and Kemalist role casted to Diyanet. Therefore, Turkish Islam is reinterpreted by the secular nationalist segment of the Turkish community as a Kemalist application of Islam.

The secular nationalist discomfort at religious groups and their "deviancy" is further supported by the claims that:

> Today in Kosovo ... conservative families mostly become religious group members. In school, for example, while telling the students about the national salvation period in Turkey, children of conservative families slam Atatürk ... We used not to hear such things among the Kosovar Turks before. Now, they denounce Atatürk for being a drinker etc ... The conservatives criticise Atatürk for drinking alcohol, for abolishing the khalifah [the Caliphate] and for changing the Arabic alphabet.
>
> (Interview LE12)

Turkey's religious groups, therefore, are blamed also for spreading hostility towards Atatürk. This is indeed in line with the conservatives' expectation from them; as one of my local respondents stated "[t]oday, the Turkish community itself invites Turkey's religious groups to Kosovo to be able to cope with the Kemalist elite" (Interview LE18). It is at this juncture that those who are perceived as acting against Atatürk or nationalism are accused of being a member of a religious group (*cemaatçi*). As seen, when it comes to the local secular cultural context, Turkey's religious groups are demonised similar to the way the so-called Wahhabis are accused of being anti-Turkist.

In sum, the cultural context becomes crucial to understanding the degree of internalisation of Turkish Islam. While conservatives mostly embrace the "Turkish Islam" defended by both Diyanet and religious groups, the secular nationalist segment of society approach Turkish Islam from a nationalist angle and, for instance, view religious groups as a threat to "Turkishness". They agree with religious groups as long as their discourse(s) and actions help them to protect their ethnic identity. When and if religious groups suggest things contrary to their secular cultural worldview, they begin to denounce such approaches. In this sense, secular nationalists are localising Turkish Islam, while the conservatives endorse it and both trends can be seen in the promotion of this by norm entrepreneurs.

Responses to Islamic Internationalism's Functioning

The ethnic Turkish community – declared boldly by almost all members without exception or hesitation – call themselves Muslim. Building on the fact that historically speaking both Albanian and Bosnian Muslims had referred to themselves as "Turk" as a synonym for "Muslim", the Turkish community view being a Turk as meaning being Muslim and argue that if Turks will disappear from Kosovo, so will Islam. However, this commitment is not reflected at the practical level with many people disinterested in certain practices discussed below. Yet they perform certain religious practices as cultural events. In this scope, for instance, they see themselves as the successors of the Ottoman religious and cultural heritage, work to protect the tekkes, celebrate Ramadan and other religious bajrams and "special nights", circumcise their male children, and partly follow religious teachings regarding dress. However, until the 1990s they showed no interest at all in writing about religion or in training their own imams or sending their children to theology faculties or madrasas. This nonetheless did not deter them from having concerns about upholding their religious identity. Their understanding of religion and religious practice is however driven by nationalism and cultural concerns and is a complex issue (see *Yeni Dönem* 10 February 2005). Here is a secular nationalist elite's take on this complexity:

> There is an attempt to Christianise Kosovo and they will succeed in this. The first and foremost step in this is wiping out the Turkish language from Kosovo. If you wipe out Turkish from Kosovo you will wipe out also the religion [Islam] ... If Turkish goes away then Islam will go away too ... [Therefore] the struggle for Turkish language is also a struggle for the religion. The most religious community in Kosovo are the Turks.
>
> (Pers. Comm. SVN4)

As is apparent, secular nationalists brand their nationalist struggle as a religious one too with the idea of "acting for the cause of Turkishness" becoming "acting for Islam". However, this framing is a relatively recent development, because such people have not historically acted in the cause of their religious identity in an activist manner. Particularly during the socialist era, there was almost an absolute disregard for religion among, in particular, the elite members of the ethnic Turkish community. A local theatre performer, accordingly, stated that:

> In the socialist era, we were as free as possible in practising our religion. Yet, we were not keen on being a practitioner and since the secularism [as suggested by Atatürk] [Turkish: *laiklik*] was apt for communism, we inevitably distanced ourselves from religion.
>
> (Interview LE3)

Here, the reason for their distancing themselves from religious practice was the socialist regime and their compliance to the regime's wishes; however, their taking of Kemalist Turkey as an example for ethnic survival also facilitated this. Therefore, on the one hand it was the socialist regime and on the other their devotion to Kemalism is what prevented them acting along their religious identity, writing about it or even learning about it. Nonetheless, by the late 1980s and throughout the 1990s, religion made a swift re-entry into the community, particularly among the elites of the Turkish community. Religious issues were discussed in the publications of the Turkish community. For instance, the old secular academic journal, Çevren began publishing papers on the Qur'an or mawlid, and also began to discuss figures such as Yunus Emre as a dervish and a poet (Çevren, Vols 85–6, 1991, Çevren, Vols 90–2, 1992). The *Tan* newspaper also began publishing columns or sections on religious issues, rituals, cultures and historical figures – all of which have recalled the Muslimness of the Turkish community in Kosovo.[13] Likewise, intellectuals wrote poems on religion and religious issues such as Ramadan or the Prophet Muhammad[14] (*Türk Yazarlar Derneği* 1996: 14, Baki 2011: 80).

By the same token, since the community did not have imams to deliver religious services in the mosques, they "got in touch with Diyanet in 1990 and requested from them to send imams and preachers to Prizren and Mamusha to deliver religious services during Ramadan" (Recepoğlu 2006: 90). They began to complain that "due to the absence of religious cadres the Kosovar Turks are devoid of Turkish sermons and khutbas, [and] the children miss out on religious education" (Ibid.: 89). It was thus in the 1990s that the Turkish community began expressing the idea that in order to survive it had to preserve its religious identity too, along with its ethnic identity.[15] Their "calls for Turkey to help", as Altay Suroy calls it, carries importance in this regard (Ibid.). Requesting imams from Turkey was followed by the community beginning to send students to Turkey to study in imam-hatip schools and theology faculties with the expectation that after completing their schooling they would return and protect the religious identity of the community (Ibid.: 90). This was a move to compensate for the abandoning of religious education and identity during the socialist era.

Due to the surfacing of concerns for religion, some local nationalists claim that "in the 1990s people became more observant in religion, [because] people saw it as a path to salvation" (Interview LE2). This cannot, however, be considered an ideological change. This is because religion became for the community a subject matter worthy of importance only after a suitable place for Atatürk in it was found. This led them to discover a religious side to Atatürk in order to justify their new position vis-à-vis religion.[16] This is similar to the community's approach to

Turkish Islam as a Kemalist religious practice. It was according to this that the journal Çevren, every time it published an issue on religion or religious identity, included articles on Atatürk and his glories alongside these (see Çevren, Vols 85–6, 1991; Çevren, Vols 90–2, 1992). Community elites also adopted a similar approach during the socialist era when they discovered a "socialist" side to Kemalist teachings. To do so, socialist-oriented Kemalists in Turkey such as Yaşar Nabi Nayır, Fazıl Hüsnü Dağlarca, Aziz Nesin were used as inspiration for the community in finding the required overlap between Kemalism and socialism (Interview LE20, Interview LE35, Recepoğlu 2006: 56–7; also see Chapter 5). Therefore, those who called Atatürk a "comrade" during the socialist era now began calling him a "model Muslim" in the 1990s. To this end, they composed poems on the "Muslimness" of Atatürk. For instance, Süleyman Brina, a professor of linguistics and a leading socialist Turkish nationalist wrote these lines in 1990:

> I said Ata* to call Sina**
> I said Ata to call Sinan***
> I said Ata to call Yunus****
> I said Ata to call civilisation.[17]

> (*Tan* 7 July 1990)

In this way, the "Muslimness" of Atatürk was constructed so as to build a safe link to justify the new-found concern for religion in the community. This is another form of branding their nationalist struggle as a religious one too, which was most visible during the 2000s (see *Yeni Dönem* 6 November 2003).

Nonetheless, by the time we begin to see the vast institutional presence of Turkey in Kosovo after the NATO intervention, the concern for religion acquired a different character. People now began to declare their commitment to Islam without reference to Atatürk. Today it is more common for one to see a hijabi-clad woman on the streets; community members attend Qur'an teaching schools in significant numbers; Holy Birth Week events are well-attended; children are sent to imam-hatip schools and theology faculties in Turkey; we also see more references to the Muslim identity of the Turks in Kosovo in literary writings emanating from the community. By the same token, it was reported by both community members and Diyanet officials that the number of people going to hajj has increased. Whether the confidence in religious practices and identity comes to mean an increase in religiosity or not is still contested. However, as a matter of fact, there are people who "previously were leading figures in the communist party ... [or] had nothing to do with the religion nor went to mosque ... now writing [books] on Islam" (Interview LE10). Confirming this, for instance, a former socialist author and poet of several poems on Tito, Enver Baki, recently published a novel titled *Adem Agha's Religious Lectures* which narrates the story of informal religious education in a Turkish-populated neighbourhood in Pristina during the socialist era (Baki 2013). The book was published by TIKA. All these therefore confirm what a local journalist argued:

> After 1999, people immediately commenced acting as Muslims ...
> Those who wrote poems, songs on socialist international [during the Yugoslav era] immediately became practising Muslims and they started promoting this ... There is an increase in the number of hijab wearers also among the Turks. It used not to be like this: old women used the traditional scarf to cover their hair. Now, girls also cover their hair ... Moreover, in wedding ceremonies female and male guests sit separately. It was not like this historically, the ceremonies were celebrated together. [Similarly], now women and men have started not to shake hands with the opposite sex ... Alcohol is now not served in ceremonies, which was a custom until 2002 ... Turkish politicians do not drink, nor serve alcohol in their events. You can no longer see them drinking publicly.
>
> (Interview LE13)

For this journalist, all of this suggests an increase in religiosity among the community. On the other hand, for some, the religiosity among the Turkish community should not be exaggerated. A conservative elite thus argued that:

> Turks rarely perform the daily prayers. This should be admitted honestly. For the last 10 years they started practising weekly Friday prayers. 10–15 years ago you would never have seen Turks in the mosques.
>
> (Interview LE6)

Whether people became more religious or not, there is an undeniable fact that Islam has become a bold frame of reference in many fields. As reviewed in Chapter 7, for instance, the Ottoman/Islamic experience of compromise and reconciliation among Muslim ethnic groups has been actively promoted as a model which should be embraced to regulate inter-ethnic affairs. Moreover, the Islamic history of the country is recalled more often and the contributions of Albanians and Bosnians to Islamic civilisation are also underlined more often, along with the Muslimness of ethnic Turks – something which is constantly emphasised. In this sense, particularly among conservatives, the "over-concern" about ethnicity among members of the Turkish community has declared a threat to the "brotherhood" among Muslim communities in Kosovo. Taken together with the fact that officials from Turkey "perform" certain identities during official visits on special occasions such as Ramadan, all this has begun to exemplify and help in the revival of what can be called "religious identity driven framing".

The prominence of religious issues, however, has not led to Islam becoming the prime identity marker for the community. Rather, there have been negative reactions. Some members of the community, particularly the secular nationalist ones, see Turkey's use of the idea of "religious brotherhood" rather than "ethnic brotherhood" when approaching the Turkish community as a threat. The community's embrace of a religious identity is also seen as a threat to the ethnic survival of the community. They even see this as a development that would destroy Turkishness in Kosovo. Accordingly, an MP from the community complained that:

> It is so sad that unfortunately we are viewed as a Muslim community. Praise be to God [Alhamdulillah] we are Muslims, we do not deny our religion, we are proud of it. Yet, we are Turks . . . It would be wrong to call us Kosovar Muslim Turks . . . because we do not differ at all from Turks living in Turkey, except as regards our place of residence.
>
> (Interview LE26)

In relation to this, any state of affairs requiring them to put their ethnic identity aside while privileging their religious identity troubles them a lot. Adopting pro-Islamic discourse to politically reconcile relations between Albanians and Turks, for instance, causes reactions and a backlash. A local nationalist reacts to the efforts of this kind as follows: 'If you say "do not call yourself Turk, rather call yourself Muslim", you only encourage Albanians to come down on our necks' (Interview LE15).

They, therefore, want to be treated and represented as an ethnic community and they fear any alternative would lead to the destruction of their ethnic identity in Kosovo. Nevertheless, there occurs a contradiction here. On the one hand, as mentioned above, they consider the fight for Turkishness as a fight for Islam while, on the other, the embracement of Islam as an identity is considered to pose a threat for their ethnic survival. Islam, therefore, is tolerated as an identity as long as it serves their nationalist causes. The secular nationalists, in a similar fashion, resort to Islamic discourse to save their ethnic identity from the adverse effects of Turkey's pro-Islamic approach. They argue that Islam does not allow Turkey to "destroy their race" and they want Turkey to stop approaching them with reference to Islam. Altay Suroy, then a member of Kosovo's Constitutional Court, wrote in a 2005 book that:

> [W]e accept that our language is a gift given to us by Allah. Therefore, we give importance to our mother tongue and we owe Him to protect and maintain such a gift. Fighting for this cause given to us by Allah is a divine aim for us.
>
> (Recepoğlu 2005: 215)

Another nationalist also argued that:

> Allah created both race and languages when creating human beings. Now they are trying to destroy the former. This is what Allah created; we did not create it [the race]. Is it not against religion [to destroy our race]?
>
> (Interview LE9)

As we can see, religion here is again used in the service of nationalism. A final discussion of this kind, this time with a Diyanet official, is instructive here:

> The importance of Diyanet for the Turkish community in Kosovo is that it delivers khutbah and sermon in the Turkish

language in the Sinan Pasha Mosque. For them, the religious messages of the talks are not necessary, what is important is that the message is given in the Turkish language.

(Interview DM1)

This is how religion and religious identity is understood and made use by the community elites. Accordingly, Islam is approached with tolerance only when it enhances the secular nationalists' cause. Otherwise use of it is interpreted as a threat.

In short, for Turkey, Islamic Internationalism has been a challenge to the long transformation of a religiously defined and organised society into a national community. In the example of Kosovar Turks, it has manifested itself as practices of transforming an ethnically organised and nationalist community into a religiously thinking and acting one, while still remaining "Turks". For the conservatives this has facilitated the prominence of the religious component of Turkish identity. For the secular nationalists, however, this functioning of the norm became a discourse which could be embraced only when it was used in the service of defending their nationalist cause and to brand their nationalist struggle as also a religious one. The real religious content, for this group, caused a backlash against it.

Conclusion

This chapter aimed to disclose the implications of post-Kemalist norms and foreign policy for the ethnic Turkish community in Kosovo. The application of the third stage and the relevant mechanisms of the framework for analysing overseas implications of domestic norms (see Fig. 4.2) has shown that such a policy from Turkey has had constitutive influences on the ethnic Turkish community. The functioning of post-Kemalist norms has, in a broader sense, created a secular nationalist versus conservative divide within the Turkish community. The response to requests for norm compliance and the internalisation of norms have been articulated within the scope of this division. Therefore, within the community, there were different and competing responses to norm internalisation attempts; while the conservatives mostly internalised post-Kemalist norms, the secular nationalists rejected them. The division, therefore, made each group grab hold of either Kemalism or post-Kemalism more tightly. In this sense, while the post-Kemalist norms became a means to replace Kemalist tendencies historically present within the community, Kemalism in turn gained a reactionary character and began to serve as the main tool to "protect" the community from the adverse effects of post-Kemalism which were, according to secular nationalists, threatening the "survival of Turkishness in Kosovo".

Based on this historic–cultural context, the functioning of Ottomania has mostly appealed to the conservatives with the result that, for this group at least, the idea of restoring positive inter-ethnic relations present during Ottoman times has been reified in the minds of many conservatives and relations with Albanians have become more positive. For secular nationalists, however, its functioning has led them to ethnicise the Ottomans against any attempt de-ethnicisation. Ottomania, therefore, could not break the dominant nationalist frames and has actually strengthened them in another sign of reactionary nationalism. Therefore, although Ottomania gained ground, its internalisation has not been completed.

Similarly, de-ethnicised nationhood could not deconstruct the dominant nationalist frames. It has in fact been counter-productive. Its functioning has caused a sharpening of nationalist discourses and frames in the scope of which nationalism has gained a reactionary character and generated a resistance against post-Kemalism. Accordingly, people now believe that their ethnic survival is jeopardised by Turkey's anti-nationalism and "anti-Turkism". Moreover, Atatürk has become a reactionary tool used to "protect national identity" and has been utilised by secular nationalists and the Turkish Tabur to prevent the internalisation of de-ethnicised nationhood in the community. On the other hand, the functioning of de-ethnicised nationhood facilitated for conservative elites to go beyond ethnicity in organising their relations with Albanians and Bosnians. Nonetheless, its constitutive influences could not save it from being the most contested and least embraced post-Kemalist norm in Kosovo.

Turkish Islam is the only norm all parts of the community accept, yet it is internalised by some and localised by others. Its localisation is done via the secular nationalist denunciations of religious groups while only accepting the Diyanet as the sole representative of a Kemalist-inspired understanding of religion. The Tabur and historical Kemalist frames have facilitated such a conclusion. Religious groups, here, are accused of changing local culture by encouraging the wearing of the hijab or by expressing hostile attitudes about Atatürk and Kemalist values. Meanwhile, the Diyanet is given the role of a "Kemalist institution" that protects both the local practice of Islam and Turkish identity. Turkish Islam, in this sense, is localised by the secular nationalist elites as a Kemalist religious practice that neither threatens existing religio-cultural practices nor Turkish identity.

Islamic Internationalism, similar to Ottomania and de-ethnicised nationhood, has also not been firmly internalised by the community, nor has it managed to break the dominant nationalist frames. Similar to the above issues, the promotion of this norm has caused a fierce reaction from secular nationalists and can thus be said to be counter-productive to the spread of post-Kemalist norms. Due to the presence of this norm, Islam and the community's Muslim identity have become bold frames of reference in many fields including politics and everyday productions of art and literature. However, the secular nationalists have used it at the service of their nationalist aims, embracing it only to brand their nationalist struggle as a battle for religion too.

The existent Kemalist frames and the Turkish Tabur, therefore, adversely affected the internalisation of post-Kemalist norms. Moreover the division caused by the presence of post-Kemalist norms within society – the division between conservatives and secular nationalists – has deepened due to the Turkish Tabur's use of Kemalism to prevent the internalisation of post-Kemalist norms. Tabur thus functioned as a counter-entrepreneur and encouraged the local elites to hold more firmly to their Kemalist cultural background as a means to resist post-Kemalist socialisation efforts. Due to the use of historical Kemalist frames regarding nationality and national history and by presenting Atatürk himself as a source and reference of resistance, post-Kemalist norms have become mostly contested and are coded as destructive.

Nevertheless, all these discursive and representative argumentation processes have also confirmed the presence and functioning of post-Kemalist norms in Kosovo.

CHAPTER 9

CONCLUSION

This book aimed to explore the implications of the post-Kemalist changes in Turkey on Outside Turks communities in the specific case of Kosovar Turks. To this end, it has offered a norm-based analysis of the constitutive relationship between domestic politics and foreign policy formation and conduct. Moreovoer, it examined the foreign policy processes and mechanisms through which domestically initiated policies in Turkey effected and were implemented in the Outside Turks locality in Kosovo. Throught this, I elucidated the domestic norms guiding the ways in which Turkey has approached "Outside Turks", traced the conduct of domestic norms-guided Outside Turks policy, and, finally. explored the implications of such policy for the Kosovar Turks. In the sections below, I draw conclusions from the analysis presented in this book and examine the main findings with reference to the research questions, then move on to the analysis of the implications of such scrutiny for the study of foreign policy and the study of norms.

Post-Kemalist Foreign Policy and Kosovar Turks

Post-Kemalist comprehension of Outside Turks

This book illustrated Turkey's radical shift from the Kemalist path and creed and has shown that due to the post-Kemalist transformation of the country, traditional Kemalist norms lost leverage against the alternative post-Kemalist ones in, for instance, their ideas about state–society relations or in imagining the Turkish nation state. In the scope of this norm change, against the ethno-cultural exclusiveness of Kemalist policies, for instance, the cultural and ethnic diversity of the country and nation was first admitted, multicultural identities became more concrete and visible in public debates, and the legal and practical barriers relating to ethno-cultural rights were mostly lifted. The post-Kemalist norms moreover brought about robust post-national and non-ethnic conceptualisations of nationhood, geography and Turkishness against the Kemalist imagining of an ethnically homogeneous Turkish identity and state. This has also influenced how the state has come to view societal links outside of Turkey. It was in this scope that the traditional Kemalist approach to Outside Turks, which has previously focused on ethnicity and building ethnic Turkish identity among the Turkish-speaking communities outside Turkey, shifted towards imagining these communities along cultural and religious lines. In this respect, this book has shown that the shift in approach to Outside Turks was generated by four domestic norms which emerged in the course of Turkey's post-Kemalist transformation: Ottomania, de-ethnicised nationhood, Turkish Islam and Islamic internationalism.

The rising promince of Ottomania was based on imagining the Ottoman Empire as providing a useful model for an inclusive framework to resolve internal socio-cultural tensions that had been generated by cultural diversity. Ottomania was presented as a cure to overcome the crises of nationalism both at home and abroad. In domestic politics, Ottomania-inspired post-Kemalist acts have been used to foster a collective Ottoman memory. It worked to open space for a more pluralist understanding of political and cultural belonging, nationality and societal relations. Ottomanist practices have thus been employed as a remedy to the Kemalist "deconstruction" of inter-societal relations and used to solve long-running disputes in Turkey such as the Kurdish issue. In dealing with Outside Turks, Ottomania manifested itself as several practices: a zeal for restoring Ottoman heritage in all former Ottoman domains, of promoting the historical and cultural bonds between Turkey and Muslim communities, and of re-erecting an imagined Ottoman identity as a culture of co-existence throughout these places. Ottomania, therefore led an imagining of Outside Turks communities as the flag-bearers and representatives of Ottoman identity and culture – rather than a purely ethnic Turkish identity.

De-ethnicised nationhood corresponds to nationalism's loss of importance as the main signifier of Turkish nationhood and its effects on reimagining Turkishness as a less boundary- and blood-line driven identification. In domestic politics, de-ethnicised nationhood manifested itself as a practice of and an effort for, for instance, uniting Turks and Kurds under an anti-nationalist, non-ethnic and pluralist definition of nation. I found out that de-ethnicised nationhood contributed to the post-Kemalist comprehension of Outside Turks as they became imagined as the holders of a non-ethnic Ottoman/Turkish identity and successors of a multi-ethnic civilisation, as opposed to imagining them as an ethno-national community and as the successor of an ethnic Turkish civilisation.

It has also been argued that "Turkish Islam" has manifested itself as a concern for the protection of the performance of a 'national Islam' among Outside Turks localities against "alien" forms of Islamic practices. This understanding derives from the idea that the contemporary practice of Islam in Turkey, refered to as "Turkish Islam", is a distinct and superior practice and a continuation of Ottoman cultural and religious heritage. Turkey has, accordingly, been thought by the entrepreneurs of the norm of Turkish Islam as bearing a responsibility for protecting its application in the former Ottoman hinterland, including but not limited to Outside Turks localities.

Islamic Internationalism, in domestic politics, is a reaction to developments brought by the Kemalist regime in terms of its policies to change people's sense of belonging to an Islamic ummah to the Turkish nation. This resulted in the loss of its practical value for the idea of ummah and its turn into empty rhetoric in the eyes of most people in Turkey. Islamic Internationalism, therefore, manifested itself as a set of post-Kemalist practices which highlighted belonging to the ummah in both domestic and foreign policies. The Outside Turks, in this respect, have been "remembered" as Muslim communities and their belonging was no longer viewed as part of a Turkish nation alone, but as tied as much to the Islamic ummah. The norm of Islamic Internationalism has thus become significant to the extent that the promotion of promoting religious unity with Outside Turks is now more important than promoting ethnic links.

In short, Ottomania and de-ethnicised nationhood have facilitated the Outside Turks' re-construction as communities with whom Turkey has strong historical and cultural ties. The ethnic ties between Turkey and Outside Turks lost leverage again in this scope. Turkish Islam and

Islamic Internationalism, on the other hand, have facilitated Outside Turks' re-imagining as "Muslim communities", whereby solidarity between Turkey and Outside Turks communities have become established along religious lines and based on religious identity, rather than along merely ethnic or national lines. Therefore, due to the functioning of these four post-Kemalist norms, Outside Turks' "Muslimness" and the cultural unity between Turkey and Outside Turks communities have gained importance, while ethnicity has lost weight in policy development.

Post-Kemalist norms' transfer to the Outside Turks locality in Kosovo

The above-reviewed policy framework suggests that Turkey's post-Kemalist Outside Turks policy – a foreign policy guided by a shift in domestic norms – was composed of practices meant to safeguard the Ottoman/Muslim identity, history and culture of Outside Turks communities. The policies therefore were constitutive in character and conclusive both in the formation and conduct of foreign policy – a fact which confirms Turkey's continued imagining of Outside Turks localities as the cultural extension of the mainland (Uzer 2010). The formation of a post-Kemalist foreign policy, or – put differently, in the translation of post-Kemalist norms into foreign policy practices or international mobilisation of post-Kemalist norms – were thus mediated by recalling Ottoman and Muslim identities. Such motive are self-evident in the foreign policy practices presented in Chapter 7; for instance, Turkey sent diplomatic convoys to visit Outside Turks localities during religious holidays (bajrams); these officials joined prayers and religious congregations, thus practising religious identity; Turkey has also taken the protection and survival of Ottoman heritage and culture in Outside Turks localities as a prime duty; the protection of the performance of Turkish/Ottoman religious practices has an important place in Turkey's policy agenda; Diyanet collaborates with local religious authorities against "alien forms of religious practices"; Diyanet customarily celebrates the Holy Birth week with mass public participation abroad; Diyanet brings children from Outside Turks communities to be educated in imam-hatib schools and theology faculties in Turkey, but also builds theology faculties and imam-hatib schools in Outside Turks localities; TIKA calls for the implementation of the "Ottoman model" as a means of resolving ethnic issues between ethnic Turks and other Muslim communities; and, finally,

Turkey directly calls the communites to work for the cause of "religious brotherhood" in Outside Turks localities.

Confirming what was suggested by the theory of how norm-induced practices function (given place in Chapter 4), the above-mentioned practices have functioned as a way to make people show endorsement to post-Kemalist norms in Outside Turks localities, along with internationally mobilising the norms guiding them. These practices thus played both diffusive and socialising roles, which were motivated by the post-Kemalist state identities. Moreover, within the structure and constraints of such identities both state and non-state actors operated. In Turkey's post-Kemalist foreign policy regarding Kosovar Turks, state institutions such as the Turkish embassy in Pristina, TIKA, the Yunus Emre Institute and Diyanet along with religious groups such as the Gülen movement, the Süleyman Efendi Group, the Menzil Group and the Erenköy Group (Osman Nuri Topbaş group) all acted in line with such identities and have played both diffusive and socialising roles. TIKA, the Yunus Emre Institute and Diyanet, and Presidency for Turks Abroad and Related Communities (YTB) (although the latter – YTB – does not have an office in Kosovo) have functioned as the most ardent supporters of the post-Kemalist cause.

Based on the above-reviewed general framework, Turkey's Ottomania-driven approach towards the Kosovar Turkish community and Ottomania's transfer to the Outside Turks locality in Kosovo, was from the very beginning had within the scope of protecting the assumed Ottoman identity of the people and reminding them of imagined Ottoman values. The Ottoman focus in this approach, therefore, had a constitutive role. Accordingly, in their approach to the Kosovar Turkish community, institutions and religious groups from Turkey not only helped Ottomania to gain international mobilisation, but also strove hard to socialise the community into its teachings. TIKA, for instance, attempted to enact the idea of the Ottomans as a "culture of the living" in Kosovo by framing the Ottoman as a useful model of dealing with cultural and ethnic diversity. The Yunus Emre Institute, in a similar vein, promoted Ottoman culture, values and identities in Kosovo with a primary emphasis on brotherhood, cultural union and solidarity between Turks and Albanians. High-level state visits from dignitaries championed the idea of Ottoman inter-ethnic accord, tolerance and a culture of co-existence, and suggested formulating relations accordingly.

In conjunction with this, local entrepreneurs praised the Ottoman model of inter-ethnic relations and acted in a multi-ethnic manner. In socialising the community into Ottomania, moreover, the figure of Mehmed Akif has been drawn on extensively as a symbol of Turkish–Albanian brotherhood and shared history and culture. The Turkish community has been encouraged to have an agenda aimed at uniting with Muslim ethnic groups while multi-ethnic associations and their production of solutions to contemporary problems of the country with reference to Ottoman experience have also been supported and promoted. All these Ottoman-driven acts have questioned the dominant nationalist cognitive frames of the Turkish community and openned more room in politico-cultural circles to discourses around 'Ottoman ethnic accord'.

De-ethnicised nationhood's translation into foreign policy practices towards the Kosovar Turks has manifested itself as an *unconcern* for ethnicity as Turkey refrained from focusing only on ethnicity and ethnic identity in its policy towards the community. For example, officials from Turkey visiting the Turkish community in Kosovo have constantly articulated their disregard for "blood" and "race-ties" with this community and have instead expressed a value for culture and history as the "cement" holding relations between them. Moreover, these officials have expressed their discomfort at the Turkish community's constant emphasis on "Turkishness" and suggested that Turkishness should not be brought to the fore all the time. In a similar vein, TIKA has persistently discouraged ethnic political mobilisation of the community when adressing inter-communal relations in Kosovo, as well as criticising the ethnic Turkish community's bold ethno-political stance, which, to TIKA, threatens the peaceful co-existence of Muslim communities in Kosovo. Additionally, religious groups from Turkey have denounced the imagining of the Turkish nation along ethnic lines. They have defended the idea that the identification "Turk" represents a heterogeneous and diverse group of Turkish-speaking *Muslim* people. In order to encourage the community to endorse a de-ethnicised nationhood, Turkey's institutions, for example, have utilised their economic wealth to promote anti-nationalist elites, associations and practices against nationalistic initiatives in the ethnic Turkish community. Local norm entrepreneurs, by the same token have also campaigned for moving beyond ethnicity.

Turkish Islam driven foreign policy practices have been found to be about making the ethnic Turkish community protect their inherited religious practices and to adopt religious practices developed in Turkey – something which may require a degree of change to the existent cultural context. The functioning of Turkish Islam, in this respect, has been observed in TIKA's concern for Ottoman religious heritage, Diyanet's emphasis on preserving historically present sects and types of worship in Kosovo, and the efforts of religious groups to sustain the cultural and spiritual legacy of the Ottoman Empire. In line with this, the utilisation of Turkish Islam has been most evident in two forms of practices. Firstly, a fierce struggle is made priority against so-called Wahhabism since it is believed that this is antagonist towards Turks and has an agenda of breaking Turkish Islam's influence in Kosovo. In relation to this, in addition to TIKA's care for Ottoman religious heritage which, it feels, makes the community immune from "alien forms of religious practices", Diyanet has also encouraged locals to send their children to imam-hatip schools and theology faculties in Turkey, rather than to those in Arab countries. This was seen as the most straightforward way to transfer Turkey's religious education structure, culture and ideas to Kosovo. Secondly, Diyanet, the Yunus Emre Institute and religious groups utilised Turkish Islamic activities such as Holy Birth Week, Sufism and Rumi events, as well as religious talks, Qur'an recitation gatherings so as to reach the community more directly. In so doing, they have heavily cooperated with the local associations from all backgrounds.

With regard to the cascade of post-Kemalist norms to Kosovo, the translation of Islamic Internationalism into foreign policy has been had through the functioning of an internationalist Muslim identity which has been about introducing frames of Muslim consciousness, solidarity and identity to the ethnic Turkish community. More precisely, this new Islamic Internationalist foreign policy towards Kosovar Turks has meant a constant underscoring of the ethnic Turkish community's religious identity and endeavoured to make them gain feelings of Islamic consciousness and Islamic brotherhood. At this juncture, Islamic internationalism has manifested itself as a set of practices aimed at transforming an ethnicity-privileging community into a religious behaving and thinking community. In this fashion, for instance, the Turkish community's over-concern for ethnicity and the dominance of ethno-politics in their policies were attacked for the sake of Islamic brotherhood in the country and of promoting the Ottoman/ Islamic experience of peaceful co-existence. Religious identity, therefore, is seen as the only grounds on which to bring Muslim communities together. The community hence was encouraged to replace ethnic-nationalism with the idea of ummah as a cure to negative relations with the majority Albanian community and with other Muslim communities in the country.

In short, post-Kemalist domestic norms are transferred to the Outside Turks locality in Kosovo through the foreign policy practices guided by post-Kemalist norms and identities, and with a motivation for safeguarding the Muslim identity, history and culture of the Outside Turks communities. This brought about a constitutive agenda for norm entrepreneurs, which led to the diffusion of post-Kemalist norms to the Outside Turks locality in Kosovo and the community's socialisation into these. This relationship generated the implementation of similar policies in both domestic politics in Turkey and in the overseas Outside Turks locality in Kosovo.

The implications of and local responses to post-Kemalist Outside Turks policy

This book has contributed to better understanding Turkey's relations with Outside Turks through developing knowledge in three domains, the first two of which were discussed above. It has been demonstrated that the implementation of post-Kemalist policies in Kosovo has been constitutive for the ethnic Turkish community. As detailed in Chapter 8 the post-Kemalist policy – and thus the functioning of post-Kemalist norms – first and foremost created a secular nationalist versus conservative divide within the Turkish community. While the conservatives mostly internalised post-Kemalist norms and adopted relevant identities, the secular nationalists rejected these. The division, moreover, made each group hold on to more tightly either to Kemalism or post-Kemalism. In this sense, while the post-Kemalist norms became a means to replace Kemalist tendencies which were historically present within the community, Kemalism in turn gained a reactionary character. It accordingly served as a means to protect the community from what it saw as the adverse affects of the post-Kemalist policies of Turkey that were threatening the survival of Turkishness in Kosovo. Similar debates were had in Turkey upon the implementation of post-Kemalist policies and disputes over what is sacred to the nation.

In Kosovo, I observed that due to Ottomania-driven activities of reworking inter-ethnic relations along Ottoman lines, relations between Turks and Albanians have been partly improved. Local Turkish associations and intellectuals have increasingly considered the Ottomans as a "joint civilisation" and have admitted the contributions made by Albanians and other nations to the building of such a civilisation. This has increased the joint and collaborative endeavours of these communities. Multi-ethnic organisations built by both communities exemplify this. As a reactionary response to it, the functioning of Ottomania has also led to secular nationalist attempts to ethnicise the Ottomans against attempts to de-ethnicise it. Ottoman artefacts accordingly have been ascribed as the symbols of Turkishness rather than an Islamic civilisation and the contributions of other groups to the development of the Ottoman Empire and culture have been rejected. Ottomania, therefore, could not break the dominant nationalist frames and in fact strengthened them and forced them into a reactionary posture.

De-ethnicised nationhood guided policies facilitated the Turkish community's transcending of ethnicity in their attempts to organise relations with Albanians and Bosnians. This has increased their ability to work on joint projects and changed intellectual production rationales into largely anti-nationalist ones. This has been the case particularly for conservatives. Nonetheless, such policies could not deconstruct the dominant nationalist frames in all the community and, in some cases, they have been counter-productive and had pro-nationalist constitutive influences. The secular nationalists have felt that post-Kemalist Turkey is a bigger threat than any other they have faced in Kosovo. They argue that because Turkey is forcing them to be anti-nationalists and to abandon their ethnic identity, it is becoming harder for them to call themselves Turks in Kosovo, something which they say is jeopardising their ethnic survival. This consideration leads them to think that only by grabbing hold of nationalism more tightly will they be able to preserve their Turkishness. Their nationalism therefore gains a reactionary character which has occasionally led secular nationalists to ultra-nationalist tendencies.

Another key finding of this research has been that, when compared to other norms, "Turkish Islam" (as a post-Kemalist policy practice) has produced more complex and ambivalent conclusions. The Turkish Islamic practices are believed to be authentic to the Turkish nation, therefore, for the most part both conservatives and the secular nationalists have welcomed these practices. The protection of Ottoman artefacts from so-called Wahhabis has made the community feel very grateful to Turkey's efforts in this regard. In the eyes of local elites, this was even cast as a move "to save Turkishness". However, some groups reacted negatively to proposed innovations that would require a change to their cultural representation of Islamic practice. This relates particularly to the wearing of hijab or the growing of the beard – a contested issue for secular nationalists who view increases in the public appearance of such practices as disturbing. They even consider these as posing a threat to Turkishness. This group has shown endorsement to Turkish Islam as long as it serves their cause of protecting ethnic identity (a form of localisation). Accordingly, teachings requiring changes to existent cultural practices are rejected. Their nationalist cognitive prior frames, identities and cultural context have been more influential in this conclusion.

My fieldwork in Kosovo has, lastly, revealed that the Islamic internationalist approach has generated practices of transforming the ethically organised and nationalist Turkish community into a religiously thinking and acting one. I observed that for conservatives, this facilitated the rise to prominence of the religious component of Turkish identity. For secular nationalists, however, it became a discourse which was embraced only to defend their nationalist causes and to brand their nationalist struggle as a religious one. This manifested itself, for instance, in their argument that efforts to protect the Turkish language were also tied to the struggle for preserving Islam in Kosovo. Nonetheless, the real religious content, which asked for the privileging of Muslim identity over ethnic identity, has been interpreted as a move aimed at dismantling Turkish ethnicity and has been rejected by secular nationalists. Such policies therefore were not sufficient to break the bold nationalist frames; rather, they caused a fierce reaction and became counter-productive. However, conservatives embraced this norm more easily.

In short, the post-Kemalist approach to Kosovar Turks was no doubt constitutive for the community, yet for the most part it was counter-productive and served the rise of nationalism with a reactionary character. Except for the conservative minority within the community, for now almost all post-Kemalist norms are rejected – except "Turkish Islam" which is modified and localised. A final point worthy of note here is that there have been two entrepreneurs which have played an imperative role in introducing post-Kemalist frames to the community and in the development of the responses to post-Kemalist policies; namely, graduates from universities in Turkey and the Turkey's military troops in Kosovo – the Turkish Tabur. Many graduates from Turkey have been at the forefront of encouraing the community to place less emphasis on ethnicity and nationalism, and to give more credit to religious identity. The Turkish Tabur, on the other hand, has contributed to the opposite – that is, to resisting post-Kemalist norms by making use of Kemalism so as to prevent the internalisation of the former. Tabur, accordingly, functioned as a counter-entrepreneur and encouraged local elites to firmly embrace their Kemalist cultural background so as to be able to resist post-Kemalist norms. Tabur promoted the idea of employing Atatürk as a source and reference of resistance through which post-Kemalist norms could be contested and considered destructive. This Kemalist resistance to post-Kemalist policies in Kosovo is similar to the process in Turkey whereby there is also a movement against post-Kemalist reconstruction of state–society relations.

In conclusion, the research has shown that the post-Kemalist changes in Turkey have had constitutive influences on the Outside Turks locality in Kosovo. The post-Kemalist norms guided the way Outside Turks are comprehended. They have been influential also in the formation and conduct of the post-Kemalist Outside Turks policy towards the Kosovar Turks, which ended up with the conveyance of relevant post-Kemalist norms and with the ethnic Turkish community's socialisation into them. Post-Kemalist policy towards the Outside Turks, however, have for the most not been welcomed by the ethnic Turkish community – particularly in nationalist circles. It has caused fierce reactions and even became counter-productive in the sense that the community embraced Kemalism so as to resist post-Kemalism. This is similar to the response given to post-Kemalist domestic norm changes in Turkey. Therefore, we can say that the application of domestic policy has had similar implications both at home and in a locality abroad as foreign policy was used to channel the relevant norms.

Norms and Foreign Policy Analysis

This book has presented a norm-based model of foreign policy analysis for the examination of the processes and mechanisms by which a domestically initiated policy can have similar implementation issues and implication effects in a locality abroad. The model verified that foreign policy intertwines domestic and international realms. This research has shown that constructivist norm analysis possesses the required tools for putting domestic and international processes back together (Kubalkova 2001: 15). The research has also demonstrated and confirmed constructivist scholarship that "the domestic arena is the place where national preferences are born and international practices are produced, reproduced and transformed" (Adler 2002: 153). These are the initial implications of our application of the theory. The analysis below presents how the proposed foreign policy framework for analysing overseas implications of domestic norms works and can bring together domestic and international localities in a unified framework through analysis of foreign policy processes.

The relationship between norms and foreign policy is determined by the role(s) and function(s) of norms and norm-induced acts. Confirming the role given to norms in mainstream constructivist literature in IR, I have seen in my own examination that norms are constitutive, creating cognitive frames which can be embraced, can shape intersubjective understandings and meanings, can reconstitute and mould conceptual categories, can generate ideational transformations, constitute identity and guide behaviour. These roles, therefore, provide foreign policy formation processes in particular with a set of value-added teachings, identities, cognitive frames and concepts to adopt and follow. Once these are followed, the second part of the foreign policy process comes into play: the conduct of the norm-induced foreign policy practice. This norm-induced policy conduct upholds several functions, five of which have been practically confirmed in this research. Accordingly, a norm-guided foreign policy act invokes the teachings of the norm guiding it, thus is a meaningful action for both the conductor and the receiver. In the same vein, a norm-guided foreign policy act invokes the identity of the conductor. Moreover, the conduct of a norm-induced act conveys the norm which is guiding it to the receiver community. Yet, it does not stop there; it urges endorsement of the norm which then creates constitutive influences for both adherents and non-adherents.

These roles and functions are thus determinative for and constitute the basis of any model or theory built on norms to analyse foreign policy processes. They are the very ground for understanding the motivation and the implications of a foreign policy conduct. The roles and functions bring together the motivation and the conductor of the policy act and enable an observer to trace the implications and influences of a conduct.

In my model, these roles and functions made possible the linking of foreign policy formation to its conduct in a continuum. In a similar degree, they facilitated my work in tracing the emergence, international mobilisation and the overseas implications and influences of domestic norms. Nonetheless, Finnemore and Sikkink's (1998) "norm life cycle" model, whereby norm survival has been formulated as a sequential three-stage processes – namely, norm emergence, norm cascade and internalisation – and on which my elaborated model is built on, has been extremely facilitative. Adopting this framework, accordingly, has enabled the linking of the roles and functions of norms and norm-induced behaviours to the norm mechanisms by which their survival could be observed.

Having been built on these grounds, below I discuss how the foreign policy analysis model for analysing the overseas implications of domestic norms worked in studying the interrelationship between the post-Kemalist domestic norms and Turkey's post-Kemalist approach to Outside Turks.

The emergence of domestic norms occurs through the political, historical, cultural, social, communicative and cognitive mechanisms and processes whereby new intersubjective understandings and cognitive frames, and new identities are constructed (confirming Katzenstein 1996b). Norm entrepreneurs, following Finnemore and Sikkink (1998), act constructively in the building of such understandings, frames and identities. Domestic norms become translated into policies through institutionalisation and the functioning of relevant identities. It is, therefore, identity politics through which domestic norms are translated into policy practices and gain international mobility and are conveyed to an overseas locality (confirming Anne-Marie Burley 1993). Nonetheless, opposed to Katzenstein (1996a), I have seen that institutionalisation is not a prerequisite and that even non-institutionalised norms embody the qualities that define actor identity. Within the structure and constraints of this identity, however, both state and non-state actors operate at home and abroad (confirming Gurowitz 2004).

The conveyance of the relevant domestic norms into an international locality and thus the conduct of domestic norms guided foreign policy take place as follows. Having been run through the norm-induced behaviours, they are the diffusion and socialisation mechanisms that provide the domestic norms with international mobilisation (cascade). Confirming Finnemore and Sikkink (1998), I have seen that these mechanisms are not a contagion process nor composed of passive courses of actions. They work rather through the involvement of both norm setter and norm taker entrepreneurs as agents of diffusion and socialisation (confirming Checkel 2001). This confirms two things. Firstly, diffusion and socialisation suggest processual web of relations and that expecting a linear or sequential set of actions is pointless. Socialisation practices therefore can be both diffusive and socialising effort, as suggested by Finnemore and Sikkink (1998). Secondly, confirming the functions of norm-induced behaviours, norm-guided acts convey the norms and call for adherence to them. Therefore, the conduct of the act itself becomes a means for both diffusion and socialisation. Nonetheless, there are certain practices facilitating the cascade. The first of these is identity politics. The identity, accordingly, continues to play an imperative role during all processes of norm cascade. To a similar degree, cultural match between the social and cultural characteristics of the domestic and international localities pave the ways for successful norm diffusion and socialisation (confirming Checkel 1999; Cortell and Davis 2000). These two are utilised by norm entrepreneurs to justify their campaigning and to promote adherence and both state and non-state actors operate within the structure and constraints of state identity and are thus involved in norm cascade and socialisation. Finally, re-institutionalising certain norm-induced practices in the target locality facilitates socialisation and increase the adherence to a norm (confirming Wiener 2007a).

The above shows how similar policies would be implemented in both domestic and international localities. The final stage of the model illustrates the implications and influences of the relevant domestic norms in an international locality after successful diffusion.

It has to be admitted that socialisation is not an instant process and neither is the internalisation of the norm by the target community. Therefore, as long as norm-guided foreign policy continues to be conducted, there will be at least three local responses to the socialisation efforts: the conveyed norm will be further internalised, the norm will continue to be rejected or the norm will be modified to create a better fit with the local context. Therefore, unless the norm becomes internalised by the entire community and becomes taken for granted, there will be continuous argumentation and validation processes regarding the norms and norm-induced policies. Those who resist will continue making the externally coming norm contested and invalidated by strengthening existing norms against these externally derived ones (confirming Weiner 2007b: 5). All these implications constitute the impact domestic norms pose in an international locality and this impact is most observable and visible when they are internalised or rejected.

To conclude, this analysis has implications for two fields in theoretical level: the study of foreign policy analysis and the study of norms. In the former, it provides the literature with a norm-informed model to understand the processes and mechanisms through which a domestically initiated policy has similar implementations and implications in a locality abroad. The model confirms the idea that foreign policy intertwines the domestic and international realms; my research has presented a way to bridge two distinct localities through foreign policy tools. For the study of norms, the research first and foremost adapted a model produced to analyse norm survival to the analysis of foreign policy. In so doing, it was necessary to bring about reflections from logic of arguing and logic of contestedness to the model so as to increase its social and communicative focuses. The original model formerly lacked such content as it originally resorted merely to the logic of appropriateness. Following this, the various roles and functions of norms and norm-guided behaviours were identified and linked to norm mechanisms (such as emergence, institutionalisation, diffusion, socialisation, internalisation) to better understand how they function. This was very necessary because only after elaborating such roles and functions could I manage to use the model as a foreign policy framework.

APPENDIX I

Türkiye Scholarships Programme of the Presidency for Turks Abroad and Related Communities
Source: http://www.turkiyeburslari.org/index.php/tr/turkiye-burslari/burs-programlari.

Türkiye Africa Undergraduate Scholarship Programme

For the citizens of Angola, Benin, Botswana, Burkina Faso, Burundi, Algeria, Djibouti, Chad, Ethiopia, Morocco, Ivory Coast, Ghana, Kenya, South Africa, Union of Comoros, Congo, Democratic Republic of Congo, Libya, Madagascar, Mali, Niger, Nigeria, Central Africa, Senegal, Tanzania, Tunisia, Uganda, Equatorial Guinea, Gabon, Gambia, Guinea, Guinea Bissau, Cameroon, Lesotho, Liberia, Malawi, Mauritius, Mauritania, Mozambique, Namibia, Seychelles, Sierra Leone, Somalia, Swaziland, Togo, Zambia, Zimbabwe, Egypt, Sudan, South Sudan, Eritrea, Rwanda, Cape Verde and Democratic Republic of São Tomé and Príncipe.

Bosphorus Undergraduate Scholarship Programme

For the citizens of Argentina, Bahrain, United Arab Emirates, Brazil, Brunei, People's Republic of China, East Timor, Ecuador, El Salvador, Indonesia, Philippines, Guatemala, South Korea, Haiti, India, Jamaica, Japan, Cambodia, Qatar, Colombia, Kuwait, Cuba, Laos, Maldives, Malaysia, Mexico, Mongolia, Myanmar, Nepal, Paraguay, Peru,

Singapore, Sri Lanka, Saudi Arabia, Chile, Thailand, Trinidad and Tobago, Oman, Uruguay, Venezuela and Vietnam.

Balkans Undergraduate Scholarship Programme

For the citizens of Albania, Bosnia Herzegovina, Bulgaria, Croatia, Montenegro, Kosovo, Macedonia, Serbia, Slovenia and Greece.

Harran Undergraduate Scholarship Programme

For the citizens of Iraq, Iran, Lebanon, Pakistan, Syria, Bangladesh, Afghanistan, Tajikistan, Jordan, Palestine and Yemen.

Black Sea Undergraduate Scholarship Programme

For the citizens of Belarus, Czech Republic, Hungary, Armenia, Estonia, Georgia, Latvia, Lithuania, Moldova, Poland, Romania, Russia, Slovakia and Ukraine.

Turkish-speaking Countries Undergraduate Scholarship Programme

For the citizens of Azerbaijan, Kazakhstan, Kyrgyzstan, Uzbekistan and Turkmenistan

Anatolian Undergraduate Scholarship Programme

For the citizens of Turkish Republic of Northern Cyprus and the non-Turkish citizens who have completed their secondary education in Turkey.

APPENDIX II

The Kemalist Oath (Our Pledge) recited every morning by primary school students

Our Pledge

"I am a Turk, honest and hardworking. My principle is to protect the younger to respect the elder, to love my homeland and my nation more than myself. My ideal is to rise, to progress. Oh Great Atatürk! On the path that you have paved, I swear to walk incessantly toward the aims that you have set. My existence shall be dedicated to the Turkish existence. How happy is the one who says 'I am a Turk!'"

APPENDIX III

Mustafa Kemal Atatürk's Address to Turkish Youth, October 20, 1927

Address to Turkish Youth

You, the Turkish youth!

Your primary duty is to forever protect and defend the Turkish independence and the Republic of Turkey.

This is the mainstay of your existence and your future. This foundation is your most precious treasure. In the future, as well, there will be malevolents, within and abroad, who will seek to deny your birthright. If, one day, you are compelled to defend your independence and the Republic, you shall not reflect on the conditions and possibilities of the situation in which you find yourself, in order to accomplish your mission.

These conditions and possibilities may appear unfavorable. The adversaries, who scheme against your independence and your Republic, may be the representatives of a victory without precedent in the World. By force or by ruse, all citadels and arsenals of our dear fatherland may have been taken, all of its armies may have been dispersed, and all corners of the country may have been physically occupied. More distressing and more grievous than all these, those who hold and exercise the power within the country may have fallen into gross error, blunder, and even treason.

These holders of power may have even united their personal interests with political ambitions of the invaders. The nation itself may have fallen into privation, and may have become exhausted and desolate.

You, the future sons and daughters of Turkey! Even under such circumstances and conditions, your duty is to redeem the Turkish independence and the Republic! The strength you shall need exists in the noble blood flowing through your veins.

APPENDIX IV

List of Interviewees

Local Elites (LE)

	Code	Location	Position	Date
1	LE1	Prizren	Media	07/05/2013
2	LE2	Prizren	Academic/Education	08/05/2013
3	LE3	Prizren	Arts	09/05/2013
4	LE4	Prizren	Media	11/05/2013
5	LE5	Prizren	Academic	12/05/2013
6	LE6	Prizren	Academic	13/05/2013
7	LE7	Prizren	Culture and Arts	15/05/2013
8	LE8	Prizren	Advocacy/Culture	17/05/2013
9	LE9	Prizren	Advocacy/Culture	18/05/2013
10	LE10	Prizren	Arts/Literature	20/05/2013
11	LE11	Prizren	Politics	23/05/2013
12	LE12	Prizren	Academic	26/05/2013
13	LE13	Prizren	Media	27/05/2013
14	LE14	Prizren	Education/Culture	02/06/2013
15	LE15	Prizren	Politics	04/06/2013
16	LE16	Prizren	Academic	05/06/2103
17	LE17	Prizren	Politics	08/06/2013
18	LE18	Prizren	Business	09/06/2013
19	LE19	Prizren	Politics	13/06/2013
20	LE20	Prizren	Academic	16/06/2013
21	LE21	Prizren	Advocacy	18/06/2013

22	LE22	Mamusha	Education	24/05/2013
23	LE23	Mamusha	Education	25/05/2013
24	LE24	Mamusha	Culture	25/05/2013
25	LE25	Mamusha	Law/Advocacy	11/06/2013
26	LE26	Pristina	Politics	28/05/2013
27	LE27	Pristina	Media/Culture	30/05/2013
28	LE28	Pristina	Politics	20/06/2013
29	LE29	Pristina	Business/Media	27/06/2013
30	LE30	Pristina	Media	29/06/2013
31	LE31	Pristina	Media	03/07/2013
32	LE32	Pristina	Education/Medicine	05/07/2013
33	LE33	Pristina	Literature/Media	09/07/2013
34	LE34	Pristina	State official	10/07/2013
35	LE35	Pristina	Education	12/07/2013
36	LE36	Pristina	Media	18/07/2013
37	LE37	Prizren	Business	05/08/2013
38	LE38	Prizren	Arts	06/08/2013

Religious Groups – Turkish NGOs (RG)

	Code	Location	Position	Date
1	RG1	Prizren	Süleymancıs	12/08/2013
2	RG2	Pristina	Gülen Cemaat	26/07/2013
3	RG3	Prizren	Gülen Cemaat	14/08/2013
4	RG4	Prizren	Erenköy Cemaat	16/08/2013
5	RG5	Prizren	Balkan RTV	17/08/2013

Diplomatic Mission (DM)

	Code	Location	Position	Date
1	DM1	Prizren	Diyanet	30/07/2013
2	DM2	Mamusha	Diyanet	02/08/2013
3	DM3	Prizren	Yunus Emre	05/08/2013
4	DM4	Pristina	Yunus Emre	19/07/2013
5	DM5	Pristina	TIKA	24/07/2013
6	DM6	Prizren	Tabur	13/08/2013
7	DM7	Pristina	Embassy	22/07/2013

Scoping Visit Notes (SVN)

	Code	Location	Position	Date
1	SVN1	Prizren	Education/Politics	13/01/2012
2	SVN2	Prizren	Politics	14/01/2012
3	SVN3	Prizren	Academic/Education	15/01/2012
4	SVN4	Prizren	Advocacy/Culture	16/01/2012
5	SVN5	Prizren	Advocacy	17/01/2012
6	SVN6	Prizren	Law/Media	18/01/2012
7	SVN7	Prizren	Politics	20/01/2012

APPENDIX V

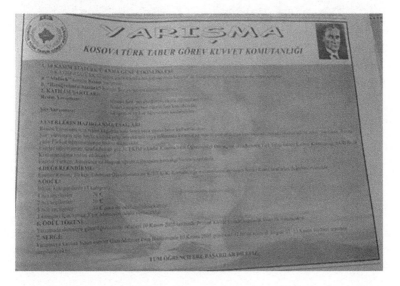

Figure A5.1 Turkish Tabur organised a poetry and painting contest in 2005 during Atatürk Commemoration Week and Teachers' Day. The theme of the Teachers' Day contest was "Atatürk as the head teacher [baş öğretmen]". To announce the contest an advertisement was published in a local newspaper (see *Yeni Dönem* 20 October 2005).

Figure A5.2 The cover photo of a video CD prepared by the Turkish Tabur. The photos on the cover show the 23 April Children's Festival organised by Turkish Tabur in 2009, in Prizren.

Figure A5.3 The poster of the 2009 Atatürk Commemoration Week jointly organised by the Turkish Tabur and a local association, Filizler Kemalist Turkish Culture and Arts Association. The text on the poster quotes Atatürk's Address to Turkish Youth: "the strength you shall need exists in the noble blood flowing through your veins".

Figure A5.4 Miscellaneous photos from the 2009 Atatürk Commemoration Week Events jointly organised by the Turkish Tabur and Filizler Kemalist Turkish Culture and Arts Association.

Figure A5.5   Miscellaneous photos from the 2009 Atatürk Commemoration Week Events jointly organised by the Turkish Tabur and Filizler Kemalist Turkish Culture and Arts Association.

Figure A5.6 The cover of the 2011 Atatürk Commemoration Week booklet. The ten days of events were funded by the Turkish Tabur.

Figure A5.7 The invitation card to the ethnic Turkish community's National Day celebration, 2013. It is on the same day as the Kemalist Children's Festival, 23 April. The design of the logo of the event consists of three crescents and six stars. Six stars represent the Kosovo's constitutionally recognised communities, while the three crescents represent Turkishness. The three crescents are also the symbols of the Nationalist Movement Party in Turkey. It was also used by the Ottoman Empire.

Figure A5.8 19 May Festival organised by the Democratic Turkish Party of Kosovo and local associations.

NOTES

Chapter 1   Introduction

1. These are the Turkish-speaking communities that reside outside of Turkey since the collapse of the Ottoman Empire. There are also Turkish speakers outside the former Ottoman Empire such as in Central Asia or Iran which are also considered as part of the "Outside Turks". I deal with these in Chapter 2. The focus here is intentionally constrained to Turkish-speaking communities in the Balkans and Cyprus who are self-identified as ethnic Turks.
2. Post-Kemalism denotes Turkey's radical shift from the Kemalist path and creed in imagining state–society relations by and after the 1990s, but particularly by 2000s.
3. The former Prime Minister of Turkey (1983–9), and the former president (1989–93).
4. The former Prime Minister of Turkey (1996–7).
5. This was declared by the Ottoman Parliament in February 1920 and later embraced by the first parliament of the Anatolian resistance government and finally by the new Republic itself.
6. A 'halaqa' is a gathering to learn about Islam, organised mostly by religious groups rather than official religious authorities.

Chapter 2   Kemalist Policy Towards the Outside Turks

1. Ahundzade proposed to the Ottoman government a plan for changing the script from Arabic to Latin (Gürbüz 2003: 507).
2. Pan-Turkism, however, was not the only response to territorial shrinking and to the vulnerabilities of the Ottoman remnant Muslim communities. Along with Pan-Turkism, Pan-Islamism and Pan-Ottomanism alike developed an interest in

the affairs of Muslim communities abroad. Pan-Ottomanism, in this sense, was aiming to re-integrate the diverse religious and ethnic communities living (or lived) under the Ottoman rule through "developing new 'cultural bonds among the whole population'" (Jacoby 2004: 73). Pan-Islamism on the other hand was resorted to as a stance of "Pan-Islamic peripheral inclusion" for gaining leverage over the institution of Caliphate in the country's wars against the Western powers (Ibid). They were however present at almost the same times and their employment depended very much on the strategic ends.

3. Hatay later became part of Turkey in 1939 after a plebiscite was held in the city–state. Hatay's annexation by Turkey was based on a nationalist motive that considered Hatay ancient Turkish territory, which would be united to the homeland. This also expressed by Kemal Atatürk (see Sarınay 1996).

4. In the scope of the agreement, along with "ethnic Turks", Muslim communities consisting of Albanians, Bosnians, Torbeshis and Pomaks were all accepted into Turkey and were equally granted Turkish citizenship (Altuğ 1991: 110, Baklacıoğlu 2010: 157, Akca 2002: 2, Çağaptay 2001: 8). Nonetheless, while these diverse migrant communities became part of the Turkish nation built inside, their co-nationals abroad were not considered part of the cross-border Turkish nation. However, Turkey never denied its responsibility towards the former (non-Turkish) subjects of the Empire with the state being imagined as the legal protector of these remnant communities. They became considered as part of Outside Turks only after the post-Kemalist transformation and with the acceptance of Outside Turks' ethnic diversity mainly from the 1990s onwards. See Chapter 3 for a detailed discussion of this shift.

5. Pan-Turkism still survives as an irredentist ideology with a motto to unite all Turkic people; however, the adherents of this ideology are mostly found only in far-right nationalist circles.

6. Another explanation for this is that Mustafa Kemal is argued to have followed a realist policy towards Outside Turks and thus refrained from interfering in the affairs of the countries with Turkish-speaking minority communities (Armaoğlu 1988: 167–8). This holds to a certain degree, but misses the intention in Turkey to also transfer Kemalist ideals to these communities.

7. These can be listed as Pan-Turkist (Landau 1995), Turanist (Oguz 2005), racist (Isyar 2005), Kemalist (Turan 1988), Anatolianist (Atabay 2002), culturalist (Ziya Gökalp) (Berkes 1959), conservative (Akgün and Çalış 2002), émigré (Soysal 2002), and diaspora (Kızılyürek 2002) Turkish nationalisms.

8. Homeland sometimes denotes Anatolia and sometimes Central Asia or Turan.

9. According to this division the Central Asian Turkic people and the culturally Turkish Muslim communities of the Balkans (Bosniaks, Pomaks, and Albanians) constitute the category of kin communities, while the Turkish speaking ethnic Turkish *minority* communities in the Balkans, Cyprus and in Iraq are the holders of the category '*soydaş*' – or those possessing the same race (For a detailed debate on this, see Karadeniz 2011: 62–72).

10. As a methodological note, confirming Fredric Barth (1969) and Rogers Brubaker (1996), ethnicity has been used as a practical category and a performative act in the example of Outside Turks communities. They become and remain Turkish through practising Turkishness. There are compulsory practices to be considered ethnic Turk by the Outside Turks communities, particularly for the Kosovar Turks, including voting for the ethnic Turkish party or sending children to Turkish-language schools.

11. In the scope of this policy, in Bulgaria, *Halk Sesi* was given a monthly subsidy of 100 *lira* in 1930, 1931, and 1933; *Rodop* was given 100 *lira* per month in 1930, *Deliorman* was given 200 *lira* monthly in 1933 and 1934; and *Özdilek* received a similar amount in 1933 (Boyar and Fleet 2008: 782–4).

12. Refers to the tenets of Kemalism, which are republicanism, nationalism populism, revolutionarism, secularism and statism.

13. Özdemir 1999: 193, Demiryürek 2003: 8, Keser 2007: 65, Nesim 1989: 335, Sonyel 1995: 176.

14. Having considered that Turkey was relinquished of all its legal responsibilities concerning Cyprus by the Treaty of Lausanne in 1923, such involvement very well shows the extent to which it's supports to and concerns for Outside Turks had reached.

15. As Rauf Denktaş, the national leader of Cyprus Turks, confessed, "Mustafa Kemal's thought on the necessity of consuming domestic goods" were the guide of their economic nationalist actions (Kızılyürek 2002: 337).

16. Turkey's national anthem was played in the Turkish schools since the establishment of the Republic of Cyprus in 1960 (Uzer 2010: 113).

17. "I am a Turk, honest and hardworking. My principle is to … love my homeland and my nation more than myself. My ideal is to rise, to progress. Oh Great Atatürk! On the path that you have paved, I swear to walk incessantly toward the aims that you have set. My existence shall be dedicated to the Turkish existence. How happy is the one who says 'I am a Turk!'"

18. Turkey supported the opening of the first Turkish secondary school in 1952 in Gümülcine, it was due to this Turkey's president Celal Bayar's name was given to the school. The second school was only opened in 1965 in İskeçe (Xanthi) (Popovic 1995: 350).

Chapter 3   Post-Kemalist Policy Towards the Outside Turks

1. JDP was established by the reformist fraction of the political Islamist Virtue Party, the legal successor to the Welfare Party closed down during the February 28 coup period.

2. A leading liberal figure in Turkey.

3. Anatolian-based small and medium scale pro-Islamist merchants and industrialists.

4. Such as Faisal Finance, Al-Baraka Group or Islamic Development Bank.
5. Such as Naqshbandis and the Gülen Movement.
6. Such an experience and its relevance to the problems Turkey was facing were brought into discussion also during the 1950s, long before Özal. What was unique about Özal was that during the 1990s Turkey was encountering a large-scale ethnopolitical armed uprising and the state was having troubles in dealing with the societal dimension of the conflict or in producing alternatives to the overtly militaristic language during this moment of crises.
7. Most of them are closed afterwards due to the lack of interest in people in learning minority languages.
8. President of Turkey, former prime minister (2003–14).
9. Its recitation in secondary schools was already removed in 2012.
10. See Aydın and Açıkmeşe (2007) for a debate on the character of Turkey's Europeanisation – whether an experience of socialisation or conditionality.
11. Former minister in charge of the YTB (2011–13).
12. Former president of the YTB (2010–14).
13. This is the official translation of "Nerede bir vatandaşımız, soydaşımız, akbaramız varsa biz oradayız" (www.ytb.gov.tr). Here, *soydaş* corresponds to *kin communities* while *akraba* to *related communities*.
14. The former president of Turkey (2007–14).
15. The name of the campaign in Turkish is as follows "Hasanlar Hans Olmasın!"
16. See http://www.turkiyeburslari.org/index.php/tr/turkiye-burslari/burs-programlari and Appendix 1 for the country list of the countries.

Chapter 4   Overseas Implications of Domestic Norms

1. A similar argument is raised by Boekle *et al.* through expressing that ideational settings "are too abstract for generating actual expectations of behaviour" (2002: 107).
2. Antje Weiner accordingly argues that in logic of arguing while "norm setting follows the logic of arguing, norm following occurs according to the logic of appropriateness" (Wiener 2007a: 53).
3. This conception is inspired from Frederick Kratochwil's valuation of norms as *action-guiding devices* (Kratochwil 1991: 5). However, Annika Björkdahl phrases what I call norm-guided behaviour as "norm-induced pattern of behaviour" (2002: 13) and norm-guided foreign policy as "norm-based foreign policy" (2002: 23). I use both phrases interchangeably.
4. Such as the conducts of states that are set in an agreement.
5. Such as the struggles centred on control over sea trade routes during the eighteenth and nineteenth centuries in the Atlantic Ocean.
6. In her response to this question, Annika Björkdahl elaborates the role norms play during the foreign policy formation not actually during the conduct (2002: 22–3). Therefore, although I consider that raising this question is a unique

attempt for Björkdahl, the response she gives ignores the conduct part of the story.

7. "[T]he mechanism through which norm leaders persuade others to adhere" to a norm (Finnemore and Sikkink 1998: 902).

8. This definitely confirms the constructivist argument of reuniting domestic and international politics divide (see Kubalkova 2001: 15).

9. It is the "mechanism through which norm leaders persuade others to adhere to norms" (Finnemore and Sikkink 1998: 902).

10. Cameron Thies, in his critique on socialisation literature argues that many of the studies are not clear whether socialisation is a process or an outcome (2003: 548). Thies is right indeed. For instance, Kai Alderson calls socialisation both as a process and as an outcome in the same paper (see Alderson 2001: 417).

11. Finnemore and Sikkink (1998) place more emphasis on the fully internalised norms such as sovereignty, market exchange or individualism.

12. Katzenstein argues that norm emergence is a communicative process (1996a: 21).

Chapter 5   Outside Turks Locality in Kosovo – Making of Kosovar Turks

1. Islam Muhafaza-i Hukuk Cemiyet (Society for the Preservation of Muslim Rights).

2. These trainings continued in Macedonia in the form of seminars even during the 1970s (Türk Öğretmenler Derneği 1996: 191).

3. See Chapter 8 for an analysis of the role of *Tan* newspaper in the building of ethnic consciousness.

4. For a detailed debate on the community's attachment to Kemalism and Atatürk see the introduction section of the Chapter 8.

5. The military base of NATO's Turkish troops in Prizren was named as Camp Sultan Murat as a reference to Ottoman Sultan Murat I, the conquerer of Kosovo, hence to Turkey's historical ties with Kosovo.

6. See Chapter 8 for the Tabur's constitutive influences on the community.

7. See Chapter 8 for a detailed discussion on the issue.

Chapter 6   Emergence of Post-Kemalist Norms Concerning Outside Turks

1. See Table 6.1 for the teachings of the post-Kemalist norms concerning Outside Turks in the conclusion section of this chapter.

2. The Ottoman concern in the country was politically expressed in the 1950s too; yet, unlike in the 1990s, Ottoman ideas never became a bold reference point nor gained political currency during the 1950s.

3. We see that this act of ethnicising reversed during the JDP era, and Ottoman history and civilisation was argued to be belonging to, for instance, Albanians, Bosnians or other nations as much as the Turks. This is also discussed in the de-ethnicised nationhood section below.

4. Davutoğlu, here, implies that multicultural and peaceful co-existence is an Ottoman norm and well experienced in the Balkans during the Ottoman era.

5. In the writing course of this book (2011–15), new developments occurred particularly in the Middle East such as the Arab revolutions, Syrian civil war, Israel's continuous offensive in Gaza strip and DAESH's (al-Dawla al-Islamiya fil Iraq wa al-Sham) taking control of vast part of territories in Iraq and Syria. Turkey's responses to these developments may suggest that Turkey diverted from the principles of "peace and harmony with the countries in the Ottoman hinterland" or "zero problems with neighbours". One may argue so because, for instance, Turkey has given support of all means to the opposition in Syria, it downgraded the diplomatic relations with Israel for its military acts in Gaza, and it was hesitant to join the coalition against the DAESH. Despite these acts, Turkey's policy makers continued uttering their intention of following the above-mentioned principles. For instance, Ahmet Davutoğlu continues arguing Turkey's historical responsibility and support towards Iraq and Syria. Turkey, as argued, accomplishes this responsibility, for instance, through hosting 1.6 million Syrian refugees since the early days of the Syrian civil war. Similarly, since December 2015, there occurs a rapprochment between Turkey and Israel. Concomitantly, the Ministry of Foreign Affairs of Turkey continues claiming their embrace of the policy of zero problem with neighbours (http://www.mfa. gov.tr/policy-of-zero-problems-with-our-neighbors.en.mfa). In tandem with the official positions, particularly the pro-Islamic groups are happy to host Syrian refugees – their brothers and sisters in religion – in Turkey and Turkey's use of force in Syria towards DAESH is politically backed in public opinion. Therefore, despite the deviations from some of the teachings, Ottomania continues to be a dominant norm.

6. Such as Mehmet Altan and Cengiz Çandar.

7. Overlap with de-ethnicised nationhood – see Table 6.1.

8. The warrant was cancelled on February 2015 and he was acquitted in line with the dismissal of the Ergenekon case (*Takvim* 10 March 2015).

9. This was a result of the removal of the abbreviation, TC–Turkish Republic– from some government departments' names. The nationalist and Kemalist groups interpreted this as a sign of the JDP's intention to change the name and/ or the regime of the country.

10. Ottomania's main teachings overlap with de-ethnicised nationhood and partly with Turkish Islam. See the Table 6.1.

11. It was to prevent the pervasion of the so-called radical Islam.

12. Here a distinction between the Turkish Islamic Synthesis and Turkish Islam is needed to be made. As a matter of fact, the former partly facilitated the latter's adoption by the secular nationalists, however, reducing Turkish Islamic practices

to the Turkish Islamic Synthesis thesis could be a mistakenly reached conclusion. While the Turkish Islamic Synthesis was a movement begun in the 1970s to promote a synthesis between Islam and Turkish nationalism and facilitated the conservatives' being comfortably nationalist (worked mostly to ethnicise Islam and Islamic history), Turkish Islam represents the historical practice of Islam in Turkey and the Ottoman Empire and suggests the incorporation of "the wisdom of Sufism with the historical experiences of modern Turkey" (Yavuz 2004: 218, Yavuz 1998, also see *Radikal* 28 May 2006).

13. In 2008, Diyanet sent more than one million copies of religious publications abroad (Korkut 2010: 133).

14. The Holy Birth Week was invented by Diyanet in the early 1990s to celebrate the birth of the Prophet Muhammed based on Gregorian calendar rather than the Islamic calendar, and today it is celebrated as an official national holiday (Bulaç 2012, *Eurasian Islamic Meeting Report* 1995: 65, for a biased yet relevant research on the issue see Toprak 2008: 142–4).

15. Member states are Bangladesh, Egypt, Indonesia, Iran, Malaysia, Nigeria, Pakistan, and Turkey.

16. The far-wing Kemalists would be an exception here, as they have constantly blamed JDP for trying to introduce Sharia to the country.

17. You can also see Tabak 2015 to learn more about the IHH's humanitarian relief and diplomacy activities and *Time Türk* 22 October 2012 for the IHH's "Once again Ummah" campaign.

Chapter 7　Cascade of Post-Kemalist Norms to Kosovo

1. Othon Anastasakis argues that Turkey's concern was more political than religious during the intervention (2012: 193). This should be borne in mind to see how religious/cultural identity politics became a prime concern in Turkey's approach to Kosovo by the time the JDP governments came to power, something which we touch on below.

2. Local elite, interview number 21. See Appendix 5 for the list of the interviewees.

3. Diplomatic mission member, interview number 5.

4. Religious group member, interview number 5.

5. Tabur's activities are dealt with in the next chapter.

6. This is also admitted by other members of the diplomatic missions and local respondents.

7. The visit took place in November 2010.

8. A city that is mainly dominated by Ottoman–Turkish culture and where many residents can speak the Turkish language regardless of their ethnic origin.

9. This is confirmed by many other respondents. See Chapter 8 for such views.

10. Sami Frasheri is a national hero for Albanians and was a pioneering figure in envisaging a free Albania, while Mehmet Akif is the poet of Turkey's national anthem.

11. This leads to negative reactions among the ethnic Turkish community and is something which we will deal with in the next chapter.
12. In September 2014, AKEA was closed down by the Kosovar government which alleged that it was promoting "radical Islam" in the country (*Kosova Haber* 23 September 2014).
13. The role of religious identity will be in detail dealt with in the Islamic Internationalism part of this chapter.
14. For another socialisation campaign this TV channel participated in, see the Islamic Internationalism part of this chapter.
15. The newspaper was founded in 1999. TIKA supported the newspaper from 2001. The newspaper closed down in 2008.
16. The former state minister of Turkey in charge of TIKA (2003–7).
17. A largely ethnic-Turkish populated village with almost no knowledge of Albanian.
18. This generates negative rections and a feeling of disgrace among Kosovar Turks and is something which we will touch on in the last chapter.
19. There is, indeed, a concrete common ground between the norm of Ottomania and de-ethnicised nationhood in making the ethnic Turkish community able to form non-nationalist relations with Muslim communities.
20. In order words, why Turkey withdrew its support is related to Yeni Dönem's nationalist aspirations.
21. An umbrella organisation bringing together several nationalistic-oriented associations of the ethnic Turkish community.
22. The deputy mayor of Prizren, also an ethnic Turk.
23. Scoping Visit Notes. See Appendix 5 for the list of the informants.
24. The respondent argues that s/he was "a Kemalist (Atatürkçü), a secular Kemalist when he first went to the imam-hatip school in Turkey" and remarks that "every single student that goes to Turkey from here {among the Turkish community} goes in as a Kemalist" (Interview LE21).
25. However, during fieldwork I learned that the majority of the Turkey alumni have returned back to their communities without a change in their approach to nationalism and Turkishness. Many of them still have a strong sense of belonging to their ethnicity. This is dealt with in detail in the next chapter.
26. Regardless of which religious groups they belong to, the local cohmmunity, particularly the Albanians and Bosnians, call the members of these groups the "Turkish hodjas".
27. Mamusha Research, Science and Education Association – Mamuşa Araştırma, Bilim ve Eğitim Derneği (MABED).
28. Turkey has sent imams to Kosovo for the past 20 years, yet during the first ten years the imams were sent only for Ramadan. Since 2005 Turkey has sent imams to be permanently based in Kosovo (Interview DM2).
29. A local, outdoor fair, organised usually for charitable purposes.
30. Reading one chapter of Qur'an on each day of Ramadan with the aim to reading it from start to finish in 30 days; this is done in groups at a mosque.

31. Salat-ul-tasbih, a prayer performed on religiously significant days.
32. A deputy prime minister and former president of the Turkish Parliament.
33. In order to exemplify the Islamic experience of the culture of peaceful co-existence, for instance, TIKA translated "A Culture of Peaceful Coextistence: Early Islamic and Ottoman Turkish Examples" written by Ekmeleddin İhsanoğlu, the former Secretary-General of the Organisation of Islamic Cooperation (OIC) (2004–14), into Albanian and published it in 2009 (İhsanoğlu 2009).
34. S/he articulated this after I asked him/her what s/he thought about ethic Turks' discomfort at Turkey's use of Islam as a "unifying policy".
35. His articulation of this is confirmed also by other members of the community (Interview LE4).
36. Our informant says this, despite the fact that the entire governing body of TÜMED consists of ethnic Turks.
37. The former Minister of Youth and Sports.
38. http://www.bezmialem.edu.tr/medya/universite-duyurular/951-16-18-mayis-balkan-genclik-forumu-etkinlikleri.

Chapter 8   Local Responses to Post-Kemalist Socialisation

1. Here, the leftist ideas and modernism are considered as teachings of (Kemalist and socialist) secularism.
2. The first political party to come from the community declared many times that the most realistic path for the Turkish community to take was to follow Atatürk's principles.
3. Zübeyde Hanım was the mother of Atatürk. Within Kemalist thought she is praised for being a "modern mother" who raised such a revolutionary leader.
4. See the following sources for coverage of commemorations of Sami Frasheri, *Yeni Dönem* 18 November 2004; *Yeni Dönem* 30 December 2004.
5. The respondent uses the word "our" here.
6. As an Albanian he means.
7. The community began publishing on Pan-Turkist issues such as "union in language, thought, and work" or "from the union in alphabet to the union in language".
8. I personally observed that many Turkish people have tattoos of Atatürk's signature on their arms or on their cars. In a similar vein, many community members have added the abbreviation TC to their Facebook profiles, following the trend in Turkey, as mentioned in Chapter 6. Finally, the meeting organised by community members in Prizren to give support to the Gezi Park anti-government protests which occurred in İstanbul in 2013 has also been in line with such trends.
9. See Chapter 6 and Appendix 2 for details of this nationalistic pledge.
10. Nationalists in Turkey had also once argued this same point with relation to their own situation.

11. To announce the contest, an advertisement was published in a local newspaper (*Yeni Dönem* 20 October 2005). See Appendix 6 for the advertisement. Regarding Teachers' Day, when 7 March was set as Teachers' Day in Kosovo in 2003, the Kosovo Turkish Teachers Association published a declaration and argued that it is unacceptable for the Turkish community to accept this. They argued that 7 March has a meaning for the Albanian majority and since Kosovo is a multi-ethnic state, each ethnic community has the right to choose its own day and thus declared that they will celebrate 24 November (of Turkey) as their own Teachers' Day (*Yeni Dönem* 27 February 2003).

12. This refers to the fact that Mustafa Kemal was born in Salonika, Greece. He was therefore from the Balkans, as are the Kosovar Turks.

13. Examples of these writings could be found at *Tan* 14 January 1989, *Tan* 10 March 1990, *Tan* 14 April 1990, *Tan* 21 April 1990, *Tan* 30 June 1990, *Tan* 8 September 1990, *Tan* 22 September 1990, *Tan* 22 December 1990, *Tan* 11 January 1991, *Tan* 29 February 1992, *Tan* 7 March 1992, *Tan* 21 March 1992, *Tan* 20 June 1992, *Tan* 11 July 1992, *Tan* 20 February 1993, *Tan* 6 March 1993.

14. Enver Baki's poem on the Prophet Muhammad was awarded honourable mention in the Holy Birth Celebrations in 1997 in Ankara, Turkey, which suggests the presence of traces of Turkish Islam among the Kosovar Turks as early as the mid-1990s (Baki 2011: 80).

15. They started publishing columns such as *Islamic culture in Kosovo is the Turkish culture!*, *We have a close concern to Islamic culture!* or *Religion is the warranty of our future* (*Tan* 2 June 1990, *Tan* 3 November 1990, *Tan* 20 March 1993 respectively).

16. In these issues of the *Tan* weekly newspaper, for instance, they published articles such as *Atatürk's revolutionary steps in the Islamic world*; *Atatürk, religion and the truths*; *Atatürk was respectful to religion and he was religious* (*Tan* 17 November 1990, *Tan* 4 April 1992, *Tan* 29 April 1992 respectively).

17. *Ata is the abbreviation of Atatürk.
   ** A Mountain in Egypt, important for religious history.
   *** Mimar Sinan, an Ottoman Muslim architect lived in sixteenth century and considered as the greatest architect in the Ottoman Empire.
   **** Yunus Emre.

BIBLIOGRAPHY

Abazi, Enika (2008). *Kosovo Independence: An Albanian Perspective*, SETA Policy Brief, Accessible online at http://setadc.org/kosovo-independence-an-albanian-persp ective/policy-papers/1082.

Abdullah, Gül, December 10, 2009, *A speech delivered during an official visit to Albania, Turgut Özal Kültür ve Eğitim Merkezi'ni ziyaret ve Epoka Üniversitesi'nin temel atma töreni'nde yaptıkları konuşma*, Arnavutluk, Accessible online at http ://www.tccb.gov.tr/konusmalar/371/56188/turgut-Özal-kultur-ve-egitim-merkezini-ziyaret-ve-epoka-universitesinin-temel-atma-toreninde-yaptikl. html.

—— February 2, 2010, *A speech delivered upon President Fatmir Sejdiu's visit to Ankara, Kosova Cumhurbaşkanı Fatmir Sejdiu'nun Onurlarına Verdikleri Akşam Yemeğinde Yaptıkları Konuşma*, Accessible online at http://www.tccb.gov.tr/konusmalar/ 371/56165/kosova-cumhurbaskani-fatmir-sejdiunun-onurlarina-verdikleri-aks am-yemeginde-yaptiklari-konusma.html.

Acharya, Amita (2004). "How ideas spread: Whose Norms Matter? Norm Localization and Institutional Change in Asian Regionalism", *International Organization*, Vol. 58, No. 2, pp. 239–75.

Adler, Emanuel (1997). "Seizing the Middle-Ground: Constructivism in World Politics", *European Journal of International Relations*, Vol. 3, No. 3, pp. 319–63.

—— (2002). *Constructivism in International Relations: Sources, Contributions, and Debates*, in Walter Carlsnaes, Thomas Risse, and Beth A. Simmons (eds), *Handbook of International Relations*, London: Sage.

Akca, Bayram (2002). "1923–1953 Arası Türk–Bulgar İlişkileri ve 1950–51 Yıllarında Muğla Vilayetine İskan Edilen Bulgar Muhacirleri", *Atatürk Araştırma Merkezi Dergisi*, Vol. 18.

Akdoğan, Yalçın (2003). *Muhafazakar Demokrasi*, Ankara: Ak Parti Yayınları.

Akgün, Sibel (2006). "Atatürk İlke ve İnkılaplarının Kıbrıs'a ve Kıbrıs Türk Kadınına Yansımaları", *Atatürk Araştırma Merkezi Dergisi, Mart-Temmuz-Kasım*, Vol. 22.

Akıllı, Erman (2013). *Türkiye'de Devlet Kimliği ve Dış Politika*, Ankara: Nobel Yayınevi.

Akpinar, Aylin (2007). *The Making of a Good Citizen and Conscious Muslim Through Public Education: The Case of Imam Hatip schools*, in Carlson et al. (eds), *Education in Multicultural Societies: Turkish and Swedish Perspectives*, London: I.B.Tauris, pp. 161–78.

Akşam, March 26, 2013, 'Ne mutlu Türküm diyene' gitti, Accessible online at http://www.aksam.com.tr/guncel/ne-mutlu-turkum-diyene-gitti/haber-180781.

—— November 16, 2013, *Yeni Türkiye ve 1920 ruhu*, Accessible online at http://www.aksam.com.tr/yazarlar/yeni-turkiye-ve-1920-ruhu-c2/haber-261622.

Akyol, Mustafa (2013). *Introducing post-Kemalist Turkey*, Accessible online at http://www.al-monitor.com/pulse/originals/2013/04/turkey-kemalism-failing-secul arism-nationalism-erdogan.html.

Alderson, Kai (2001). "Making sense of State Socialization", *Review of International Studies*, 27:3, pp. 415–33.

Altan, Mehmet (2013). *2. Cumhuriyet'in neresindeyiz?*, *Radikal*, October 29, Accessible online at http://www.radikal.com.tr/turkiye/2_cumhuriyetin_neres indeyiz-1157839.

Altınok, Mehtap (2012). "Interview with President Abdullah Gül (Cumhurbaskani Abdullah Gül ile Roportaj)", *Arti90*, April, pp. 4–9.

—— (2013a). "PM Erdoğan:You are Never Alone (Basbakan Erdoğan: Sizler Asla Yalniz Degilsiniz)", *Arti90*, January, pp. 6–9.

—— (2013b). "Head of the Presidency for Turks Abroad and Related Communities Kemal Yutnac tells about the Presidency (YTB Baskani Kemal Yurtnaç Kurumu Anlatiyor)", *Arti90*, January, pp. 12–15.

Altuğ, Yılmaz (1991). "Balkanlardan Anayurda Yapılan Göçler", *Belleten–Türk Tarih Kurumu*, Vol. 55, No. 212, pp. 109–20.

Altunya, Eylem (2003). "The Kosovo Crisis and Turkey (1991–2001)", Unpublished PhD Thesis, Bilkent Univesity, Ankara.

Anastasakis, Othon (2012). *Turkey's Assertive Presence in Southeast Europe: Between Identity Politics and Elite Pragmatism*, in Öktem, Kadıoğlu, and Karlı (eds), *Another Empire? A Decade of Turkey's Foreign Policy under the Justice and Development Party*, İstanbul: Bilgi University Press, pp. 185–208.

Anzerlioğlu, Yonca (2006). "Bükreş Büyükelçisi Hamdullah Suphi ve Gagauz Türkleri", *Bilig, Güz*, No. 39, pp. 31–51.

Aras, Bulent and Omer, Caha (2000). "Fethullah Gülen and His Liberal "Turkish Islam" Movement", *Middle East Review of International Affairs*, Vol. 4, No. 4, pp. 30–42.

Aras, Tevfik Rüştü (1932). A *Parliamentary speech on "Türkiye Cumhuriyeti ile İran Hükümeti arasında aktedilen uzlaşma, adlî tesviye ve hakem muahedesinin ta'sdiki hakkında 1/324 numaralı kanun lâyihası ve Hariciye ve Adliye encümenleri mazbataları"*, TBMM – Zabıt Ceridesi, Devre 4, Cilt 9, İçtima 1, Altmış Beşinci İnikat, 18–6-1932 Cumartesi. Accessible online at http://www.tbmm. gov.tr/tutanaklar/TUTANAK/TBMM/d04/c009/tbmm04009065.pdf.

Arti90, January, 2012.

—— April, 2012.

Aşıkferki, Ferhat (1996). *Türk Öğretmenler Derneği*, Prizren.

Aslan, Ali (2013). "Problematizing Modernity in Turkish Foreign Policy: Identity, Sovereignty and Beyond", *Review of International Law and Politics*, No. 33, pp. 27–57.

Atam İzindeyiz Booklet (2009). "Filizler Türk Kültür Sanat Derneği Atam İzindeyiz – Atatürk'ü Anma Haftası 01–10 Kasım 2008", Prizren.

Atasoy, Yıldız (2005). *Turkey, Islamists, and Democracy: Transition and Globalization in a Muslim State*, London: I.B.Tauris.

Atmaca, Metin (2012). "Harar: the anathomy of a Muslim city in East Africa", *Arti90*, January, pp. 78–81.

Avrasya Bülteni, July 2003, "Başbakan Yardımcısı ve Dışişleri Bakanı Abdullah Gül'ün TIKA'yı ziyareti", *July*, Vol. 24.

―― October 2003, "Moğolistan Ankara Büyükelçini Panidjunai Khaliun ile Görüşmeleri", *October*, Vol. 15, pp. 6–7.

―― February 2005, "Dışişleri Bakanı Abdullah Gül'ün İsrtail ve Filistin Temasları", *February*, Vol. 31, p. 3.

―― October 2005, "TIKA 14. Yılında", *October*, Vol. 39, p. 3.

―― January–February 2006, "TIKA savaşın küstürdüğü gençleri bir araya getiriyor", Vol. 42, p. 22.

―― May 2006.

―― June 2006, "Bilge Kağan Karayolu/Büyük Öğrenci Projesi", *June*, Vol. 47, pp. 9–16.

―― July 2006, "Başbakan Erdoğan Türkoloji öğrencileriyle buluştu/TIKA ve Islam Kalkınma Bankası", Vol. 48, pp. 1–5/11–12.

―― February 2008, "TIKA Heyeti Yemen'de", *February*, Vol. 63, pp. 18–25.

―― August 2009, "Sudan'daki Osmanli Eserleri Restore Ediliyor", Vol. 82, p. 18.

―― November 2009.

―― September 2010, "Haberler", *September*, Vol. 95, pp. 4–7.

Axelrod, Robert (1986). "An Evolutionary Approach to Norms", *The American Political Science Review*, Vol. 80, No. 4, pp. 1095–1111.

Ayan, Ergun (2011). "Kafkasya ve Türkistan'da Ulus–Devletler Sistematiğinin Oluşma Süreci", *ODU Sosyal Bilimler Araştırma Dergisi*, Vol. 2, No. 3, pp. 7–33.

Aydın, Mehmet (2008). "Diyanet's Global Vision", The Muslim World, Vol. 98, pp. 164–71.

Aydın, Mustafa and Açıkmeşe, A. Sinem (2007). "Europeanization through EU conditionality: understanding the new era in Turkish foreign policy", *Journal of Southern Europe and the Balkans*, Vol. 9, No. 3, pp. 263–74.

Aydın, Suavi (1995). "Etnik bir Ad Olarak Türk Kavramının Sınırları ve Genişletilmesi Üzerine", *Birikim Dergisi*, Vol. 71–2, pp. 50–64.

Babacan, Ali, January 13, 2009, A speech delivered at the Kosovo Parliament, *T.C. Dışişleri Bakanı Sayın Ali Babacan'ın Kosova Meclisi Genel Kurulu'nda Yaptığı Konuşma*, 13.01.2009, Accessible online at http://pristine.be.mfa. gov.tr/ShowSpeech.aspx?ID=578.

Baki, Enver (2011). *Priştine'nin Eski Sokakları – Şiirler*, Gerçek Derneği, Priştine: Bahçe Yayınları.

―― (2013). *Adem Ağa'nın Din Dersleri*, Priştine: Trend.

Bâkiler, Yavuz Bülent (2010). *Üsküp'ten Kosova'ya*, 14. Baskı, İstanbul: Türk Edebiyat Vakfı.

Baklacıoğlu, Nurcan Özgür (2010). *Dış Politika ve Göç- Yugoslavya'dan Türkiye'ye Göçlerde Arnavutlar (1920–1990)*, İstanbul: Derin Yayınları.

Balcer, Adam (2012). *Turkey as a stakeholder and contributor to regional security in the Western Balkans*, in Canan-Sokullu, Ebru (ed.), *Debating Security in Turkey, Challenges and Changes in the Twenty-First Century*, Lanham: Lexington Books, pp. 219–36.

Balci, Bayram (2003). "Fetullah Gülen's Missionary School in Central Asia and their role in the Spreading of Turkism and Islam", *Religion, State and Society*, Vol. 31, No. 2, pp. 151–77.

Balkan Insight, November 4, 2010, *New Chapter in Kosovo–Turkey Relations Needed*, Accessible online at http://www.balkaninsight.com/en/article/kosovo-turkey-historic-ties.

—— September 20, 2012, *Turkey Pledges Military Aid For Kosovo*, Accessible online at http://www.balkaninsight.com/en/article/turkey-pledges-military-help-to-kosovo.

Banac, Ivo (1984). *The National Question in Yugoslavia: Origins, History, Politics*, New York: Ithaca.

Bardakçı, Murat (2009). *Ayyy, siz yoksa Türk müsünüz? Ne kadar ayıp*, Haber Türk Gazetesi, April 24, 2009, Accessible online at http://www.haberturk.com/yazarl ar/murat-bardakci/218187-ayyy-siz-yoksa-turk-musunuz-ne-kadar-ayiiip.

Barth, Fredrik (1969). "Introduction", in Barth, Fredrik (ed.), *Ethnic Groups and Boundaries: The Social Organization of Cultural Difference*, London: Allen & Unwin.

Baymak, Ethem (1987). *Süreyya Yusuf: Yaşamı, Sanatı, Yapıtları*, Pristine: Tan Yayınları.

—— (2013). *Türkçem Rumeli'nin Onur Bayrağı – Balkan Türk Şiiri Üzerine İncelemeler*, Prizren: RKS.

Beamer, Glenn (2002). "Elite Interviews and State Politics Research", *State Politics and Policy Quarterly*, Vol. 2, No. 1: pp. 86–96.

Beckingham, Charles Fraser (1957). "Islam and Turkish Nationalism in Cyprus", *Die Welt des Islams, New Series*, Vol. 5, Issue 1/2, pp. 65–83.

Bekir, Bozdağ (2012). *A Parliamentary speech, Başbakan Yardımcısı Bozdağ'ın Bütçe Konuşması, TBMM Plan–Bütçe Komisyonu Konuşması*, Accessible online at http://www.bekirbozdag.com.tr/haberler/78-haberler/152-basbakan-yard-mc-s-bozdag-n-buetce-konusmas.

Bennett, Andrew and Elman, Colin (2007). "Case Study Methods in the International Relations Subfield", *Comparative Political Studies* 40: 170–95.

Berger, Thomas U. (1996). *Norms, Identity, and National Security in Germany and Japan*, in Peter Katzenstein (ed.), *The Culture of National Security*, New York: Columbia University Press, pp. 317–56.

Bernstein, Steven (2000). "Ideas, Social Structure and the Compromise of Liberal Environmentalism", *European Journal of International Relations*, Vol. 6, No. 4, pp. 464–512.

Beşir, Atalay (2006). *A Parliamentary speech*, TBMM Tutanak Dergisi, Birleşim 36, 18.12.2006, pp. 392–3.

—— (2007). *A Parliamentary speech*, TBMM Tutanak Dergisi, Birleşim 55, 25.01.2007, pp. 227–33.

Beylur, Suat (2012). "Somali: A sample for Turkey's involvements", *Arti90*, April, pp. 76–7.

Bishop, R. (2005). *Freeing ourselves from neocolonial domination in research*, in Denzin and Lincoln (eds), *The Sage handbook of qualitative research*, London: Sage.

Bizden, Ali (1997). *Kıbrıs'ta güç/iktidar mücadelesinin değişen yüzü: Kıbrıs(lı/Türk). Milliyetçiliği*, Birikim, Mayıs, pp. 79–91.

Björkdahl, Annika (2002). "Norms in International Relations: Some Conceptual and Methodological Reflections", *Cambridge Review of International Affairs*, Vol. 15, No. 1, pp. 9–23.

Boekle, Henning, Rittberger, Volker and Wagner, Wolfgang (2002). *Constructivist Foreign Policy Theory*, in Rittberger, Volker (ed.), *German foreign policy since unification: theories and case studies*, Manchester: Manchester University Press, pp. 105–40.

Bojkov, J. Victor (2004). "Bulgaria's Turks in the 1980s", *Journal of Genocide Research*, Vol. 6, No. 3, pp. 343–69.

Börklü, Meşkure Yılmaz (1999). "Türkiye Cumhuriyeti'nin takip ettiği Dış Türkler Politikası", Unpublished PhD Thesis, Selçuk University, Konya.

Boyar, Ebru and Fleet, Kate (2005). "Mak[ing} Turkey and the Turkish revolution known to foreign nations without any expense: propaganda films in the early Turkish Republic", *Oriente Moderno, Nuova serie*, Anno 24 (85), No. 1, pp. 117–32.

——— (2008). "A Dangerous Axis: The "Bulgarian Müftü", the Turkish Opposition and the Ankara Government, 1928–1936", *Middle Eastern Studies*, Vol. 44, pp. 775–89.

Bozkurt, Ismail (1998). *Kıbrıs Türklerinde Altay ve Avrasya Yansımaları*, A paper presented in Uluslararası Daimi Altay Bilimleri Konferansı (PIAC). 41'inci Yıllık Toplantısı, 5–10 July, Helsinki.

Brubaker, Rogers (1996). *Nationalism Reframed: Nationhood and the National Question in the New Europe*, New York: Cambridge University Press.

Bryman, Alan (1988). *Quantity and Quality in Social Research*, London: Routledge.

Bucholtz and Hall (2005). "Identity and interaction: a sociocultural linguistic approach", *Discourse Studies*, Vol. 7 (4–5): 585–614.

Bulaç, Ali (2012). *AK Parti, "Muhafazakar demokrasi" ve İslamcılık (4)*, October 2, 2012, Accessible online at http://www.dunyabulteni.net/?aType=yazarHaber& ArticleID=18552.

Bulgarian Helsinki Committee (2003). *The Human Rights of Muslims in Bulgaria in Law and Politics since 1878*, Sofia, Accessible online at http://miris.eurac.edu/mu gs2/do/blob.pdf?type=pdf&serial=1075393805246.

Bulut, Arslan, June 7, 2013, *Taksim için bayrak sohbeti!*, Accessible online at http:// www.yenicaggazetesi.com.tr/taksim-icin-bayrak-sohbeti-27035yy.htm.

Bulut, Esra (2004). "The Role of Religion in Turkish Reactions to Balkan Conflicts", *Turkish Policy Quarterly*, Vol. 3, No. 1, pp. 1–13.

——— (2006). "'Friends, Balkans, Statesmen Lend Us Your Ears': The Trans-State and State in Links between Turkey and the Balkans", *Ethnopolitics*, Vol. 5, No. 3, pp. 309–26.

Burley, Anne-Marie (1993). *Regulating the World: Multilateralism, International Law, and the Projection of the New Deal Regulatory State*, in Ruggie, John (ed.), *Multilateralism Matters, the Theory and Praxis of an Institutional Form*, New York: Columbia University Press.

Burris, A. Gregory (2007). "The Other from Within: Pan-Turkist Mythmaking and the Expulsion of the Turkish Left", *Middle Eastern Studies*, Vol. 43, No. 4, pp. 611–24.

Buttanrı, Müzeyyen (2005). "Bulgaristan Türk Edebiyatı", *Eskişehir Osmangazi Üniversitesi Sosyal Bilimler Dergisi*, Vol. 6, No. 2, pp. 27–45.

Çağaptay, Soner (2009). "The AKP's Foreign Policy: The Misnomer of "Neo-Ottomanism"," *Turkey Analyst*, Vol. 2, No. 8, 24 Nisan 2009, Accessible online at http://www.silkroadstudies.org/new/inside/turkey/2009/090424B.htm.

——— (2012a). "How Does the New Turkey Think?", *Hurriyet Daily News*, April 30, Accessible online at http://www.washingtoninstitute.org/policy-analysis/view/ how-does-the-new-turkey-think.

—— (2012b). Kemalism is dead, but not Ataturk, CNNWorld, May 2, Accessible online at http://globalpublicsquare.blogs.cnn.com/2012/05/02/kemalism-is-dead-but-not-ataturk/.

Çakır, Ruşen, Bozan, İrfan, and Talu, Balkan (2004). İmam Hatip Liseleri: Efsaneler ve Gerçekler, İstanbul: Tesev Yayınları.

Çalış, Şaban (1996). "The role of identity in the making of modern Turkish foreign policy", Unpublished PhD Thesis, University of Notthingham.

—— (2001). Hayalet Bilimi ve Hayali Kimlikler: Neo-Osmanlılık, Özal ve Balkanlar, Konya: Çizgi.

Çelik, Dilek Yalçın (2008). Kosova'da Çağdaş Türk Edebiyatı (1951–2008), Prizren: Doğru Yol Türk Kültür Sanat Derneği Yayınları.

Çetinsaya, Gökhan (1999). "Rethinking Nationalism and Islam: Some Preliminary Notes on the Roots of "Turkish–Islamic Synthesis" in Modern Turkish Political Thought", The Muslim World, Vol. 89, Issue 3–4, pp. 350–76.

Çevren Bilim/Kültür Dergisi, Vols 85–6, Year 28, September–December, 1991.

—— Vols 90–2, Year 29, July–December, 1992.

Checkel, T. Jeffrey (1997). "International Norms and Domestic Politics: Bridging the Rationalist – Constructivist Divide", European Journal of International Relations, Vol. 3, No. 4, pp. 473–95.

—— (1999). "Norms, Institutions, and National Identity in Contemporary Europe", International Study Quarterly, Vol. 43, pp. 83–114.

—— (2001). "Why Comply? Social Learning and European Identity Change", International Organization, Vol. 55, No. 3, pp. 553–88.

—— (2005). "International Institutions and Socialization in Europe: Introduction and Framework", International Organization, Vol. 59, No. 4, pp. 801–26.

CHP, September 13, 2012, Hatay Milletvekili Dudu: "Çocuklarımızın dünyalarından Atatürk'ü ve Türkiye Haritasını silmeye çalışıyorlar", Accessible online at http://www.chp.org.tr/?p=85239.

Çiçek, Yıldıray (2013). AKP'den Kurtulmak Türklüğün ve İslam'in Zaferi Olacaktir, Ortadogu Gazetesi, January 29, Accessible online at http://www.ortadogu gazetesi.net/makale.php?id=12581.

Çitak, Zana (2010). Between "Turkish Islam" and "French Islam": The Role of the Diyanet in the Counseil Français du Culte Musluman, Journal of Ethnic and Migration Studies, 36:4, pp. 619–34.

Çolak, Yılmaz (2006). "Ottomanism vs. Kemalism: Collective memory and cultural pluralism in 1990s Turkey", Middle Eastern Studies, Vol. 42, No. 4, pp. 587–602.

Cortell, Andrew and Davis, James (2000). "Understanding the Domestic Impact of International Norms", International Studies Review, Vol. 2, No. 1, pp. 65–87.

Creswell, J.W. (2007). Qualitative inquiry and research method: Choosing among five approaches, Sage, Thousand Oaks.

Criss, Nur Bilge (2010). "Dismantling Turkey: The will of the people?", Turkish Studies, Vol. 11, No. 1, pp. 45–58.

Dağ, Rahman (2016). The Failure of the State (Re)Building Process in Iraq, in E. Akcali (ed.), Neoliberal Governmentality and the Future of the State in the Middle East and North Africa, London: Palgrave Macmillan.

Dağı, İhsan (2005). "Transformation of Islamic Political Identity in Turkey: Rethinking the West and Westernization", Turkish Studies, Vol. 6, No. 5, pp. 21–37.

—— (2010). "Remembering the architect of change: Turgut Özal", *Today's Zaman*, Accessible online at http://www.todayszaman.com/columnist/ihsan-dagi/remembering-the-architect-of-change-turgut-ozal_207805.html.

Dağıstan, Adil (2002). "Hamdullah Suphi'nin Romanya Büyükelçiliği ve Gagauz Türkleri", *Atatürk Araştırmaları Merkezi Dergisi*, Vol. 18, No. 54.

Davutoğlu, Ahmet (2010a). "Turkish Vision of Regional and Global Order: Theoretical Background and Practical Implementation, Keynote Lecture at the Conference on Turkey's Foreign Policy in a Changing World at the University of Oxford", *May 1, 2010, transcripted and published by Political Reflection Magazine*, Vol. 1, No. 2, pp. 37–50.

—— November 15, 2012, *Statement by Mr. Ahmet Davutoğlu, Minister of Foreign Affairs of Turkey, at the 39th Session of the OIC Council of Foreign Ministers, 15 November 2012, Djibouti*, Accessible online at http://www.mfa.gov.tr/statement-by-mr_-ahmet-Davutoğlu_-minister-of-foreign-affairs-of-turkey_-at-the-39th-session-of-the-oic-council-of-foreign-m.en.mfa.

—— February 4, 2013, *Statement by H.E. Ahmet Davutoğlu, Minister of Foreign Affairs of the Republic of Turkey at the Ministerial Meeting Preparatory to the Twelfth Session of the Islamic Summit Conference*, 4 February 2013, Cairo, Accessible online at http://www.mfa.gov.tr/statement-by-h_e_-ahmet-davuto%C4%9Flu_-minister-of-foreign-affairs-of-the-republic-of-turkey-at-the-ministerial-meeting-preparatory-to-the-twelfth-session-of-the-islamic-summit-conference_-4-february-2013_-cairo.en.mfa.

Demirtas-Coskun, Birgul (2008). "Systemic changes and State Identity: Turkish and German Responses", *Insight Turkey*, Vol. 10, No. 1, pp. 31–54.

—— (2010). "Kosova'nın Bağımsızlığı ve Türk Dış Politikası (1990–2008)", *Uluslararası İlişkiler*, Vol. 7, No. 27, pp. 451–86.

Demiryürek, Mehmet (2003). "Kıbrıs'ta bir 150'lik: Sait Molla (1925–1930)", *Atatürk Araştırma Merkezi Dergisi, Kasım*, Vol. 19, No. 57.

Denzin, Norman and Lincoln, Yvonna (2005). *The SAGE Handbook of Qualitative Research*, London: Sage.

Dere, Ali (2008). "The PRA of Turkey: The Emergence, Evolution and Perception of its Religious Services Outside of Turkey", *The Muslim World*, Vol. 98, pp. 291–301.

Deringil, Selim (1994). *Denge Oyunu – 2. Dünya Savaşı'nda Türkiye'nin Dış Politikası*, İstanbul: Tarih Vakfı Yurt Yayınları.

Derviş, Fetnan (2010). *Tarih 5*, Pristine: Libri Shkollor.

DHA, April 16, 2013, *Diyanet İşleri Başkanlığı Kosova'da Kutlu Doğum Haftası Programı Düzenledi*, Accessible online at http://www.dha.com.tr/diyanet-isleri-baskanligi-kosovada-kutlu-dogum-haftasi-programi-duzenledi_457088.html.

Dilligil, Turhan (1994). *Erbakancılık ve Erbakan*, Ankara: Onur.

Diyanet Faaliyet Raporu, 2006, Accessible online at diyanet.gov.tr.

—— 2011, Accessible online at diyanet.gov.tr.

—— 2012, Accessible online at diyanet.gov.tr.

Doğru Yol 30. *Yıl Monografisi (1981). Doğru Yol Kültür ve Güzel Sanatlar Derneği (1951–1981)*, 30. Yıl Monografisi, Prizren.

Doğru Yol Derneği 60. Yıl Kataloğu, 2012.

Dünya, April, 14, 2012, *Kosova – Türkiye ilişkisi kıskandırıyor*, Accessible online at http://www.dunya.com/kosova-turkiye-iliskisi-kiskandiriyor-151562h.htm.

Dünya Bizim, August 16, 2012, *Prizren'de AKEA ne yapıyor, Ramazan nasıl?*, Accessible online at http://www.dunyabizim.com/?aType=haberYazdir&Articl eID=10712&tip=haber.

Duran, Burhanettin (2013). "Understanding the AK Party's Identity Politics: A Civilizational Discourse and its Limitations", *Insight Turkey*, Vol. 15, No. 1, pp. 9–109.

Eminov, Ali (1986). "Are Turkish-speakers in Bulgaria of ethnic Bulgarians?", *Journal of Muslim Minority Affairs*, Vol. 7, No. 2, pp. 503–18.

Ensonhaber, April 3, 2013, *Abdullah Gül: Osmanlı Türklük diye dayatmamış*, Accessible online at http://www.ensonhaber.com/abdullah-gul-imparatorluklar-turkluk-diye-dayatmamis-2013–04–03.html.

Eralp, Doğa Ulaş (2010). *Kosovo and Turkey: What Lies Ahead?*, SETA Policy Brief, Accessible online at http://arsiv.setav.org/Ups/dosya/52482.pdf.

Erdeha, Kamil (1998). *Yüzellilikler yahut Milli Mücadelenin Muhasebesi*, İstanbul: Tekin Yayınları.

Erdenir, Burak (2012). "Türkiye'nin Siyasi Reform Sürecinde Avrupa Birliği'nin Demokratik Koşulluluğu", *Amme İdaresi Dergisi*, Vol. 45, No. 4, pp. 95–117.

Eurasian Islamic Meeting Report (1995). *The First Eurasian Islamic Meeting held in Ankara, Turkey on 23–26 October 1995*, Accessible online at diyanet.gov.tr.

—— (1998). The Third Eurasian Islamic Meeting held in Ankara, Turkey on 25–29 May 1998, Accessible online at diyanet.gov.tr.

—— (2000). *The Fourth Eurasian Islamic Meeting held in Sarajevo, Bosnia–Herzegovina on 25–28 July 2000*, Accessible online at diyanet.gov.tr.

Fearon, D. James (1998). "Domestic Politics, Foreign Policy, and Theories of International Relations", *Annual Reviews of Political Science*, Vol. 1, pp. 289–313.

Feroze, Muhammad Rashid (1976). *Islam and secularism in post-Kemalist Turkey*, Islamabad: Islamic Research Institute.

Finnemore, Martha (1993). "International Organizations as teachers of norms: the United Nations Educational, Scientific, and Cultural Organization and science Policy", *International Organization*, Vol. 47, No. 4, pp. 565–97.

—— (1996a). *Humanitarian Intervention*, in Katzenstein, Peter (ed.), *The Culture of National Security–Norms and Identity in World Politics*, New York: Columbia University Press.

—— (1996b). "Norms, culture, and world politics: insights from sociology's institutionalism", *International Organizations*, Vol. 50, No. 2, pp. 325–47.

Finnemore, Martha and Sikkink, Kathryn (1998). "International Norm Dynamics and Political Change", *International Organization*, Vol. 52, No. 4, pp. 887–917.

Flick, Uwe (2004). *Constructivism*, in Flick, *et al.*, (ed.) *A Companion to Qualitative Research*, London: Sage.

—— (2009). *An Introduction to Qualitative Research*, London: Sage.

Florini, Ann (1996). "The Evolution of International Norms", *International Studies Quarterly*, Vol. 40, pp. 363–89.

Flyvbjerg, Bent (2006). "Five Misunderstandings about Case-Study Research", *Qualitative Inquiry*, Vol. 12, No. 2, pp. 219–45.

Galliers, D. Robert (1991). *Choosing Appropriate Information Systems Research Approaches: A Revised Taxonomy*, Nissen *et al.* (eds) *Information Systems Research:*

Contemporary Approaches and Emergent Traditions, Elsevier Science Publishers, North Holland, pp. 327–45.

Gangloff, Sylvie (2001). "The Weight of Islam in the Turkish Foreign Policy in the Balkans", *Turkish Review of Balkan Studies*, Vol. 5, pp. 91–102.

—— (2004). "Turkish Policy Towards the Conflict in Kosovo: The pre-eminnce of national political interests", *Balkanologie*, Vol. 8, No. 1, pp. 105–22.

Gercek Gundem, April 7, 2013 *T.C ibaresi neden kaldırılıyor?*, Accessible online at http://arsiv.gercekgundem.com/?p=537671.

Gergen, J. Kenneth (1994). *Realities and Relationships: Soundings in Social Construction*, Cambridge, MA: Harvard University Press.

Goertz, Gary and Diehl, F. Paul (1992). "Toward a Theory of International Norms: Some Conceptual and Measurement", *The Journal of Conflict Resolution*, Vol. 36, No. 4, pp. 634–64.

Goldstein, Judith and Keohane, Robert (1993). *Ideas and Foreign Policy: An Analytical Framework*, in Goldstein and Keohane (eds), *Ideas and Foreign Policy*, Ithaca: Cornell University Press.

Gourevitch, Peter (2002). *Domestic Politics and International Relations*, in Handbook of international relations, London: Sage, pp. 309–28.

Grigoriadis, N. Ioannis (2007). "Türk or Türkiyeli? The reform of Turkey's minority legislation and the rediscovery of Ottomanism", *Middle Eastern Studies*, Vol. 43, No. 3, pp. 423–38.

—— (2009). *The Trials of Europeanization: Turkish Political Culture and the European Union*, Basingstoke: Palgrave Macmillan.

Guba, G. Egon and Lincoln, S. Yvonna (2005). *Paradigmatic Controversies, Contradictions, and Emerging Confluences*, in Denzin, K. Norman and Lincoln, S. Yvonna, *The Sage Handbook of Qualitative Research*, 3rd edn, Sage Publications, pp. 191–216.

Gürbey, Gülistan (2006). *The urgency of post-Nationalist perspectives: "Turkey for the Turks" or an open society? On the Kurdish Conflict*, in Hans-Lukas Kieser (ed.), *Turkey beyond nationalism*, London: I.B.Tauris, pp. 155–63.

Gurowitz, Amy (2006). "The Diffusion of International Norms: Why Identity Matters", *International Politics*, Vol. 43, pp. 305–41.

Haber 7, April 5, 2008, 3. Uluslararası Lale Festivali başladı, Accessible online at http://www.haber7.com/kultur/haber/311065–3-uluslararasi-lale-festivali-basl adi.

—— April 16, 2013, *Erdoğan: Türklük Anayasa'dan çıkarılamaz*, Accessible online at http://www.haber7.com/partiler/haber/1014734-erdogan-turkluk-anayasadan-cikarilamaz.

—— September 15, 2013, *Türkler gelmeden önce azraili bekliyorduk*, Accessible online at http://www.haber7.com/guncel/haber/1074050-turkler-gelmeden-once-azraili-bekliyorduk.

Haberartiturk, April 3, 2013, *Abdullah Gül; 'Türk'tür' diye bir şey yok'*, Accessible online at http://haberartiturk.com/Haber/abdullah-gul--turk-tur–diye-bir-sey-yok-.html.

HaberTurk, December 12, 2013, *Klavye'deki Türklük*, Accessible online at http://www.haberturk.com/yazarlar/murat-bardakci/903007-klavyedeki-turkluk.

Hablemitoğlu, Necip (1999). *Kemal'in Öğretmenleri*, Yeni Hayat, Kasım.

Hafız, Nimetullah (1989). *Yugoslavya'da Çağdaş Türk Edebiyatı Antolojisi, Cilt 1*, Ankara: Kültür Bakanlığı Yayınları.

Hanrieder, F. Wolfram (1967). "Compatibility and Consensus: A Proposal for the Conceptual Linkage of External and Internal Dimensions of Foreign Policy", *The American Political Science Review*, pp. 971–82.

Harrison, Ewan (2004). "State Socialization, International Norm Dynamics and the Liberal Peace", *International Politics*, Vol. 41, pp. 521–42.

Hatay, Mete (2008). "The problem of pigeons: orientalism, xenophobia and a rhetoric of the 'local' in north Cyprus", *The Cyprus Review*, Vol. 20, No. 2, pp. 145–72.

Herman, G. Robert (1996). *Identity, Norms, and National Security: The Societ Foreign Policy Revolution and the End of the Cold War*, in Katzenstein, Peter (ed.), *The Culture of National Security-Norms and Identity in World Politics*, New York: Columbia University Press.

Hill, Christopher and Light, Margot (1985). *Foreign Policy Analysis*, in Light, Margot and Groom A.J.R. (eds), *International Relations: A Handbook of Current Theory*, London: Pinter Publishers, pp. 156–73.

Hopf, Ted (1998). "The Promise of Constructivism in International Relations Theory", *International Security*, Vol. 23, No. 1, pp. 171–200.

Höpken, Wolfgang (1997). *From Religious Identity to Ethnic Mobilization: The Turks of Bulgaria Before, Under, and Since Communism*, in Poulton, Hugh and Taji-Farouki, Suha, Muslim Identity and the Balkan State, London: Hurst & Company.

Hrabak, Bogumil (2003). *Dzemijet: Organizacija Muslimana Makedonije, Kosova, Metohije i Sandjaka 1919–1928*, Beograd: VMD.

Hüdaverdi, Nevzat (2001). *Prištine'de Türkçe Eğitim (1951–2001)*, Prištine: Kosova Açık Toplum Vakfı.

Hür Haber, November 27, 2007, *'Türküm demek ayıp hale geldi'*, Accessible online at http://www.hurhaber.com/haberarsiv/turkum-demek-ayip-hale-geldi/ 86389.

Hurriyet Daily News, June 19, 2012, *Magazine Journalists to honor Ahmet Kaya*, Accessible online at http://www.hurriyetdailynews.com/magazine-journalists-to-honor-ahmet-kaya.aspx?pageID=238&nID=23473&NewsCatID=383.

Hürriyet, September 17, 2012, *Ulusculukla hesaplaşma zamanı geldi*, Accessible online at http://www.Hürriyet.com.tr/gundem/21483551.

—— February 18, 2013, *Erdoğan: Milliyetçilik ayak altında*, Accessible online at http ://www.Hürriyet.com.tr/gundem/22621388.asp.

—— July 13, 2013, *Yargıtay'dan 'Kürdistan' ismine onay*, Accessible online at http:// www.hurriyet.com.tr/gundem/23718266.asp.

—— November 5, 2013, *Devlet nişanları değişti*, Accessible online at http://www. hurriyet.com.tr/gundem/25075783.asp.

—— November 6, 2013, *Diyarbakır'da o tabela kaldırıldı*, Accessible online at http ://www.hurriyet.com.tr/gundem/25060087.asp.

—— December 27, 2014, *İşte Ak Parti'nin seçim şarkısı*, Accessible online at www. hurriyet.com.tr/Haber?id=27851580.

IHA, September 25, 2014, *IŞİD'le mücadeleye CHP'den destek*, Accessible online at http://www.iha.com.tr/haber-isidle-mucadeleye-chpden-destek-394293/.

IHH, 2012, http://www.ihh.org.tr/tr/main/pages/gelir-gider/86.

İhsanoğlu, Ekmeleddin (2009). *Kultura E Bashkëjetesës, Pristine:TIKA. Translated by Musli Ymeri and Xhabir Hamiti*, The book was originally published by IRCICA Publications in Istanbul in 2004.

Ingebritsen, Christine (2002). "Norm Entrepreneurs: Scandavia's Role in World Politics", *Cooperation and Conflict: Journal of Nordic International 'studies Association*, Vol. 37, No. 1, pp. 11–23.

İsmail, Sabahattin (2001a). "Atatürk'ün Kıbrıs'a ve Kıbrıs Türklerine Verdiği Önem – 1", *Bölüm, Müdafaa-i Hukuk*, No. 36 (August).

—— (2001b). "Atatürk'ün Kıbrıs'a ve Kıbrıs Türklerine Verdiği Önem – 2, Bölüm", *Müdafaa-i Hukuk*, No. 37 (September).

Jacobsen, John Kurt (1996). "Are All Politics Domestic? Perspectives on the Integration of Comparative Politics and International Relations Theories", *Comparative Politics*, Vol. 29, No. 1, pp. 93–115.

Jacoby, Tim and Tabak, Hüsrev (2015). "Islam, Nationalism and Kurdish Ethnopolitics in Turkey", *Peace Review: A Journal of Social Justice*, Vol. 27, No. 3, pp. 346–53.

Jepperson, Ronald, Wendt, Alexander and Katzenstein, Peter J. (1996). *Norms, Identity, and Culture in National Security*, in Peter J. Katzenstein (ed.), *The Culture of National Security*, pp. 33–75. New York: Columbia University Press.

Johnston, I. Alastair (1996). *Cultural Realism and Strategy in Maoist China*, in Katzenstein, Peter (ed.), *The Culture of National Security-Norms and Identity in World Politics*, New York: Columbia University Press.

Kadıoğlu, Ayşe (2007). "Denationalization of Citizenship? The Turkish Experience", *Citizenship Studies*, Vol. 11, No. 3, pp. 283–99.

Kadirbeyoglu, Zeynep (2009). *Changing Conceptions of citizenship in Turkey*, in Bauböck *et al.* (eds), *Citizenship Policies in the New Europe*, Amsterdam: Amsterdam University Press, pp. 419–40.

Kapstein, B. Ethan (1995). "Is realism dead? The domestic sources of international politics", *International Organizations*, Vol. 49, No. 4, pp. 751–74.

Karadeniz, Radiye Funda (2011). "Türk Dış Politikası'nda "Dış Türkler": Karşılaştırmalı Teorik Bir Çalışma", Unpublished PhD Thesis, Marmara University, Istanbul.

Karakoç, Ercan (2001). "Atatürk'ün Dış Türkler Politikası", Unpublished Master's Thesis, Kocaeli: Gebze Yüksek Teknoloji Enstitüsü.

Karpat, H. Kemal (1995). "The Turks of Bulgaria: The Struggle for National-Religious Survival of a Muslim Minority", *Nationalities Papers*, Vol. 23, No. 4, 725–48.

Katzenstein, Peter (1993). *Coping with Terrorism: Norms and Internal Security in Germany and Japan*, in Judith Goldstein and Robert O. Keohane (eds), *Ideas and Foreign Policy: Beliefs, Institutions and Political Change*, pp. 265–95, Ithaca: Cornell University Press, 1993.

—— (ed.) (1996a). *The Culture of National Security- Norms and Identity in World Politics*, New York: Columbia University Press.

—— (1996b). *Cultural Norms and National Security*, Ithaca and London: Cornell University Press.

Katzenstein, Peter, Keohane, Robert, and Krasner, D. Stephen (1998). "International Organization and the Study of World Politics", *International Organization*, Vol. 52, No. 4, pp. 645–85.

Kemmis, Stephen and Wilkinson, Merwyn (1998). *Participatory action research and the study of practice*, in Atweh, Bill, Kemmis, Stephen, Weeks, Patricia (eds), *Action research in practice: Partnerships for social justice in education*, New York: Routledge, pp. 21–36.

Keser, Ulvi (2007). "Genç Türkiye Devleti'nin Cumhuriyet Kazanımları ve Bunların Kıbrıs Türk Toplumuna Yansımaları", *ÇTTAD*, Vol. 6, No. 14, Spring, pp. 41–84.

Kier, Elizabeth (1996). *Culture and French Military Doctrine*, in Katzenstein, Peter (ed.) *The Culture of National Security-Norms and Identity in World Politics*, New York: Columbia University Press.

Killoran, Moira (1998). "Good Muslims and "Bad Muslims," "Good" Women and Feminists: Negotiating Identities in Northern Cyprus (Or, the Condom Story)", *Ethos*, Vol. 26, Issue 2, pp. 183–203.

Kirişçi, Kemal (2006). *National Identity, asylum and immigration: The EU as a vehicle of post-national transformation in Turkey*, in Hans-Lukas Kieser (ed.), *Turkey beyond nationalism*, London: I.B.Tauris, pp. 183–99.

—— (2009). *Mirage or Reality: Post-National Turkey and Its Implications for Immigration*, Robert Schuman Centre for Advanced Studies, CARIM Research Reports, 2009/14.

Kızılyürek, Niyazi (2002). *Rauf Denktaş ve Kıbrıs Türk Milliyetçiliği*, in Bora, Tanıl (ed.), *Modern Türkiye'de Siyasi Düşünce – Milliyetçilik*, İstanbul: İletişim, pp. 309–24.

Kızılyürek, Niyazi and Gautier Kızılyürek, Sylvaine (2004). "The politics of identity in the Turkish Cypriot community and the language question", *International Journal of Sociology of Language*, No. 168, pp. 37–54.

KKTC Constitution (1983). *Constitution of the Turkish Republic of Northern Cyprus*, Accessible online at http://www.cypnet.co.uk/ncyprus/main/polsyst/constitution/.

Klotz, Audie (1995). *Norms in International Relations: The Struggle against Apartheid*, Ithaca, NY: Cornell University Press.

Knaus, Gerald (2010). *Multikulti and the future of Turkish Balkan Policy*, December, 4, Accessible online at http://www.esiweb.org/rumeliobserver/2010/12/04/multikulti-and-the-future-of-turkish-balkan-policy/.

Köksal, Yonca (2010). "Transnational networks and kin states: the Turkish minority in Bulgaria, 1878–1940", *Nationalities Papers*, Vol. 38, No. 2, pp. 191–211.

Korkut, Şenol (2010). *The Diyanet of Turkey and Its Activities in Eurasia after the Cold War*, Acta Slavica Iaponica, Tomus 28, pp. 117–39.

Koro, Bedrettin (2011). *Kosova Cumhuriyeti İlköğretim Okullarinin Tarih Dersi Müfredatinda ve Ders Kitaplarinda Mustafa Kemal Atatürk*, 7. Uluslararası Atatürk Kongresi, 17–22. Ekim 2011, Makedonya, Atatürk Araştırma Merkezi Başkanlığı [ATAUM] and Makedonya Bilimler ve Sanatlar Akademisi (MANU). Information regarding the conference is accessible online at http://www.atam.gov.tr/etkinlikler/vii-uluslararasi-ataturk-kongresi-17–22-kasim-2011-makedonya.

Kösebalaban, Hasan (2005). "The Impact of Globalization on Islamic Political Identity: The Case of Turkey", *World Affairs*, Vol. 168, No. 1, pp. 27–37.

Kosova Haber, November 3, 2010, *Erdoğan Prizrenlilere Seslendi*, Accessible online at http://www.kosovahaber.com/?page=2,9,3530.

—— November 9, 2010, *Semazenlerden Muhteşem Gösteri*, Accessible online at http://www.kosovahaber.com/?page=2,11,3622.

—— March 1, 2011, *Kosova'da Okullardaki Ders Haritalarında 'Kürdistan' ve Ermenistan Yazısı*, Accessible online at http://www.kosovahaber.com/?page=2,38,5477.

—— March 9, 2011, *Mehmet Akif Ersoy Günleri Cuma Başlıyor*, Accessible online at http://www.kosovahaber.com/?page=2,11,5621.

—— March 12, 2011a, *Mehmet Akif, Türk–Arnavut Kardeşliğinin Sembolü*, Accessible online at http://www.kosovahaber.com/?page=2,11,5673.

—— March 12, 2011b, *Priştine'de Mehmet Akif Ersoy'u Anma Sempozyumu Düzenlendi*, Accessible online at http://www.kosovahaber.com/?page=2,11, 5682.

—— August 22, 2011, *Ozan: Yanlış ve Önyargılı İfadeler Değiştirilmeli*, Accessible online at http://www.kosovahaber.com/?page=2,9,8138.

—— August 26, 2011, *Kosova Türk–Arnavut İlişkilerini Tartışıyor*, Accessible online at http://www.kosovahaber.com/?page=2,9,8199.

—— August 27, 2011, *Davutoğlu Kosova'nın Toprak Bütünlüğünü ve Egemenliğini Bir Kez Daha Teyit Etti*, Accessible online at http://www.kosovahaber.com/?page=2,9,8217.

—— December 19, 2011, *Kosova'da Mevlana Günleri Panel ile Devam Etti*, Accessible online at http://www.kosovahaber.com/?page=2,11,9972.

—— December 25, 2011, *Mevlana Haftası, Tasavvuf Konseriyle Sona Erdi*, Accessible online at http://www.kosovahaber.com/?page=2,11,10072.

—— April 26, 2012, *Kosova'daki Müslümanlar, Kardeşlik Örneği*, Accessible online at http://www.kosovahaber.com/?page=2,11,12251.

—— September 23, 2014, *AKEA ve 10'dan fazla STK Kapatildi*, Accessible online at http://www.kosovahaber.net/?page=2,12,26479.

——Accessible online at http://www.kosovahaber.com/?page=2,11,22634.

Kosova Port, November 3, 2010a, *Tarihi Prizren'de Tarihi Gün*, Accessible online at http://www.kosovaport.com/?p=770.

—— August 11, 2012, *Gilan'da Alaaddin Medresesi'nin açılışını Bozdağ Yaptı*, Accessible online at http://www.kosovaport.com/?p=26306.

—— August 12, 2011, *Arınç'tan Prizren'de Önemli Mesajlar*, Accessible online at http://www.kosovaport.com/?p=11132.

—— August 19, 2011, *Bakan Dincer KDTP iftarinda*, Accessible online at http://www.kosovaport.com/?p=11422.

—— August 27, 2011b, *Davutoğlu: Kosovali Kardeşlerimiz Ailemiz, Kosova Silamizdir*, Accessible online at http://www.kosovaport.com/?p=11737.

—— August 28, 2011, *Davutoğlu Mehmet Akif Ersoy'un Köyünü Ziyaret Etti*, Accessible online at http://www.kosovaport.com/?p=11794.

—— August 16, 2012, *Kosova'daki Kasabaya Obiliç'in İsminin Verilmesine Tahammül Edemiyoruz*, Accessible online at http://www.kosovaport.com/?p=26531.

—— September 5, 2012, Davutoğlu: *Arnavut Kökenli 28 Başbakanımız Vardı*, Accessible online at http://www.kosovaport.com/?p=27414.

—— June 3, 2013, Erdoğan: *Priştine'de Büyük Bir Cami İnşa Edeceğiz*, Accessible online at http://www.kosovaport.com/?p=39754.

—— June 21, 2014, Priştine'de yeni caminin yapımı görüşüldü, Accessible online at http://www.kosovaport.com/pristinede-yeni-caminin-yapimi-gorusuldu/.

Kosova'dan Çanakkale'ye, (2008). *Kosova'dan Çanakkale'ye Makalelerle, Anılarla, Şiirlerle, Törenlerle ve Belgelerle 1915 Savaşı*, Prizren: Bal-Tam Yayınları.

Köstüklü, Nuri (2011). "TMT Öncesi Kıbrıs Türkleri'nin Durumuna Dair Türkiye'nin Kıbrıs Konsolosluğunca Hazırlanan Bir Rapor ve Düşündürdükleri", *Atatürk Araştırma Merkezi Dergisi*, No. 81, pp. 533–43.

Kowert, A. Paul and Legro, W. Jeffrey (1996). *Norms, Identity, and Their Limits: A Theoretical Reprise*, in Katzenstein, Peter (ed.), *The Culture of National Security- Norms and Identity in World Politics*, New York: Columbia University Press.

Krasner, D. Stephen (ed.) (1983). *Introduction*, International Regimes, Ithaca, NY: Cornell University Press.

Krasniqi, Gëzim (2011). "The 'forbidden fruit': Islam and politics of identity in Kosovo and Macedonia", *Southeast European and Black Sea Studies*, Vol. 11, No. 2, pp. 191–207.

Kratochwil, V. Fredrich (1991). *Rules, norms, and decisions: on the conditions of practical and legal reasoning in international relations and domestic affairs*, Cambridge: Cambridge University Press.

Kratochwil, Friedrich and Ruggie, G. John (1986). "International Organization: a state of art on an art of the state", *International Organization*, Vol. 40, No. 4, pp. 753–75.

Kreiser, Klaus (2002). "Public Monuments in Kemalist and Post-Kemalist Turkey", *Journal of Turkish Studies*, Vol. 26, No. 2, pp. 43–60.

Kubalkova, Vendulka (2001). *Foreign Policy, International Politics, and Constructivism*, in Vendulka Kubalkova (ed.), *Foreign Policy in a Constructed World*, New York: E. Sharpe.

Küçükcan, Talip (1999). "Re-claiming identity: Ethnicity, Religion, and Politics among Turkish Muslims in Bulgaria and Greece", *Journal of Muslim Minority Affairs*, Vol. 19, No. 1, 1999.

Kutay, Cemal (1993). *Atatürk Olmasaydı*, İstanbul: Kazancı Kitap Tic.

Laciner, Sedat (2001). "From Kemalism to Ozalism, the Ideological Evolution of Turkish Foreign Policy", Unpublished PhD thesis, London: King's College University of London.

Lampe, R. John (1996). *Yugoslavia as History: Twice there was a country*, Cambridge: Cambridge University Press.

Landau, M. Jacob (1995). *Pan-Turkism – From irredentism to cooperation*, London: Hurst & Company.

Landman, Nico (1997). *Sustaining Turkish Islamic Loyalities: The Diyanet in Western Europe*, in Poulton, Hugh and Taji-Farouki, Suha (eds), *Muslim Identity and the Balkan State*, London: Hurst & Company.

Legro, W. Jeffrey (1997). "Which norms matter? Revisiting the "failure" of internationalism", *International Organization*, Vol. 51, No. 1, pp. 31–63.

Light, Margot (1994). *Foreign policy analysis*, in Groom, A.J.R. and Light, Marton (ed.), *Contemporary International Relations: A Guide to Theory*, London: Pinter, pp. 93–108.

Maoz and Russett (1991). *Normative and structuralc auses of democraticp eace, 1946– 1986*, Paper presented at the Annual meeting of the Peace Science Society (International), Ann Arbor, Michigan.

Mardin, Şerif (2005). *Turkish Islamic Exceptionalism Yesterday and Today: Continuity, Rupture and Reconstruction in Operational Codes*, Turkish Studies, 6:2, pp. 145–65.

Mehmet Aydın (2006). *A Parliamentary speech*, TBMM Tutanak Dergisi, Birleşim 53, 24.01.2006, pp. 164–95.

Mehmet Özay, Dünya Bülteni, June 24, 2013, *Türkiye'nin Malezya'daki bağları, 'Malezya Müslüman Öğrenciler Birliği' Genel Sekreteri Muhammed Raimi ile Malezya ve Türkiye'yi konuştuk*, Accessible online at http://www.dunyabulteni.net/rop ortaj/264404/turkiyenin-malezyadaki-baglari.

Mehmetçik Kosova'da (2002). *Mehmetçik Kosova'da Booklet*, Yayına Hazırlayanlar Zeynel Beksaç, Raif Kirkul, Prizren: Kosova Türk Yazarlar Derneği Yayınları.

——— (2009). *Mehmetçik Kosova'da Booklet*, Kosova Türk Temsil Heyet Başkanlığı Yayını.

Meral, Akşener (1997). *A Parliamentary speech*, TBMM Tutanak Dergisi, Birleşim 60, 25.02.1997, pp. 142–3.

Mertens, D.M. (1998). *Research methods in Education and Psychology: Integrating diversity with quantitative and qualitative approaches*, Thousand Oaks: Sage Publications.

Milliyet, November 19, 2013, Erdoğan'dan önemli açıklamalar, Accessible online at http://siyaset.milliyet.com.tr/erdogan-dan-onemli-aciklamalar/siyaset/detay/1794452/default.htm.

Müftüler-Bac, Meltem (2005). "Turkey's Political Reforms and the Impact of the European Union", *South European Society & Politics*, Vol. 10, No. 1, pp. 16–30.

Mynet, April 3, 2013, *Türküm demekten korkar oldum*, Accessible online at http://www.mynet.com/haber/guncel/turkum-demekten-korkar-oldum-687186–1.

Nesim, Ali (1989). "Kıbrıs Türklerinde Atatürk İlke ve İnkılapları, Atatürk Araştırma Merkezi Dergisi", Vol. 5, No. 14, pp. 326–43.

Nevzat, Altay (2005). *Nationalism amongst the Turks of Cyprus: The first wave*, Oulu: Oulu University Press.

Odell, S. John (2001). "Case Study Methods in International Political Economy", *International Studies Perspectives*, 2, pp. 161–76.

Öge, Akin (2009). "Türkiye'de resmi miliyetçiliğin "Türklük" kavrayışı: "Dış Türklerden Sorumlu" Devlet Bakanlığı ve Türk İşbirliği ve Kalkınma İdaresi Başkanlığı (TİKA). incelemesi", Unpublished Masters Thesis, Yıldız Technical University, Istanbul.

Öksüz, Hikmet (2001). "Batı Trakya Basınında Atatürkçü Bir Gazete", *Inkılap (1930–1931). Atatürk Araştırma Merkezi Dergisi*, Vol. 17, No. 40.

Öktem, Kerem (2010). *New Islamic actors after the Wahhabi intermezzo: Turkey's return to the Muslim Balkans*, European Studies Centre, University of Oxford. Working paper.

——— (2012). "Global Diyanet and Multiple Networks: Turkey's New Presence in the Balkans", *Journal of Muslims in Europe*, Vol. 2012, No. 1, pp. 27–58.

Onar, Nora Fisher (2009). "Echoes of a Universalism Lost: Rival Representations of the Ottomans in Today's Turkey", *Middle Eastern Studies*, Vol. 45, No. 2, pp. 229–41.

Öniş, Ziya (1997). "The Political Economy of Islamic Resurgence in Turkey: The Rise of the Welfare Party in Perspective", *Third World Quarterly*, Vol. 18, No. 4, pp. 743–66.

Onuf, G. Nicholas (1989). *World of Our Making: Rules and Rule in Social Theory and International Relations*, Columbia, University of South Carolina Press.

Onur, Öymen (2005). *A Parliamentary speech*, TBMM Tutanak Dergisi, Birleşim 106, 01.06.2005, pp. 245–9.

Oran, Baskın (1991). *Türk-Yunan İlişkilerinde Batı Trakya Sorunu*, Ankara: Bilgi Yayınları.

——— (2001). "Kemalism, Islamism, and Globalizaiton: A study on focus supreme loyalty in Globalizing Turkey", *Southeast European and Black Sea Studies*, Vol. 1, No. 3, pp. 20–50.

——— (2004). "Azınlık Hakları ve Kültürel Haklar Raporu'nun Bütün Öyküsü", *Birikim*, No. 188, pp. 17–25.

——— (2011). "The issue of 'Turkish' and 'Türkiyeli' (Turkey National; from Turkey)", January 11, 2011, *Today's Zaman*, Accessible online at http://www.todayszaman.com/news-232143-the-issue-of-%E2%80%9Cturkish%E2%80%9D-and-%E2%80%9Cturkiyeli%E2%80%9D-turkey-national-from-turkey.html.

Orhan, Merva (2012). "Cruelty in Arakan (Arakan'da Zulum)," *Arti90*, July, pp. 78–9.

Osman, Durmuş (2009). *A Parliamentary speech*, TBMM Tutanak Dergisi, Birleşim 82, 28.04.2009, pp. 245, 296–7.

Özdalga, M. Elizabeth (2006). "The Hidden Arab: A Critical Reading of the Notion of 'Turkish Islam'", *Middle Eastern Studies*, Vol. 42, No. 4, pp. 551–70.

Özdemir, Suzan (1999). "Atatürk Devriminin Diğer Ülkeler Üzerindeki Etkileri", Unpublished PhD Thesis, İstanbul: İstanbul Üniversitesi Atatürk İlkeleri ve İnkılapları Enstitüsü.

Özdoğan, İbrahim (2007). *A Parliamentary speech, TBMM Tutanak, Dergisi*, Birleşim 117, 30.05.2007, pp. 133–6.

Park, Susan and Vetterlein, Antje (2010). *Owning Development Creating Policy Norms in the IMF and the World Bank*, Cambridge: Cambridge University Press.

Popovic, Aleksandre (1995 [1986]). *Balkanlarda İslam (L'Islam balkanique: les musulmans du sudest europeen dans la période postottomane)*, İstanbul: İnsan Yayınları.

Poulton, Hugh (1997b). *Turkey as a Kin-State: Turkish Foreign policy towards Turkish and Muslim Communities in the Balkans*, in Poulton, Hugh and Taji-Farouki, Suha (eds), *Muslim Identity and the Balkan State*, London: Hurst & Company.

Price, Richard and Reus-Smit, Christian (1998). "Dangerous Liaisons? Critical International Theory and Constructivism", *European Journal of International Relations*, Vol. 4, No. 3, pp. 259–94.

Pristina.be.mfa.gov.tr.

Putnam, D. Robert (1988). "Diplomacy and domestic politics: the logic of two-level games", *International Organization*, Vol. 42, No. 3, pp. 427–60.

Radikal, October 12, 2005, *Kosovalılara Üç Nasihat*, Accessible online at http://www.radikal.com.tr/haber.php?haberno=166712.

——— May 28, 2006, *Türk-İslam sentezi ideolojisinin failini tanımak*, by Çiler Dursun, Accessible online at http://www.radikal.com.tr/ek_haber.php?ek=r2&haberno=5895.

——— April 15, 2009, *Genelkurmay'dan açılım: Türk değil Türkiye halkı*, Accessible online at http://www.radikal.com.tr/politika/genelkurmaydan_acilim_turk_degil_turkiye_halki-931193.

——— April 17, 2009a, *Başbuğ'a Encümen-i Daniş'ten destek*, Accessible online at http://www.radikal.com.tr/turkiye/basbuga_encumen_i_danisten_destek-931603.

——— April 17, 2009b, *Başbuğ AKP'li Kürt milletvekillerini umutlandırdı*, Accessible online at http://www.radikal.com.tr/politika/basbug_akpli_kurt_milletvekillerini_umutlandirdi-931625.

—— May 5, 2012, *Bayramda resmi törene son*, Accessible online at http://www. radikal.com.tr/turkiye/bayramda_resmi_torene_son-1087029.

—— September 30, 2013, *İşte demokrasi paketinin içeriği*, 'Anadilde Mektebi Sultani' modeli, Accessible online at http://www.radikal.com.tr/turkiye/iste_ demokrasi_paketinin_icerigi-1153164.

—— September 30, 2013a, *İşte demokrasi paketinin içeriği*, Accessible online at http:// www.radikal.com.tr/turkiye/iste_demokrasi_paketinin_icerigi-1153164.

—— September 30, 2013b, *Başbakan Erdoğan 'Demokratikleşme Paketi'ni açıkladı,* Accessible online at http://www.radikal.com.tr/politika/basbakan_erdogan_ demokratiklesme_paketini_acikliyor-1153198.

—— November 20, 2013, *Serdar Ortaç: Kendimden tiksiniyorum*, Accessible online at http://www.radikal.com.tr/turkiye/serdar_ortac_kendimden_tiksiniyorum-1161984.

—— January 2, 2015, *Cumhuriyet tarihinde bir ilk! Yeni kilise yapılması kararı alındı*, Accessible online at www.radikal.com.tr/politika/basbakan_davutoglundan_ bir_ilk_yesilkoyde_kilise_yapilmasi_talimati-126414.

Recepoğlu, Altay Suroy (2004). *Kosova Türkçe veya Kimlik Mücadelesi*, Prizren: Siprint Basımevi.

—— (2005). *Kosova Türk Toplumunun ve Üyelerinin Hakları*, Prizren: Özel Yayın.

—— (2006). *Kosova'da Türk Olmak*, Prizren: Özel Yayın.

—— (2007). *Kosova'nın Türk Dernekleri ve Kuruluşları (1951–2006)*, Prizren: Siprint Basımevi.

Reşat, Doğru (2008). *A Parliamentary speech,* TBMM Tutanak Dergisi, Birleşim 30, 18.12.2008, pp. 312–14.

Reus-Smit, Christian (2005). *Constructivism*, in Burchill, Scot *et al.*, *Theories of International Relations*, 3rd edn, Basingstoke: Palgrave.

Richards, David (1996). "Elite Interviewing: Approaches and Pitfalls", *Politics*, Vol. 16, No. 3, pp. 199–204.

Risse, Thomas (1999). *The Power of Human Rights: International Norms and Domestic Change*, Cambridge: Cambridge University Press.

Risse, Thomas (2000). "'Let's Argue!': Communicative Action in World Politics", *International Organization*, Vol. 54, No. 1, Winter, pp. 1–39.

Risse, Thomas and Sikkink, Kathryn (1999). *The socialization of International Norms into domestic practices: introduction,* in Risse *et al.* (eds), *The Power of Human Rights: International Norms and Domestic Change*, Cambridge: Cambridge University Press.

Risse-Kappen, Thomas (1994). "Ideas do not float freely: Transnational Coalitions, Domestic Structures, and the End of the Cold War", *International Organization*, Vol. 48, No. 2, pp. 185–214.

—— (ed.) (1995). *Bringing Transnational Back In: Non-state actors, Domestic Structures, and International Institutions*, Cambridge: Cambridge University Press.

Robins, Philip (1997). "Turkish foreign policy under Erbakan", *Survival: Global Politics and Strategy*, Vol. 39, No. 2, pp. 82–100.

Robson, Colin (1993). *Real World Research – A resource for Social Scientists and Practitioner-Researchers*, Oxford: Blackwell.

Rose, Gideon (1998). "Neoclassical Realism and Theories of Foreign Policy", *World Politics*, No. 51, pp. 144–72.

Rosenau, James (1987). *New Directions and Recurrent Questions in the Comparative Study of Foreign Policy*, in Charles F. Hermann *et al.* (ed.), *New Directions in the Study of Foreign Policy*, Boston: Allen & Unwin.

Rubasam, December 15, 2012, *TIKA'dan Kosova'da Sivil Toplumu Destekleyen Proje*, Accessible online at http://www.rubasam.com/NewsDetail.Asp?News ID=1822&Title=T%DDKA%92DAN-KOSOVA%92DA-S%DDV%DDL-TOPLUMU-DESTEKLEYEN-PROJE.

Sabah, July 5, 1999, *Şükür Kavuşturana*, p. 1.

—— January 21, 2013, *PM Erdoğan says No to Ethnic Nationalism*, Accessible online at http://english.sabah.com.tr/National/2013/01/21/pm-Erdoğan-says-no-to-ethnic-nationalism.

—— November 21, 2013, *Abdullah Gül during an inaugural address at the Economic and Commercial Cooperation of the Organization of Islamic Cooperation's (COMCEC)*, Accessible online at http://english.sabah.com.tr/national/2013/11/21/pres ident-gul-if-we-do-not-come-up-with-a-solution-others-will.

Safçı, Nazan and Koro, Bedrettin (2008). *Kosova'da Türkçe Eğitimde Öğretmen Kadrosu*, Prizren: Ngbl Beratiç.

Şahin, G. Mustafa (2010). "Turkey and Neo-Ottomanism: Domestic Sources, Dynamics, and Foreign Policy", Unpublished PhD Thesis, Florida International University.

Samanyoluhaber, July 27, 2012, *AK Parti, anayasada 'vatandaş' açılımı yaptı*, Accessible online at http://www.samanyoluhaber.com/politika/Turkluk-ifades inin-yerine-bu-gelecek/805264/.

—— April 5, 2013, *İşte parti parti yeni anayasa tasarıları!*, Accessible online at http://www.samanyoluhaber.com/politika/Iste-parti-parti-yeni-anayasa-tas arilari/984076/.

Sarınay, Yusuf (1996). *Atatürk'ün Hatay Politikası I (1936–1938)*, Atatürk Araştırma Merkezi Dergisi, 12:34. Accessible online at http://www.atam.gov.tr/ dergi/sayi-34/ataturkun-hatay-politikasi-i-1936-1938.

Schutt, K. Russell (2012). *Investigating the Social World: The Process and Practice of Research*, 7th edn, Thousand Oaks: Sage Publications.

Simons, Helen (2009). *Case study Research in Practice*, London: Sage Publication.

Snyder, Jack (1991). *Myths of Empire: Domestic Politics and International Ambition*, Ithaca: Cornell University Press.

Solberg, Anne Ross (2007). "Balkan Muslims and Islam in Europe", *SudostEuropa*, Vol. 55, No. 4, pp. 429–62.

Sonyel, R. Salâhi (1995). "İngiliz Yönetiminde Kıbrıs Türklerinin Varlık Savaşımı (1878–1960)". *Belleten*, Vol. 59, No. 224, pp. 133–90.

Sozcu, February 25, 2013, *Türk bayrağı, Türkiye bayrağı oldu*, Accessible online at http://sozcu.com.tr/2013/gundem/turk-bayragi-turkiye-bayragi-oldu-235103/.

—— August 28, 2013, *O ödül artık yok*, Accessible online at http://sozcu.com.tr/ 2013/gundem/o-odul-artik-yok-362397/.

Stake, E. Robert (1995). *The Art of Case Study Research*, London: Sage Publications.

T24, November 05, 2012, *Bekir Bozdağ: Büyük bir dramla büyük bir asimilasyonla karşı karşıyayız*, Accessible online at http://t24.com.tr/haber/bozdag-yurt-dis indaki-sahipsiz-turk-cocuklari-hristiyanlastiriliyor/216741.

Tabak, Hüsrev (2011). "Political and Ideological Profiling of Muslims in Inter-War Yugoslavia", Unpublished MA Dissertation, University College London: School of Slavonic and East European Studies.

—— (2015). "Broadening the Nongovernmental Humanitarian Mission: The IHH and Mediation", *Insight Turkey*, Vol. 17, No. 3, pp. 193–215.

Takvim, March 10, 2015, *Bedrettin Dalan Türkiye'ye döndü*, Accessible online at http://www.takvim.com.tr/guncel/2015/03/10/bedrettin-dalan-turkiyeye-dondu.

Tan, January 8, 1971.

—— January 14, 1989.

—— November 12, 1989.

—— March 10, 1990.

—— April 14, 1990.

—— April 21, 1990.

—— June 2, 1990.

—— June 30, 1990.

—— July 7, 1990.

—— September 8, 1990.

—— September 22, 1990.

—— November 3, 1990.

—— November 17, 1990.

—— December 22, 1990.

—— January 11, 1991.

—— February 29, 1992.

—— March 7, 1992.

—— March 21, 1992.

—— April 29, 1992.

—— May 30, 1992.

—— June 20, 1992.

—— July 11, 1992.

—— August 29, 1992.

—— November 21, 1992.

—— February 20, 1993.

—— March 6, 1993.

—— March 20, 1993.

Taraf, October 14, 2011, *Türklük yerine yurttaşlık gelsin*, Accessible online at http://taraf.com.tr/haber/turkluk-yerine-yurttaslik-gelsin.htm.

Taşpınar, Ömer (2008). *Turkey's Middle East Policies: Between Neo-Ottomanism and Kemalism*, Carnegie Papers, No. 10, Washington, DC.

—— (2013a). *The Big Picture of post-Kemalist Turkey (1)*, November 3, Accessible online at http://www.todayszaman.com/columnists/omer-taspinar-330501-the-big-picture-of-post-kemalist-turkey-1.html.

—— (2013b). *The Big Picture of post-Kemalist Turkey (2)*, November 10, Accessible online at http://www.todayszaman.com/columnist/omer-taspinar_331057_the-big-picture-of-post-kemalist-turkey-2.htmlTan, April 04, 1992.

Tataroglu, Elif, April 10, 2013, *İktidarın "lale" inadı*, Accessible online at http://arsiv.gercekgundem.com/?c=70650.

Tepe, Sultan (2000). "A Kemalist-Islamist movement? The nationalist action party", *Turkish Studies*, Vol. 1, No. 2, pp. 59–72.

Thies, Cameron (2003). "Sense and sensibility in the study of state socialisation a reply to Kai Alderson", *Review of International Studies*, Vol. 29, No. 4, pp. 543–50.

TIKA Dünyası, June 2012, "Interview with Bekir Bozdağ", Vol. 1, pp. 17–21.

—— December 2012, "Interview with Ahmet Davutoğlu", Vol. 2, pp. 20–6.

TIKA Faaliyet Raporu 2005, Accessible online at tika.gov.tr.
—— 2006, Accessible online at tika.gov.tr.
—— 2007, Accessible online at tika.gov.tr.
—— 2008, Accessible online at tika.gov.tr.
—— 2009, Accessible online at tika.gov.tr.
—— 2010, Accessible online at tika.gov.tr.
—— 2011, Accessible online at tika.gov.tr.
TIKA Haber, January 23, 2012, *Sultan Murad Türbesi Kompleksinde Çalışmalar Tamamlandı*, Accessible online at http://www.tika.gov.tr/haber/sultan-murat-tu rbesi-kompleksinde-calismalar-tamamladi/164.
TIKA Kosova Proje ve Faaliyetleri, 2006–7.
TIKA: Kosovo – Projects and Activities Booklet, 2009.
Time Türk, November 7, 2009, *İşte 'Kürt açılımı'*, Accessible online at http://www.timeturk.com/tr/2009/11/07/iste-kurt-acilimi.html.
—— October 22, 2012, *Interview: Bülent Yıldırım 'Yeniden ümmet' seferini anlattı*, Accessible online at http://www.timeturk.com/tr/2012/10/22/bulent-yildirim-yeniden-ummet-seferini-anlatti.html.
Tocci, Nathalie (2005). "Europeanization in Turkey: Trigger or Anchor for Reform?", *South European Society & Politics*, Vol. 10, No. 1, pp. 73–83.
Today's Zaman, June 18, 2012, *MGD to bestow special award in memory of singer Ahmet Kaya*, Accessible online at http://www.todayszaman.com/newsDetail_getNews ById.action?newsId=283941.
—— October 28, 2013, *Kurdish singer Ahmet Kaya among winners of Presidential Grand Awards*, Accessible online at http://www.todayszaman.com/news-329958-kurdis h-singer-ahmet-kaya-among-winners-of-presidential-grand-awards.html.
Toktaş, Şule and Bülent, Aras (2009). "The EU and Minority Rights in Turkey", *Political Science Quarterly*, Vol. 124, No. 4, pp. 697–720.
Tokyay, Menekse, October 17, 2011, *Ottomania on the rise in Turkey*, Accessible online, http://www.setimes.com/cocoon/setimes/xhtml/en_GB/features/setimes/articles/2011/10/17/reportage-01.
Toprak, Binnaz (1984). *Politicization of Islam in a Secular State: The National Salvation Party in Turkey*, in Said Amir Arjomand (ed.), *From Nationalism to Revolutionary Islam*, Albany: SUNY Press, pp. 119–33.
—— (1990). *Religion as a State Ideology in a secular Setting: The Turkish–Islamic Synthesis*, in Wagstaff, Malcom (ed.), *Aspects of Religion in Secular Turkey*, University of Durham Occasional Paper Series, No. 40, pp. 10–15.
—— (2008). *Türkiye'de farklı olmak: din ve muhafazakarlık ekseninde ötekileştirilenler*, Bosphorus University Scientific Research Proect, Istanbul: Bogazici University Press, Accessible online at http://www.osiaf.org.tr/images/basin/pdf/turkiyede_farkli_olmak.pdf.
Topsakal, Cem and Koro, Bedrettin (2007). *Kosova'da Yaşayan Türkçe Eğitim*, Prizren: Bay Yayınları.
TRT Turk, July 27, 2012, *Ak Parti'nin yeni Anayasa taslağında Türklük tanımı yok*, Accessible online at http://www.trtturk.com.tr/haber/ak-partinin-yeni-anayasa-taslaginda-turkluk-tanimi-yok.html.
Tüfekçi, Özgür (2012). "Another Last Eurasianist: Davutoğlu's Eurasianist Rhetoric", *Caucasus International*, Vol. 2, No. 3, Autumn, pp. 101–9.
—— (2016a). *The Foreign Policy of Modern Turkey: Power and the Ideology of Eurasianism*, London: I.B.Tauris.

—— (2016b). *Turkish Eurasianism: Roots and Discourses*, Tüfekci, Özgür, Tabak, Hüsrev, Akıllı, Erman (eds), Eurasian Politics and Society: Issues and Challenges, Newcastle Upon Tyne: Cambridge Scholars Publishing.

Türk Öğretmenler Derneği (1996). *Monografi 1951–1996: Özgeçmişler, Belgeler, Fotoğraflar*, Prizren.

—— (1996). *Türk Yazarlar Derneği: Belgeler, Bilgiler, Eserler*, Prizren: BAF.

Türkçem Dergisi, May 2013, Year 15, Number 150.

Turkish Official Gazette (2010). *The law on the foundation of the Presidency for Turks Abroad and Related Communities*, Article 5978, 24/03/2010, Gazette No: 27544.

Tüzün, Süleyman (1998). "İkinci Dünya Savaşı yıllarında Türk iç politikasında dış Türkler meselesi (1939–1945)". Unpublished PhD Thesis, Hacettepe University, Ankara.

Uğur, Etga (2004). "Intellectual roots of 'Turkish Islam' and approaches to the 'Turkish Model'", *Journal of Muslim Minority Affairs*, Vol. 24, No. 2, pp. 327–45.

Ulusal, Kanal, July 27, 2012, *Türklük kalkıyor, vatandaşlık geliyor*, Accessible online at http://www.ulusalkanal.com.tr/gundem/turkluk-kalkiyor-vatandaslik-gel iyor-h4496.html.

Üstel, Füsun (1996). *Türk Ocakları ve Dış Türkler*, in Vaner, Semih (ed.), *Unutkan Tarih – Sovyet sonrası Türkdilli Alan*, İstanbul: Metis Yayınları, pp. 53–65.

Uysal, Faruk (2004). *Kosova Dosyası*, Avrasya Bulteni, Vol. 23, Accessible online at http://www.tika.gov.tr/yukle/dosyalar/AvBulteni/Av23.pdf.

Uzer, Umut (2010). *Identity and Turkish Foreign Policy: The Kemalist Influence in Cyprus and the Caucasus*, London: I.B.Tauris.

Walton, F Jeremy (2010). *Practices of Neo-Ottomanism: Making Space and Place Virtuous in Istanbul*, Orienting Istanbul: Cultural Capital of Europe?, pp. 88–103.

Waltz, Kenneth (1996). "International Politics is not Foreign Policy", *Security Studies*, Vol. 6, No. 1, pp. 54–7.

Warning, Martina and Kardaş, Tuncay (2011). "The Impact of Changing Islamic Identity on Turkey's New Foreign Policy", *Alternatives Turkish Journal of International Relations*, Vol. 10, No. 2–3, pp. 123–40.

Wendt, Alexander (1992). "Anarchy is what states make of it: the social construction of power politics", *International Organization*, Vol. 46, No. 2, pp. 391–425.

—— (1999). *Social Theory of International Politics*, Cambridge: Cambridge University Press.

White, Brian (1992). *Analysing Foreign Policy: Problems and Approaches*, in Clarke, Michael and White, Brian (ed.), *Understanding Foreign Policy – The Foreign Policy Systems Approach*, Worcester: Edward Elgar, pp. 1–26.

White, Jenny (2013). *Muslim Nationalism and the New Turks*, Princeton: Princeton University Press.

Wiener, Antje (2007a). "The Dual Quality of Norms and Governance beyond the State: Sociological and Normative Approaches to "Interaction"", *Critical Review of International Social and Political Philosophy*, Vol. 10, No. 1, pp. 47–69.

—— (2007b). "The Contested Meanings of Norms", *Comparative European Politics*, Vol. 5, pp. 1–17.

—— (2009). "Enacting meaning-in-use: qualitative research on norms and international relations", *Review of International Studies*, Vol. 35, pp. 175–93.

Wiener, Antje and Puetter, Uwe (2009). "The Quality of Norms is What Actors Make of It- Critical Constructivist Research on Norms", *Journal of International Law and International Relations*, Vol. 5, No. 1, pp. 1–16.

www.balkanrtv.com.

www.bezmialem.edu.tr/medya/universite-duyurular/951–16–18-mayis-balkangenclik-forumu-etkinlikleri.

www.mfa.gov.tr/policy-of-zero-problems-with-our-neighbors.en.mfa.

www.pristine.be.mfa.gov.tr.

www.turkiyeburslari.org/index.php/tr/turkiye-burslari/burs-programlari.

www.ytb.gov.tr.

Xupolia, Ilia (2011). "Cypriot Muslims among Ottomans, Turks and two world wars", *Boğaziçi Journal*, Vol. 25, No. 2, pp. 109–20.

Yanık, Lerna (2006). "Millet, Milliyet ve Milliyetçilik: Soğuk Savaş'ın Sonunda Türk Dış Politikasından bir Kesit", *Doğu Batı*, Vol. 39, No. 4, pp. 188–206.

Yavan, Nuri (2012). "Türkiye'nin Yurt Dışındaki Doğrudan Yatırımları: Tarihsel ve Mekânsal Perspektif", *Bilig*, Vol. 63, pp. 237–70.

Yavuz, Hakan (1998). "Turkish Identity and Foreign Policy in Flux: The Rise of Neo-Ottomanism", *Critique*, No. 12, pp. 19–42.

—— (2000). "Cleansing Islam from the Public Sphere", *Journal of International Affairs*, Vol. 54, pp. 21–42.

—— (2004). *Opportunity Spaces, Identity, and Islamic Meaning in Turkey*, in Quintan Wiktorowicz (ed.), *Islamic Activism: A Social Movement Theory Approach*, Bloomington: Indiana University Press, pp. 270–88.

—— (2009). *Secularism and Muslim Democracy in Turkey*, Cambridge: Cambridge University Press.

Yavuz, Yenel (2012). "Kardesler Bayramda Bulustu-Hasrtet Giderildi", *Arti90*, October, pp. 68–9.

Yeni Dönem, November 1, 2001.

—— November 15, 2001.

—— January 17, 2002.

—— March 21, 2002.

—— April 18, 2002.

—— April 25, 2002.

—— September 5, 2002.

—— February 27, 2003.

—— November 6, 2003.

—— May 20, 2004.

—— November 18, 2004.

—— December 30, 2004.

—— February 10, 2005.

—— April 21, 2005.

—— October 20, 2005.

Yeni Kosova, October 31, 2013, *Kosova Türklerinin Dil-sizliğ-i ve Hak-sızlık-ları (by Ergin Jable)*. Accessible online at http://www.yenikosova.com/kosova-turklerinin-dilsizligii-ve-haksizliklari/.

Yeni Safak, October 12, 2013, *Türklükle uğraşmanın adı demokrasi değil*, Accessible online at http://yenisafak.com.tr/politika-haber/turklukle-ugrasmanin-adi-demokrasi-degil-13.10.2013–573263.

Yeniçağ, April 23, 2013, *Türk'üm Özür Dilerim*, Column by Arslan Tekin, Accessible Online at http://www.yenicaggazetesi.com.tr/turkum-ozur-dilerim-26516yy. htm.

—— May 22, 2013, *Millilik düşmanlığı, Atatürk ve AKP*, Accessible online at http://www.yg.yenicaggazetesi.com.tr/yazargoster.php?haber=26850.

Yiğit-Yüksel, Dilek (2009). "Kıbrıs'ta Türk Milli Mücadelesi (1914–1958)." *ÇTTAD*, Vol. 8, No. 18–19, Spring, pp. 161–84.

Yin, Robert (2003). *Case Study Research – design and methods*, London: Sage Publications, 3rd edn.

YTB News (August 2013). *Başbakan Yardımcımız Bekir Bozdağ, Bayram Namazını Bulgaristan'da Soydaşlarımızla Birlikte Kıldı*, Accessible online at http://www.ytb.gov.tr/index.php/soydas-ve-akraba-topluluklar/965–2013080802.html.

Yunus Emre Bulletin, Octrober 2011, Vol. 10. Official Publication of the Yunus Emre Institute.

Yurtnaç, Kemal (2012). *Turkey's New Horizon: Turks Abroad and Related Communities*, Centre for Strategic Research, SAM Papers, No. 3, Accessible online at http://sam.gov.tr/turkeys-new-horizon-turks-abroad-and-related-communities/.

Yusuf, Süreyya (1976). *Yugoslavya Turk Siiri*, Pristine: Tan Yayınları.

Zakaria, Fareed (1992). "Realism and Domestic Politics", *International Security*, Vol. 17, No. 1, pp. 177–98.

Zaman, October 26, 2013, *Bahçeli: 36 etnik milleti biliyor da açıklamıyorsan 'namert kere namertsin'*, Accessible online at http://www.zaman.com.tr/gundem_bahceli-36-etnik-milleti-biliyor-da-aciklamiyorsan-namert-kere-namertsin_2157683. html.

—— November 7, 2013, *Diyarbakır'da 'Ne mutlu Türk'üm diyene' tabelası kaldırıldı*, Accessible online at http://www.zaman.com.tr/gundem_diyarbakirda-ne-mutlu-turkum-diyene-tabelasi-kaldirildi_2163460.html.

Zürcher, Erik Jan (1999). "The vocabulary of Muslim nationalism", *International Journal of the Sociology of Language*, Vol. 137, Issue 1, pp. 81–92.

INDEX